T0224907

A COMPOSITIONAL APPROACH TO
PERFORMANCE MODELLING

Distinguished Dissertations in Computer Science

Edited by
C.J. van Rijsbergen, University of Glasgow

The Conference of Professors of Computer Science (CPCS), in conjunction
with the British Computer Society (BCS), selects annually for publication
up to four of the best British PhD dissertations in computer science. The
scheme began in 1990. Its aim is to make more visible the significant
contribution made by Britain – in particular by students – to computer
science, and to provide a model for future students. Dissertations are
selected on behalf of CPCS by a panel whose members are:

C.B. Jones, Manchester University (Chairman)
S. Abramsky, Imperial College, London
D.A. Duce, Rutherford Appleton Laboratory
M.E. Dyer, University of Leeds
G. Nudd, University of Warwick
V.J. Rayward-Smith, University of East Anglia
I. Wand, University of York
M.H. Williams, Heriot-Watt University

A COMPOSITIONAL APPROACH TO PERFORMANCE MODELLING

JANE HILLSTON
University of Edinburgh

CAMBRIDGE
UNIVERSITY PRESS

CAMBRIDGE UNIVERSITY PRESS
Cambridge, New York, Melbourne, Madrid, Cape Town, Singapore, São Paulo

Cambridge University Press
The Edinburgh Building, Cambridge CB2 2RU, UK

Published in the United States of America by Cambridge University Press, New York

www.cambridge.org
Information on this title: www.cambridge.org/9780521571890

© Cambridge University Press 1996

First published 1996
This digitally printed first paperback version 2005

A catalogue record for this publication is available from the British Library

ISBN-13 978-0-521-57189-0 hardback
ISBN-10 0-521-57189-8 hardback

ISBN-13 978-0-521-67353-2 paperback
ISBN-10 0-521-67353-4 paperback

Contents

Table of Notation

$\mathcal{C}$	set of possible components
$\mathcal{A}$	set of possible action types
$\mathcal{A}ct$	set of possible activities
$\mathcal{A}(C)$	set of current action types of component C
$\mathcal{A}ct(C)$	multiset of current activities of C
$\mathcal{A}ct(C_i \mid C_j)$	multiset of current activities of C_i with derivative C_j
$\vec{\mathcal{A}}(C)$	complete action type set of C
τ	unknown action type
$\top$	unspecified activity rate
w_i	weight of a passive activity
$r_\alpha(C)$	apparent rate of action type α in component C
$ds(C)$	derivative set
$\mathcal{D}(C)$	derivation graph
Sys_P	the system component represented by P
$\mathcal{C}/\cong$	set of equivalence classes induced by $\cong$ on $\mathcal{C}$
$\mathcal{C}/\mathcal{R}$	set of equivalence classes induced by $\mathcal{R}$ on $\mathcal{C}$
$(\alpha, r).P$	activity prefix
$P + Q$	component choice
$P \bowtie_L Q$	cooperation between P and Q on the set of action types L
$P \parallel Q$	parallel composition of P and Q, cooperation on $\emptyset$
P/L	activities of P with types in L appear as unknown type
$E\{P/X\}$	every occurrence of X in E is replaced by P
$\tilde{X}, \tilde{P}$	indexed sets of variables and components respectively
$A \stackrel{\text{def}}{=} P$	defining equation for the constant A
$Id_\mathcal{C}$	identity function on components
$P \equiv Q$	syntactic equivalence
$P = Q$	P is isomorphic to Q
$C \leq P$	C is a compact form of P
$P \approx Q$	P is weakly isomorphic to Q
$P \sim Q$	P is strongly bisimilar to Q
$P \cong Q$	P is strongly equivalent to Q
$\overline{P}$	the compact form of component P
$\widehat{P}$	the lumped component of P
$V_{(\tau,r)}(C)$	visible (τ, r)-derivative of C
$\mathcal{A}ct_\cong(T)$	lumped activity set
$ds(\mathcal{S})/\cong$	lumped derivative set
$\mathcal{D}_\cong(\mathcal{S})$	lumped derivation graph
$\vec{\mathcal{A}}ct_\cong(\mathcal{S})$	complete lumped activity set

$\mathbb{R}^+$ set of activity rates, $\{x \mid x > 0; x \in \mathbb{R}\} \cup \{\top\}$
$\mathbb{N}$ natural numbers, $\{1, 2, 3, \dots\}$

$F_a(t)$ probability distribution function associated with a
$f_a(t)$ probability density function associated with a

X_i state in a Markov process
$\mathbf{Q}$ infinitesimal generator matrix
q_{ij} transition rate between state X_i and X_j
$\Pi(\cdot)$ steady state probability distribution
$\Pi_j(\cdot)$ conditional steady state probability distribution
$X_{[j]}$ aggregated state in a Markov process

x_n state in a generalised semi-Markov process (GSMP)
s active element in a GSMP
$p(x_i, s, x_j)$ transition probability in a GSMP

$q(C)$ exit rate from component C
$q(C_i, C_j)$ transition rate from C_i to C_j
$q(C_i, C_j, \alpha)$ conditional transition rate via activities of type α
$q(C, \alpha)$ conditional exit rate via activities of type α
$q[C, S]$ total transition rate from C to the set of derivatives S
$q[C, S, \alpha]$ total conditional transition rate via activities of type α

$p(C, a), p(C, \alpha)$ conditional probabilities that C completes a, or an activity of type α
$p(C_i, C_j)$ transition probability from C_i to C_j
$p[C, S]$ total transition probability from C to the set of derivatives S
$p[C, S, \alpha]$ total conditional transition probability via activities of type α

ρ_i reward associated with derivative C_i
R total reward

$\uplus$ multiset union
$\{\!| \dots |\!\}$ multiset delimiters

Preface

This book is, in essence, the dissertation I submitted to the University of Edinburgh in early January 1994. My examiners, Peter Harrison of the Imperial College, and Stuart Anderson of the University of Edinburgh, suggested some corrections and revisions. Apart from those changes, most chapters remain unaltered except for minor corrections and reformatting. The exceptions are the first and final chapter.

Since the final chapter discusses several possible directions for future work, it is now supplemented with a section which reviews the progress which has been made in each of these directions since January 1994. There are now many more people interested in stochastic process algebras and their application to performance modelling. Moreover, since these researchers have backgrounds and motivations different from my own some of the most interesting new developments are outside the areas identified in the original conclusions of the thesis. Therefore the book concludes with a brief overview of the current status of the field which includes many recent references. This change to the structure of the book is reflected in the summary given in Chapter 1. No other chapters of the thesis have been updated to reflect more recent developments. A modified version of Chapter 8 appeared in the proceedings of the 2nd International Workshop on Numerical Solution of Markov Chains, January 1995.

I would like to thank my supervisor, Rob Pooley, for introducing me to performance modelling and giving me the job which brought me to Edinburgh initially. Many colleagues on the IMSE project provided stimulating discussions which influenced this work. My second supervisor, Julian Bradfield, provided support and advice in large quantities for which I am very grateful. Many other people also influenced this work through helpful comments, discussions and encouragement; they include Graham Birtwistle, Stephen Gilmore, Peter King, James McKinna, Faron Moller, Michael Rettelbach, Ben Strulo and Nico van Dijk. Stephen also provided the tools which made constructing and solving the large models in Chapter 4 possible.

I would never have finished this thesis without the support, encouragement and distractions provided in appropriate proportions by my parents and many friends, during the four and a half years it took to complete.

I am grateful to David Miles and Juliet Sheppard at Kingston Business School who arranged for my first year tuition fees to be paid. The final two years of my work were supported by a SERC studentship.

Jane Hillston
December 1995

Chapter 1

Introduction

Performance modelling is concerned with the capture and analysis of the dynamic behaviour of computer and communication systems. The size and complexity of many modern systems result in large, complex models. A compositional approach decomposes the system into subsystems that are smaller and more easily modelled. In this thesis a novel compositional approach to performance modelling is presented. This chapter presents an overview of the thesis. The major results are identified.

A significant contribution is the approach itself. It is based on a suitably enhanced process algebra, PEPA (Performance Evaluation Process Algebra). As this represents a new departure for performance modelling, some background material and definitions are provided in Chapter 2 before PEPA is presented. The chapter includes the motivations for applying process algebras to performance modelling, based on three perceived problems of performance evaluation. The recent developments of timed and probabilistic process algebras are unsuitable for performance modelling. PEPA, and related work on TIPP [1], represent a new area of work, *stochastic process algebras* [2]. The extent to which work on PEPA attempts to address the identified problems of performance evaluation is explained. The chapter concludes with a brief review of TIPP and other related work.

Chapter 3 presents PEPA in detail. The modifications which have been made to the language to make it suitable for performance modelling are explained. An operational semantics for PEPA is given and its use to generate a continuous time Markov process for any PEPA model is explained. Thus it is demonstrated that PEPA may be used as a paradigm for specifying Markov models. At the end of the chapter the relationship between PEPA and established performance modelling paradigms is discussed.

A compositional approach offers potential for complex systems to be modelled systematically. Separate aspects or components of a system may be considered in detail individually, but subsequently in a more abstract form as the interactions between them are developed. The benefits of the compositional approach to model construction provided by PEPA are demonstrated in Chapter 4. The modelling study presented investigates the characteristics of various *multi-server multi-queue* (MSMQ) systems. These systems, an extension of classical polling systems, have been shown to be useful representations of many local area network architectures, with ring topologies and scheduled access, in which more than one node may transmit simultaneously. However, they are not readily amenable to queueing theory solution. These systems are straightforward to model using PEPA and exact analysis based on solution of the underlying Markov process is carried out in each case. These case studies also demonstrate how the size of the state space of this underlying process grows rapidly as the dimensions and complexity of the modelled system increase. The remainder of the thesis addresses this problem. It is demonstrated that the compositional structure of PEPA models can also benefit model simplification techniques.

Model simplification and state space aggregation have been proposed as means to tackle the problems of large performance models. These techniques, particularly aggregation, are typically applied at the level of the Markov process rather than the modelling paradigm. This means that the whole state space of the process must be constructed before it can be reduced. In Chapter 5 these techniques of model simplification and aggregation are presented in terms of notions of equivalence between modelling entities. A framework is developed for analysing such notions of equivalence. It is explained how this framework may also be applied to the *bisimulation* relations defined for process algebras.

A process algebra incorporates an apparatus for reasoning about the structure and behaviour of the model. Such an apparatus is not usually available in Markovian based modelling paradigms. The next three chapters of the thesis present three model simplification techniques for PEPA models which take advantage of this apparatus together with the compositional nature of the language. These techniques avoid the construction of the state space of the original model. In each case the integrity of the performance measures to be derived from the model can be guaranteed. They represent the major contribution of the thesis. Each is illustrated using one of the MSMQ models presented in Chapter 4.

Based on the operational semantics of the language four different notions of equivalence for PEPA are developed. These are considered within the framework presented in Chapter 5. For each equivalence its properties in the context of a process algebra, and its implications for the underlying Markov process, are studied. Three of these equivalences are shown to be congruences and all are complementary to the compositional nature of the models considered.

The strongest notion of equivalence for PEPA components, *isomorphism*, is presented in Chapter 6. This is a structural equivalence, similar to the equivalence between Markov processes discussed in Chapter 5. Nevertheless it is the basis of equational laws which may be used to transform the presentation of a model, and so make it amenable to simplification. A weaker form of this equivalence, *weak isomorphism*, is the basis of one of the model simplification techniques—state space reduction via the amalgamation of states. This takes advantage of judicious use of PEPA abstraction mechanisms, provided certain insensitivity conditions are satisfied. Although weak isomorphism is not a congruence for PEPA it is shown to be preserved by some combinators of the language. This means that the model simplification technique it provides can be applied compositionally in some circumstances. These circumstances are identified. It is proved that the integrity of the performance measures to be derived from the model is guaranteed.

The other two equivalence relations developed are based on the process algebra notion of bisimulation. The first, *strong bisimilarity*, is presented in Chapter 7. A *strong bisimulation* aims to capture the notion of indistinguishability under observation used in many process algebras. Two components are strongly bisimilar if they are able to perform the same activities, resulting in derivatives which are strongly bisimilar. Strong bisimilarity is the largest relation satisfying the conditions of a strong bisimulation relation. It is shown that the relation does not ensure exact equivalence of behaviour. However, circumstances in which a strongly bisimilar component may be substituted within a model, resulting in a simpler model, are identified.

The other notion of equivalence in the bisimulation style, *strong equivalence*, is presented in Chapter 8. This is developed analogously to a *probabilistic bisimulation* used in probabilistic extensions of process algebras. However, transition rates, already embedded in the PEPA labelled transition system as activity rates, are used instead of probabilities. The relation again aims to capture a notion of equivalent observed behaviour, but the observation is now assumed to be less detailed than in strong bisimilarity. The resulting relation is closely allied to the notion of lumpability in the underlying Markov process. The use of strong equivalence to partition the state space as a basis of exact aggregation is outlined. The conditions under which the integrity of the performance measures is guaranteed are discussed.

Finally, in Chapter 9, the results of the thesis are summarised. The direction for further work and the future development of PEPA are discussed as they appeared at the end of the thesis. The book concludes with a review of the extent to which these outlined objectives have been addressed by more recent work, and a summary of current work on stochastic process algebras and their application to performance modelling.

Chapter 2

Background

2.1 Introduction

This chapter presents the background material for the thesis. The field of performance modelling is introduced and the standard paradigms for specifying stochastic performance models, queueing networks and stochastic Petri nets, are reviewed. In Section 2.3 process algebras are introduced, and some of the extensions into timed and probabilistic processes are considered in the following subsections. In particular we describe the Calculus of Communicating Systems (CCS), and various extended calculi based upon it.

We present the motivation for applying process algebras to performance modelling in Section 2.4. This outlines the objectives of the work presented in the remainder of the thesis. Finally, in Section 2.5, some related work, involving process algebras and performance evaluation, is discussed.

2.2 Performance Modelling

Performance evaluation is concerned with the description, analysis and optimisation of the dynamic behaviour of computer and communication systems. This involves the investigation of the flow of data, and control information, within and between components of a system. The aim is to understand the behaviour of the system and identify the aspects of the system which are sensitive from a performance point of view.

In performance modelling an abstract representation, or *model*, of the system is used to capture the essential characteristics of the system so that its performance can be reproduced. A performance study will address some objective, usually investigating several alternatives—these are represented by values given to the parameters of the model. The model will be evaluated to determine its behaviour and performance measures under the current set of parameter values. Evaluation may take place via the solution of a set of equations by some analytical, possibly numerical, technique or via the simulation of the model. Analytical models are usually based on stochastic models and throughout the rest of the thesis the term *performance modelling* will apply to stochastic models solved analytically unless otherwise stated. There are two established notations for constructing such models—queueing networks and stochastic Petri nets. These are described in Sections 2.2.1 and 2.2.2 respectively. In many cases these underlying stochastic models are assumed to be Markov processes.

The size and complexity of many modern systems result in large complex models. This is problematical for both model construction and model solution, and has led to an interest in compositional approaches to performance modelling. These approaches decompose a system into subsystems that are smaller and more easily modelled. Several authors have advocated the adoption of software engineering style structuring techniques for performance model construction [3, 4, 5, 6].

Finding techniques for the solution of large Markov chains, whose state spaces are finite but exceedingly large, has been a major preoccupation of performance analysis research for many years [7]. Standard numerical techniques cannot cope with such models—a problem often referred to as *state space explosion*. Compositional approaches which would be applicable to model solution as well as model construction, allowing separate solution of submodels, have been sought.

In this thesis we offer a technique which allows subsystems to be modelled separately although the model must be considered as a single entity for the purposes of solution. However, we also present some approaches to model simplification which may be applied to the subsystem models in isolation but which are guaranteed not to affect the integrity of the whole model. Thus, although compositional solution is not, in general, feasible, a large model may be tackled in a systematic way and formally manipulated to reduce it to a manageable size.

2.2.1   Queueing Networks

The use of queueing networks for performance modelling is well-established. In this section we briefly introduce the main ideas and some terminology which will be useful later in the thesis. More details can be found in any one of the many books written on the subject, for example [8, 9, 10, 11, 12].

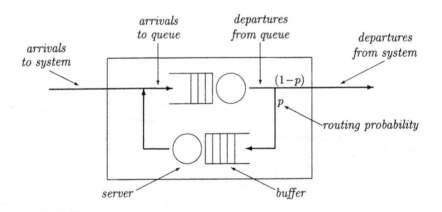

Figure 2.1: A Simple Open Queueing Network

A queue consists of an arrival process, a buffer where customers await service and one or more servers representing a resource which must be retained by each customer for some period before leaving the queue. The queue may be characterised by five factors: the arrival rate, the service rate, the number of servers, the capacity of the buffer and the queueing discipline. The first four of these characteristics may be concisely represented using *Kendall's notation* for classifying queues. In this notation a queue is represented as $A/S/c/m/N$:

A denotes the arrival process; usually M, to denote Markov (exponential), G, general, or

D, deterministic distributions. Identifiers for other distributions, such as H_k (hyper-exponential with parameter k), may also be used.

S denotes the service rate and uses the distribution identifiers as above.

c denotes the number of servers available to provide service to the queue.

m denotes the capacity of the buffer, infinite by default. Customers who arrive when the buffer is full may be lost or blocked.

N denotes the customer population, also infinite by default.

The last two classifiers may be omitted in the default case. The queueing discipline determines how a server selects a customer from the queue for next service. For example, the discipline might be *first-come-first-served* (FCFS) in which the customer who has been waiting longest is served next, or *processor sharing* (PS) in which the service capacity is shared by all the customers present at the queue.

A queueing network is a directed graph in which the nodes are queues, often called *service centres* in this context, each representing a resource in the system being modelled. Customers, representing the jobs in the system, flow through the system and compete for these resources. The arcs of the network represent the topology of the system, and together with *routing probabilities*, determine the paths that customers take through the network. Depending on the demand for the resources and the service rate that the customers experience, contention over a resource may arise leading to the formation of a queue of waiting customers.

The state of the system is typically represented as the number of customers currently occupying each of the service centres. There may be a number of different *classes* of customers each exhibiting different characteristics within the network. In this case the state is the number of customers of each class at each service centre. A network may be *closed*, *open* or *mixed* depending on whether a fixed population of customers remain within the system; customers may arrive from, or depart to, some external environment; or there are classes of customers within the system exhibiting open and closed patterns of behaviour respectively.

A large class of queueing networks have been shown to have a straightforward and computationally efficient solution [13]. Although this class excludes some interesting and important system features, when applicable they allow performance measures to be derived without resorting to the underlying Markov process. The solution of these models, often termed a *product form* solution, allows individual queues within a network to be considered separately. Based on this, relatively simple algorithms exist for computing most performance measures based directly on the parameters of the queueing network.

2.2.2 Stochastic Extensions of Petri Nets

Petri nets are directed graphs with two types of node, *places* and *transitions*, and unidirectional arcs between them. *Tokens* move between places according to the firing rules imposed by the transitions. A transition can *fire* when each of the places connected to it has at least one token; when it fires, the transition removes a token from each of these places and deposits a token in each of the places it is connected to.

The state of the system is denoted by the number of tokens at each place in the network. This is termed the *marking* of the net. A Petri net is defined by its structure and an *initial marking* which is the initial placement of tokens. The *reachability set* is the set of all possible markings that a net may exhibit, starting from the initial marking and following the firing rules. This is used to form the *reachability graph* in the natural way.

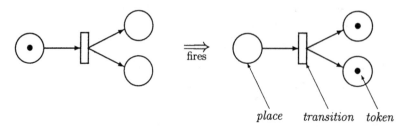

Figure 2.2: A Simple Petri Net Firing

Various timed and stochastic extensions of Petri nets have been proposed for performance modelling [14, 15, 16, 17, 18, 19, 20, 21]. Amongst the most influential have been the stochastic Petri nets (SPNs) proposed by Molloy [22] and their subsequent refinement by Ajmone Marsan *et al.*, generalised stochastic Petri nets (GSPNs) [17].

In SPNs an exponentially distributed firing rate (possibly dependent on the marking) is associated with each transition. Once a transition is enabled (each input place is marked) a drawing is made on the distribution to define a delay before the transition will fire; if the transition is still enabled at the end of that time it then fires. Molloy showed that the reachability graph underlying such nets is isomorphic to a Markov process when this delay is exponentially distributed [16]. Thus SPNs provide an alternative means of specifying the stochastic models used for performance modelling. Moreover they are able to easily express some of the features not readily modelled in queueing networks such as multiple resource usage. Performance measures are usually extracted from the models via numerical solution of the underlying Markov process. There has been some work on product form solutions for SPNs, for example [23], but these rely on restrictive conditions on the structure of the net.

In GSPNs the transitions of the net are partitioned into two subsets—*timed* transitions which behave like the transitions in SPNs, each with an exponentially distributed firing time, and *immediate* transitions which fire immediately upon being enabled. It is assumed that all enabled immediate transitions fire before any timed transitions. Consequently the reachability graph of a GSPN can be partitioned into *tangible* and *vanishing* markings. Ajmone Marsan *et al.* showed that since no time elapses in vanishing markings they can be eliminated prior to the solution of the embedded Markov chain. Thus immediate transitions are disregarded during model solution. GSPN models have been used widely for performance analysis, for example [24, 25, 26]. As well as immediate transitions GSPNs also sometimes include inhibitor arcs. Such extensions to the notation often make it possible to express a model more concisely but they have been shown not to increase the modelling power of GSPNs [27].

Stochastic activity networks (SAN), introduced by Movaghar and Meyer [19], are also of interest because, like PEPA, they place emphasis on the activities of the system. Although similar to GSPNs these nets, intended for performability modelling (joint consideration of the performance and the availability of a system), have more structure. As well as immediate transitions and inhibitor arcs they include *gates* and *cases* which introduce more sophisticated firing rules into the net. In [28] the authors introduce an abstract underlying model, the *stochastic activity system*, which may be used to reason about the SAN. In [5] the use of compositional techniques for SAN is investigated. Work on SAN is discussed in more detail in Section 5.3.

2.3 Process Algebras

Process algebras are mathematical theories which model concurrent systems by their algebra and provide apparatus for reasoning about the structure and behaviour of the model. Examples include the Calculus of Communicating Systems (CCS) [29], Communicating Sequential Processes (CSP) [30], and the Algebra of Communicating Processes (ACP) [31]. A system is characterised by its active components and the *interactions*, or *communications*, between them. Unlike queueing networks or Petri nets there is no notion of *entity* or *flow* within a model. However, in recompense, compositional reasoning is an integral part of the language.

In CCS the active components of a system are called *agents* or *processes* and these undertake *actions*, representing the discrete actions of the system. Any action may be internal to an agent or may constitute the interaction or communication between neighbouring agents. Agents may proceed with their internal actions simultaneously, but it is important to note that this behaviour is given an interleaving semantics. Combinators of the language make it possible to construct an agent which has a designated first action (prefix); has a choice over alternatives (choice); or has concurrent possibilities (composition). In PEPA prefix and choice are retained but composition is replaced by *cooperation*.

Like many other process algebras, CCS is given an operational semantics, in the style of Plotkin [32], using a labelled transition system. From this a *derivative tree*, or *graph*, in which language terms form the nodes and transitions are the arcs, may be constructed. This structure is a useful tool for reasoning about agents and the systems they represent. It is the basis of the *bisimulation* style of equivalence. The actions of an agent characterise it, so two agents are considered to be equivalent if they are observed to perform exactly the same actions. Strong and weak forms of equivalence are defined depending on whether the internal actions of an agent are also considered to be observable. Bisimulation and related notions of equivalence are presented in more detail in Section 5.2.

CCS models have been used extensively to establish the correct behaviour of systems, both with respect to a given specification and in the more abstract sense. This is sometimes termed *functional* or *qualitative* modelling. Behavioural properties such as *fairness* and freedom from *deadlock* are investigated, in contrast to the quantitative values extracted from performance models.

In the following sections we discuss some of the extensions which have been made to process algebras to incorporate time and probability. Most of these can be exemplified by an extension of CCS. When we want to refer to a process algebra without such extensions we will sometimes find it convenient to refer to it as a *pure* process algebra.

2.3.1 Timed Extensions of Process Algebras

In pure process algebras time is abstracted away within a process so that all actions are assumed to be instantaneous and only relative timing is represented via the traces of the process. The simplest way in which time may be incorporated into such an algebra is by making it synchronous. In synchronous calculi, such as SCCS [33], it is assumed that there is an implicit global clock, and one action must occur at each clock tick. However in order to model the real time behaviour of systems a more sophisticated representation of time is needed.

Time may be represented explicitly in a process algebra by allowing an agent to witness periods of delay, of specified lengths, in addition to witnessing actions, as in Temporal

CCS (TCCS) [34]. In TCCS actions are still assumed to be instantaneous, and the time domain is taken to be the natural numbers. The language is given an operational semantics with two different types of transition: action transitions and time transitions. Observation equivalence may be defined as before but with the additional condition that any period of delay experienced by one agent must also be possible for the other agent.

An alternative approach is taken in Real Time ACP [35]. Here an *absolute* time is associated with each *event*, where an event is the completion of an action by a process. It is also possible to specify a relative time for each action, or an interval during which an event must occur. Such intervals lead to the introduction of an integration operator since it represents a choice over a continuum of alternatives.

2.3.2   Probabilistic Process Algebras

Process algebras will often be used to model systems in which there is uncertainty about the behaviour of a component but, like time, this uncertainty will be abstracted away so that all choices become nondeterministic. Probabilistic extensions of process algebras allow this uncertainty to be quantified because nondeterministic choice is replaced by a probabilistic choice. In this case a probability is associated with each possible outcome of a choice.

The operational semantics for probabilistic process algebras are given in terms of probabilistic labelled transition systems, labelled transition systems in which probabilities are associated with the transitions. These systems may be classified as being *reactive* or *generative* . In a reactive system the probabilities of the transitions of an agent may depend on the environment in which the agent is placed. In a generative system the transition probabilities are independent of the environment. In effect, in the reactive case a probability distribution is defined over the possible derivatives of an agent given that a particular action is performed and in the generative case a probability distribution is defined over the possible actions of the agent.

In [36] Jou and Smolka describe a language PCCS which is similar to SCCS but with probabilistic choice replacing nondeterministic choice. Another extension of SCCS is Tofts' WSCCS [37] which uses weights to assign probabilities. Here nondeterministic choice is replaced by probabilistic and prioritised choice.

Probabilistic process algebras have been proposed as a more suitable way of testing equivalence between a system's specification and its implementation [38]. Two processes are probabilistically bisimilar, or equivalent, if their visible behaviour will be the same with probability $1 - \varepsilon$, where ε is an arbitrary small number. Another alternative is the use of preorders which express the idea that one process may be probabilistically better than another [39]. In this case it is necessary to show that a system's implementation improves on its specification. Thus if the specification allows 0.05 probability of breakdowns, an implementation which ensures that the probability of breakdown is less than 0.04 will be satisfactory.

2.4   Process Algebra for Performance Modelling

In this section we present some of the motivations for investigating the use of process algebras for performance modelling. These can be regarded as arising from three distinct problems of performance analysis which have been identified in recent years.

Integrating Performance Analysis into System Design: Several authors have pointed out the importance of the timely consideration of performance aspects of a planned system [40, 41, 42, 3, 43, 6, 2]. However, most have also highlighted the limited extent to which this occurs in practice.

Representing Systems as Models: The restricted expressiveness of queueing networks has been highlighted by recent developments in computer and telecommunication systems.

Model Tractability: Solving models of the size and complexity necessary to model many modern systems is often beyond the capabilities of contemporary techniques and equipment. This has led to considerable interest in model simplification and aggregation techniques, for example [25, 7, 44, 45].

The adoption of a process algebra as a performance modelling paradigm has implications for each of these problems, as explained below. We consider the use of process algebras as a design methodology; the style in which process algebras express systems; and the apparatus provided by process algebras for manipulating models.

2.4.1 Process Algebras as a Design Methodology

The process algebra style of system description is close to the way that designers think about systems, and is gaining acceptance as a design methodology [46, 47], particularly in the area of communication system and protocol design. Using a process algebra based language for performance modelling introduces the possibility of a closer integration of performance analysis into design methodologies. Performance models can be formed by the annotation of existing system descriptions for design, as recent work with LOTOS has shown [42, 48]. This has clear implications for both the practice of performance evaluation and the verification of models against designs.

The use of system description formalisms for performance modelling has been investigated by several researchers. Examples include SDL (Specification and Description Language) in [49, 42], ACP in [50] and Estelle in [51, 42, 52].

Not only does the use of such a formal description language allow the integration of performance modelling into the design process but, as most of the authors point out, it presents the possibility of qualitative (or functional) and quantitative modelling using the same system description. An alternative approach to this integration of modelling aspects is presented by Pooley [53] (Section 2.5.4). This is similar to earlier work within the CUPID project [54, 55] (Section 2.5.1), in which CCS is used as a canonical representation language.

2.4.2 The "Cooperator" Paradigm and Hierarchical Models

A process algebra description represents a system as a collection of active agents who co-operate to achieve the behaviour of the system. This *cooperator paradigm* (as opposed to *operator* and *operand*) is appropriate for modelling many modern computer systems. These systems do not readily fit the traditional models of sequential flow of control and resource allocation, as captured by the established performance modelling paradigms. For example, in distributed systems and communications networks components have autonomy and the framework is one of cooperation. In a process algebra model all system elements have equal status; the model defines their individual behaviours and how they interact.

Similar expressiveness is offered by the stochastic extensions of Petri nets [17, 18, 28]. However, in addition process algebras include mechanisms for composition and abstraction, as well as apparatus for compositional reasoning, which are missing from performance modelling techniques [56, 4]. These mechanisms, which are an integral part of the language, facilitate the systematic development of large models with hierarchical structure.

The process algebra style of system description will be fully illustrated by a case study introduced in Chapter 4. The system studied, a polling system with multiple servers, cannot be solved exactly using conventional queueing network models. Moreover we will see in subsequent chapters that the structure introduced in the system description, reflecting the structure of the system itself, has useful implications for solution of the underlying Markov process.

2.4.3   Structure within Models

Model simplification and aggregation techniques are often based on conditions phrased in terms of the underlying Markov process or its generator matrix. For very large systems the size of the state space may prohibit the generation and storage of the complete Markov process [44].

The structure inherent in process algebra models offers the possibility of introducing model simplification and aggregation techniques based on the system description rather than the underlying stochastic model. Moreover the compositionality of the process algebra allows these techniques to be applied to part of the model whilst maintaining the integrity of the model as a whole.

The formal definition of the process algebra provides the basis for comparing and manipulating models within a formal framework. In particular we will develop notions of equivalence based on this formal definition which will allow one model, or part of a model, to be substituted for another whilst retaining the same observable behaviour. These notions of equivalence will be presented in Chapters 6, 7 and 8 and form the main results of the thesis.

2.4.4   The Work Presented in This Thesis

The work presented in this thesis concentrates on the compositionality offered by a particular process algebra, PEPA, and its benefits for performance modelling. It is shown that this language supports a compositional approach to model construction, resulting in models which are easy to understand and readily modified. Moreover, it is also demonstrated that the structure provided within a model can be exploited for model manipulation and simplification. In particular model simplification techniques which avoid the generation of the complete state space of the underlying stochastic process are presented. As these techniques are formally defined, in terms of the operational semantics of PEPA, they offer potential for automation or machine-assistance of model simplification.

The thesis does not address the problem of using the compositional structure of a model during its solution although this appears to be a promising area for future research.

2.5   Related Work

Some related work is now reviewed, showing how process algebras have been applied to performance modelling. The approaches adopted vary considerably. Most of the work presented has originated in the area of performance modelling, and has been motivated by the attractive features of process algebras.

2.5.1 Early Work on Protocol Specification

Early work arose from the consideration of correctness of communication protocols and the recognition that timing behaviour was often disregarded during protocol design only to cause problems subsequently [54].

Columbia's Unified Protocol Implementation and Design (CUPID) environment was an ambitious project, started in the early 1980's, aiming at the integration and automation of protocol design and implementation tools [54]. Central to the approach was a single representation of the system, developed in an algebraic form, based on value passing CCS. From this canonical representation alternative views of the system could be developed to address different objectives during the development process. Moreover the translation into a different representation was formally defined and consistency between different representations guaranteed.

For example, in order to carry out performance analysis, in [54] the authors define a formal procedure to map each port of an agent to a distribution function specifying the delay corresponding to the associated action. Sequential composition (prefix) is mapped onto convolution and choice is mapped onto the convex combination of the respective distributions. In order to calculate performance measures an execution tree (derivative tree) is formed and the appropriate distribution is associated with each branch together with the probability that the branch is executed. An alternative approach to performance evaluation is via the use of a simulation model developed by associating suitable terms from an algebra of routines with each agent in the canonical representation. In subsequent work, [55], the canonical representation was revised to be a variant of CCS, in which a strict one-to-one correspondence between conjugate ports is enforced and synchronising τ actions are labelled by the action they replace.

Later work by Zic, [57], advocates the use of a variant of Timed CSP for performance analysis of protocol specifications. In this approach *stochastic determinism* is introduced as an operator over the traces generated by Timed CSP processes. This generative probabilistic choice ensures fairness and allows reasoning about the probability of event sequences such as breakdowns and failures. In this way it is proposed that designers may specify acceptable error probabilities and use the specification to ensure that these are not exceeded.

2.5.2 TIPP

The work on the language TIPP (TImed Process for Performance Evaluation), developed in Herzog's group at Erlangen, is the closest to the work presented in this thesis. This work has been motivated by a desire to encourage the timely consideration of performance characteristics of developing systems, particularly distributed systems [4]. Herzog recognised that process algebras are well-suited to modelling such systems due to their inherent compositionality.

The initial work was carried out with a process algebra EXL which was a variant of CSP in which a random variable is associated with each event and a probabilistic choice operator replaces non-deterministic choice [4]. This language evolved into TIPP.

The language captures three basic patterns of interaction of behaviours—sequential execution, rivalry and concurrent execution—and these are represented by the combinators of the language—prefix, choice and parallel composition respectively. A distribution function F_a is associated with each action a, and is regarded as a fixed property of the action, i.e. all instances of a have the same distribution function. In general no assumptions are made about the nature of the distribution function but in later papers a subset of the language, in which all times are assumed to be exponentially distributed, is discussed [1]. The core language also includes a hiding operator and a recursion operation. Extended versions of the language have also been studied and these included probabilistic choice, sequential combination (;) and asymmetric synchronisation.

The operational semantics of the language is given in terms of transitions labelled by the action, the distribution of its delay and a natural number called the *start reference counter*. This is used to indicate the number of completed lifetimes an interrupted process has witnessed. These additional labels are unnecessary when the restriction to exponential distributions is made. Unlike work with PEPA, it is assumed that the semantic rules generate a graph as in CCS, rather than a *multigraph*. Thus in order to maintain the correct behaviour with respect to the probability distributions simultaneous instances of the same action are distinguished by supplementary labels [2]. When necessary these *left* and *right* labels may be concatenated in the natural way.

For the general language, the approach to performance analysis is similar to CUPID. Timing information is extracted from an execution graph of the model. Time distributions are attached to the arcs of this execution graph which is derived from the operational semantics. The execution time for any subtree can be calculated from the probability of the corresponding trace and the execution time for each branch, using the convolution and the convex combination of the distribution functions. A steady state analysis of an underlying stochastic process may be used when the distributions are all assumed to be exponential.

Work on TIPP has demonstrated the practicality of the process algebra approach to performance modelling. It has been shown that models developed in TIPP can be successfully used to derive functional and timing properties of systems such as a communication protocol and a multiprocessor system [1, 2].

2.5.3   CCS+

In [58] an extension of CCS is developed with the objective of reasoning about simulation models representing the performance of a system. This language, CCS+, is intended to give the semantics of simulation models thus providing more support for the rigorous development of simulation models than has been previously available.

The language is given an operational semantics in terms of three transition systems representing probabilistic, action and time evolution. Probabilistic evolution resolves probabilistic choices and assigns values to random variables representing delays within the system by drawing from appropriate distributions. Action evolution, resulting in *labelled* transitions, represents the computation of the system. The real time variables in the language represent simulation time, not computation time, and this is updated by time evolution.

It is intended that the language may be used to establish properties of a simulation once it has been written or to transform it into some more desirable form using formal rules at the syntactic level. Strong and weak bisimulation are defined for the language and are used for these purposes. A relationship between CCS+ expressions and generalised semi-Markov processes (GSMP) , a low-level representation sometimes used to reason about simulations, has been established.

2.5.4 Relating DEMOS to TCCS and WSCCS

Another use of process algebras in relation to discrete event simulation models is exemplified in the work of Pooley [59] and Birtwistle *et al.* [60]. This work aims at incorporating the analysis of functional properties of systems into the development of discrete event simulation models. In Pooley's approach a concise graphical notation is used as a high level representation of the system. This graph may then be automatically transformed into a program in the process interaction simulation language DEMOS [61], suitable for simulating the system and deriving performance characteristics. Alternatively it may be transformed into a TCCS expression which can be analysed to investigate the functional properties of the system, such as liveness. In Birtwistle *et al.*'s work, a more direct approach is taken deriving CCS expressions from simulation programs.

2.5.5 Performance Equivalence as a Bisimulation

A recent paper by Gorrieri and Rocetti [62] reports some preliminary work using a timed process algebra for performance modelling. A fixed time, specified as a natural number, is associated with each action. It is assumed that each agent has a local clock which it updates each time an action is completed. Whenever a synchronisation action occurs between two agents their clocks are brought into agreement. This corresponds to an assumption that the first agent arriving at the synchronisation will wait for the second. A bisimulation is defined if they are capable of the same actions in the same period of time—this is termed *performance equivalence*. Unfortunately this relation is not a congruence.

Chapter 3

Performance Evaluation Process Algebra

3.1 Introduction

This chapter presents the Performance Evaluation Process Algebra (PEPA). This language has been developed to investigate how the compositional features of process algebra might impact upon the practice of performance modelling. Section 3.2 outlines the major design objectives for the language. Most of the rest of the chapter is taken up with the subsequent informal and formal descriptions of the language, and a description of its use as a paradigm for specifying Markov models. Some simple examples are presented to introduce the reader to the language and its use in describing systems. This establishes PEPA as a formal system description technique. Presentation of more complex examples is postponed until Chapter 4.

The use of PEPA for performance modelling is based on an underlying stochastic process. It is shown that, under the given assumptions, this stochastic process will be a continuous time Markov process. Generating this Markov process, solving it and using it to derive performance results are presented and illustrated by a simple example. The relationship between PEPA and established performance modelling paradigms is discussed in Section 3.6.

3.2 Design Objectives for PEPA

An objective when designing a process algebra suitable for performance evaluation has been to retain as many as possible of the characteristics of a process algebra whilst also incorporating features to make it suitable for specifying a stochastic process. The aim is to develop a language in which the performance evaluation features can be regarded as an extension, offering the potential for the "basic" process algebra to be used as a design formalism with the performance model being developed by annotation of the design.

Several features of process algebras are regarded as being essential:

Parsimony: Process algebras are simple languages with only a few elements. This parsimony means that it is easy to reason about the language and provides a great deal of flexibility to the modeller. In PEPA the basic elements of the language are *components* and *activities*—these correspond to *states* and *transitions* in the underlying stochastic model.

Formal Definition: The language is given a structured operational semantics, providing a formal interpretation of all expressions. The notions of equivalence which are subsequently developed are based on these semantic rules. This gives a formal basis for the comparison and manipulation of models and components, and introduces the possibility of developing tools to automate, or semi-automate, these tasks.

Compositionality: The model structure provided by the compositional nature of process algebras, and the ability to reason about that structure, have already been highlighted in Section 2.4.3 as a major motivation for investigating the use of such a language for performance modelling. In PEPA the *cooperation* combinator forms the basis of composition. In the later chapters of the thesis we show that model simplification and aggregation techniques can be developed which are complementary to this combinator. This means that part of a model can be simplified in isolation, if its interaction with the rest of the system is modelled by such a combinator, and replaced by the simplified component without jeopardising the integrity of the whole model.

The main attribute which is missing from a process algebra such as CCS, and which is necessary for performance evaluation, is the *quantification* of time and uncertainty. The time associated with actions in CCS, for example, is implicit and the models are nondeterministic. In performance models, in order that performance measures can be extracted from the model, it is important that timing behaviour and uncertainty be quantifiable. This is achieved in PEPA by associating a random variable with each activity, representing its duration. This is presented in more detail in Section 3.3 when the language is described. A delay is thus inherent in each activity in the model and the timing behaviour of the system is captured. Moreover since the duration is a random variable, *temporal uncertainty* [28], the uncertainty of how long an action will take, is represented. As in probabilistic process algebras, nondeterministic branching is replaced by probabilistic branching—here the probabilities are determined by a race condition between the enabled activities. This represents so-called *spatial uncertainty*, the uncertainty about what will happen next within a system.

Thus adapting the process algebra to make it suitable for performance modelling is achieved by introducing a random variable for each activity within the system. Clearly, this may be regarded as an annotation of the pure process algebra model. The construction is analogous to the association of a duration with the firing of a timed transition in GSPNs and the other stochastic extensions of Petri nets.

3.3   The PEPA Language

In this section we describe the language PEPA in some detail, starting with an informal outline of the language and the syntax. Some examples of PEPA terms and their intended interpretation are presented.

3.3.1   Informal Description

In PEPA a system is described as an interaction of *components* and these components engage, either singly or multiply, in *activities*. The components will correspond to identifiable parts in the system, or roles in the behaviour of the system. They represent the active units within a system; the activities capture the actions of those units. For example, a queue may be considered to consist of an arrival component and a service component which interact to form the behaviour of the queue.

A component may be atomic or may itself be composed of components. Thus the queue in the above example may be considered to be a component, composed of the atomic arrival and service components. We assume that there is a countable set of possible components, $\mathcal{C}$. Each component has a behaviour which is defined by the activities in which it can engage. Actions of the queue might be *accept*, when a customer enters the queue, *service*, or *loss*, when a customer is turned away from a full buffer.

When talking about PEPA we use the term *activity* to distinguish it from the usual process algebra notion of an instantaneous *action*. Every activity in PEPA has an associated duration which is a random variable with an exponential distribution. In this thesis the term *action* will relate to the behaviour of the system.

Each activity has an *action type* (or simply *type*). We assume that each discrete action within a system is uniquely typed and that there is a countable set, $\mathcal{A}$, of all possible such types. Thus the action types of a PEPA term correspond to the actions of the system being modelled. If there are several activities within a PEPA model which have the same action type then they represent different instances of the same action by the system.

There are situations when a system is carrying out some action (or sequence of actions) the identity of which is unknown or unimportant. To capture these situations there is a distinguished action type, τ, which can be regarded as the *unknown* type. Activities of this type will be private to the component in which they occur. These activities are not instantaneous—each instance of an activity with action type τ will have an associated duration, as with any other type. However, unlike all other types, multiple instances of τ type activities within a PEPA model do not necessarily represent the same action by the system.

Since an exponential distribution is uniquely determined by its parameter, the duration of an activity, an exponentially distributed random variable, may be represented by a single real number parameter. This parameter is called the *activity rate* (or simply *rate*) of the activity; it may be any positive real number, or the distinguished symbol ⊤, which should be read as *unspecified*.

Throughout the thesis we adopt the following conventions:

- Components will be denoted by names which start with a large roman letter; for example, P, *System* or C_j.

- Activities will be denoted by single roman letters taken from the beginning of the alphabet; for example, a, b, or c.

- Action types will be denoted by small greek letters, such as α, β, etc., or by names which start with a small roman letter, such as *task*, *serve* or use_2.

- Activity rates will be denoted by single roman letters taken from towards the end of the alphabet, typically r, but also r_i, s, t etc. Occasionally the greek letters μ and λ will designate rates when a queue is being considered (the service rate and arrival rate respectively).

- The characters L, K, and M will typically be used to denote subsets of $\mathcal{A}$.

Thus each activity, a, is defined as a pair (α, r) where $\alpha \in \mathcal{A}$ is the action type and r is the activity rate. It follows that there is a set of activities, $Act \subseteq \mathcal{A} \times \mathbb{R}^+$, where $\mathbb{R}^+$ is the set of positive real numbers together with the symbol ⊤.

Some Terminology

When the behaviour of the system is determined by a component P the system is said to *behave as* P. The action types which the component P may next engage in are the *current action types* of P, a set denoted $\mathcal{A}(P)$. The activities which the component P may next engage in are the *current activities* of P, a multiset denoted $\mathcal{A}ct(P)$.

Note the distinction we make between action types and activities: the dynamic behaviour of a component depends on the number of instances of each enabled activity and therefore we consider *multisets* of activities as opposed to *sets* of action types. Throughout the rest of the thesis we will assume that collections of action types are sets, and collections of activities are multisets, unless otherwise stated.

When enabled an activity, $a = (\alpha, r)$, will delay for a period determined by its associated distribution function, i.e. the probability that the activity a happens within a period of time of length t is $F_a(t) = 1 - e^{-rt}$. We can think of this as the activity setting a timer whenever it becomes enabled. The time allocated to the timer is determined by the rate of the activity. If several activities are enabled at the same time each will have its own associated timer. When the first timer finishes that activity takes place—the activity is said to *complete* or *succeed*. This means that the activity is considered to "happen": an external observer will witness the event of an activity of type α. An activity may be *preempted*, or *aborted*, if another one completes first.

For each $a \in \mathcal{A}ct(P)$ there is some component P' which describes the behaviour of the system when P has completed a. This component P' is not necessarily distinct from P. We write $P \xrightarrow{a} P'$, or $P \xrightarrow{(\alpha, r)} P'$ to denote the completion of activity a and the subsequent behaviour of the system as P'. A more precise definition of $\xrightarrow{a}$ will be given in Section 3.3.7.

3.3.2 Syntax

Components and activities are the primitives of the language PEPA; the language also provides a small set of combinators. As explained in the previous section the behaviour of a component is characterised by its activities. However, this behaviour may be influenced by the environment in which the component is placed. The combinators of the language allow expressions, or terms, to be constructed defining the behaviour of components, via the activities they undertake and the interactions between them.

The syntax for terms in PEPA is defined as follows:

$$P ::= (\alpha, r).P \mid P + Q \mid P \bowtie_L Q \mid P/L \mid A$$

The names of these language constructions and their intended interpretations are presented in some detail below.

Prefix: $(\alpha, r).P$

Prefix is the basic mechanism by which the behaviours of components are constructed. The component $(\alpha, r).P$ carries out activity (α, r), which has action type α and a duration which is exponentially distributed with parameter r (mean $1/r$). The time taken for the activity to complete will be some Δt, drawn from the distribution. The component subsequently behaves as component P. If the component is $(\alpha, r).P$ at some time t, the time at which it completes (α, r) and becomes P, enabling all the activities in $\mathcal{A}ct(P)$, will be $t + \Delta t$. When $a = (\alpha, r)$ the component $(\alpha, r).P$ may be written as $a.P$.

It is assumed that there is always an *implicit resource*, some underlying resource facilitating the activities of the component which is not modelled explicitly. Thus the time elapsed before activity completion represents use of this resource by the component. For example, this resource might be bandwidth on a communication channel, processor time or CPU cycles within a processor, depending on the system and the level at which the modelling takes place.

Choice: $P + Q$

The component $P + Q$ represents a system which may behave either as component P or as Q. $P + Q$ enables all the current activities of P and all the current activities of Q, i.e. $Act(P+Q) = Act(P) \uplus Act(Q)$ (where $\uplus$ denotes multiset union). Whichever enabled activity completes it must belong to either $Act(P)$ or $Act(Q)$. Note that this is true even if P and Q are capable of the same activity since we distinguish between instances of an activity. In this way the first activity to complete distinguishes one of the components, P or Q. The other component of the choice is discarded. The continuous nature of the probability distributions ensures that the probability of P and Q both completing an activity at the same time is zero. The system will subsequently behave as P' or Q' respectively, where P' is the component which results from P completing the activity, and similarly Q'.

It is important to note that there is an underlying assumption that P and Q are competing for the same implicit resource. Thus the choice combinator represents competition between components.

Cooperation: $P \bowtie_L Q$

The cooperation combinator is in fact an indexed family of combinators, one for each possible set of action types, $L \subseteq \mathcal{A}$. The set L, the *cooperation set*, determines the interaction between the components P and Q. Thus it is possible that the component $P \bowtie_L Q$ will have quite different behaviour from the component $P \bowtie_K Q$, if $L \neq K$.

The cooperation set defines the action types on which the components must synchronise or *cooperate*. In contrast to choice, it is assumed that each component in a cooperation has its own implicit resource and that they proceed independently with any activities whose types do not occur in the cooperation set L. However activities with action types in the set L require the simultaneous involvement of both components (both resources) in an activity of that type. The unknown action type, τ, may not appear in any cooperation set.

All activities of P and Q which have types which do not occur in L will proceed unaffected. These are termed *individual* activities of the components. In contrast *shared* activities, activities whose type does occur in L, will only be enabled in $P \bowtie_L Q$ when they are enabled in both P and Q. Thus one component may become blocked, waiting for the other component to be ready to participate. These activities represent situations in the system when the components need to work together to achieve an action. In general both components will need to complete some work, corresponding to their own representation of the action. This means that a new *shared* activity is formed by the cooperation $P \bowtie_L Q$, replacing the individual activities of the individual components P and Q. This activity will have the same action type as the two contributing activities and a rate reflecting the rate of the slower participant, i.e. the expected duration of a shared activity will be greater than or equal to the expected durations of the corresponding activities in the cooperating components.

If an activity has an unspecified rate in a component, the component is *passive* with respect to that action type. This means that although the cooperation of the component may be required to achieve an activity of that type the component does not contribute to the work involved. An example might be the role of a channel in a message passing system: the *cooperation* of the channel is essential if a transfer is to take place but the transfer involves no work (consumption of implicit resource) on the part of the channel. This may be regarded as one component *coopting* another.

When the set L is empty, $\underset{L}{\bowtie}$ has the effect of parallel composition, allowing components to proceed concurrently without any interaction between them. This situation will arise quite frequently, especially in systems with repeated components. Therefore we introduce the more concise notation $P \parallel Q$ to represent $P \underset{\emptyset}{\bowtie} Q$. We will refer to $\parallel$ as the *parallel* combinator. Note, however, that this is only a syntactic convenience—no expressiveness is added to the language by its inclusion.

Hiding: P/L

The component P/L behaves as P except that any activities of types within the set L are *hidden*, meaning that their type is not witnessed upon completion. Instead they appear as the unknown type τ and can be regarded as an internal delay by the component.

Hiding does not have any effect upon the activities a component may engage in individually, but it does affect whether these activities can be fully witnessed externally. Normally, when an activity is completed an external observer can see the type of the completed activity. The observer will also have been aware of the delay while the activity took place, the length of time since the previous activity completed. A hidden activity is witnessed only by its delay and the unknown type, τ. Moreover such an activity cannot be carried out in cooperation with any other component. In effect the action type of a hidden activity is no longer externally accessible, to an observer or to another component. However the duration of an activity is unaffected if it is hidden.

Constant: $A \overset{\text{def}}{=} P$

We assume that there is a countable set of *constants*. Constants are components whose meaning is given by a defining equation such as $A \overset{\text{def}}{=} P$ which gives the constant A the behaviour of the component P. This is how we assign names to components (behaviours).

Suppose E is a component *expression* which contains a *variable* X. Then $E\{P/X\}$ denotes the component formed when every occurrence of X in E is replaced by the component P. More generally an indexed set of variables, $\tilde{X}$, may be replaced by an indexed set of components $\tilde{P}$, as in $E\{\tilde{P}/\tilde{X}\}$.

The precedence of the combinators provides a default interpretation of any expression. Hiding has highest precedence with prefix next, followed by cooperation. Choice has the lowest precedence. Brackets may be used to force an alternative parsing or simply to clarify meaning.

Brackets may also be used to clarify the meaning of a combination of components such as $P \underset{L}{\bowtie} Q \underset{K}{\bowtie} R$. Here the intended *scope* of the cooperation sets, L and K, is unclear. If the component is $(P \underset{L}{\bowtie} Q) \underset{K}{\bowtie} R$, R may then proceed independently for any action types in $L \setminus K$ and P and R must cooperate for any action types in K. However if the component is $P \underset{L}{\bowtie} (Q \underset{K}{\bowtie} R)$, R must cooperate with P to achieve action types in L and P may proceed independently for action types in $K \setminus L$. Thus brackets delimit the intended scope of the cooperation set. When brackets are missing we assume that the cooperation combinator associates to the left.

Consequently the cooperation between several different components using differing cooperation sets may be regarded as being built up in layers or *levels*, each cooperation combining just two components, those components possibly being formed from cooperations between components at a lower level. For example, the component

$$\left((P_1 \bowtie_{L} P_2) \bowtie_{M} P_3 \right) \bowtie_{K} \left(P_4 \bowtie_{N} P_5 \right)$$

can be regarded at the top level as $Q_1 \bowtie_{K} Q_2$ where, at the lower level, if $\equiv$ denotes syntactic equivalence, $Q_1 \equiv Q_3 \bowtie_{M} P_3$ and $Q_2 \equiv P_4 \bowtie_{N} P_5$, and at the lowest level $Q_3 \equiv P_1 \bowtie_{L} P_2$. Components at the lowest level, which do not contain a cooperation will sometimes be referred to as *atomic components*. Those at the top level will be referred to as *top-level components*.

3.3.3 Execution Strategies and the Exponential Distribution

A *race condition* governs the dynamic behaviour of a model whenever more than one activity is enabled. This means that we may think of all the activities attempting to proceed but only the "fastest" succeeding. Of course which activity is fastest on successive occasions will vary due to the nature of the random variables determining the durations of activities.

The race condition has the effect of replacing non-deterministic branching (as in CCS) with probabilistic branching. The probability that a particular activity completes will be given by the ratio of the activity rate of that activity to the sum of the activity rates of all the enabled activities. We may take advantage of this to represent a single action in a system by more than one activity in the corresponding PEPA model, if the action has more than one possible outcome.

For example, a component engaging in an action of type α with mean duration $1/r$, may have two different possible outcomes resulting from the action. In the PEPA model of the component this single action would be represented by two separate activities. The activity rates of these activities would be adjusted to capture the probabilities of the different outcomes. Thus a system which will perform an action of type α at rate r and then, with probability 1/3, behave as component P, and with probability 2/3, behave as component Q, will be represented by a PEPA component enabling two type α activities:

$$(\alpha, \frac{r}{3}).P + (\alpha, \frac{2r}{3}).Q$$

Whenever an activity completes, the behaviour of the model may change, as it takes on the behaviour of the resulting component. Any other activities which were simultaneously enabled will be preempted. This may have the effect of *aborting* the activity, or merely *interrupting* it, if it is also enabled in the new component.

Where the simultaneously enabled activities were sharing the same implicit resource the effect of the completion of one activity can be regarded as *preemptive restart with resampling*. In a preemptive restart strategy an activity which is preempted by the completion of another activity abandons its spent lifetime and starts another lifetime whenever it is next enabled (possibly at once). Without resampling the restarted activity will retain information about the abandoned lifetime and when next enabled restart another lifetime with exactly the same duration. If there is resampling whenever the activity is restarted it will make a fresh drawing from the distribution governing the lifetime, starting a lifetime with a new, randomly selected duration[1]. This means that any subsequent enabling of a preempted activity must

---

[1]Throughout the rest of the thesis *preemptive restart* will mean *preemptive restart with resampling* unless otherwise stated.

be regarded as a fresh attempt by that activity to acquire the resource and complete its work. An example of this would be activities which compete within a choice.

On the other hand the effect of preemption on simultaneously enabled activities working on different implicit resources will be *preemptive resume*. In a preemptive resume strategy a preempted activity will remember its spent lifetime and whenever it is next enabled it will resume from that point, only completing the remaining portion of its lifetime. The progress of the activity may be regarded as being interrupted by the completion of an activity in another component. However, whenever the activity is re-enabled it will *continue* from the point at which it was interrupted. This implies that information about the remaining lifetime of each such preempted activity must be retained. This strategy is applicable to the case of activities which are simultaneously enabled by different components within a cooperation.

Fortunately we can take advantage of the memoryless property of the exponential distribution: the time to the next event is independent of when the last event occurred. In other words how much longer the activity will wait before completing is independent of how long it has waited already. This allows a blurring of the distinction between the *preemptive restart* and the *preemptive resume* execution strategies and means that it is not necessary to retain information about the remaining lifetime of an activity in either case, as long as exponentially distributed delays are assumed for all activities.

3.3.4 Examples

In this section we present three simple examples, illustrating how the language may be used to describe systems.

Multiple Server Queue as a Single Component

Consider an $M/M/c/N$ queue, a queue with c servers and a buffer with capacity N, where $N > c$. We assume that customers arrive at a rate λ. As the queue is modelled as a single component we do not represent the customers directly but we assume that, when it is not full, the queue will engage in an *accept* activity at rate λ, representing the acceptance of a customer into the queue. When the queue is full, since the arrival process will not be suspended, the queue will be involved in a *loss* activity, losing a customer at rate λ. The service rate of each server is assumed to be μ so that when there are i customers in the queue, it will engage in a *serve* activity at rate $i\mu$, if $i \leq c$, and rate $c\mu$, when $c \leq i < N$. Let Q_i denote the component representing the behaviour of the queue when there are i customers present (including those in service).

$$Q_0 \stackrel{\text{def}}{=} (accept, \lambda).Q_1$$

$$\vdots \qquad \vdots$$

$$Q_i \stackrel{\text{def}}{=} (accept, \lambda).Q_{i+1} + (serve, i\mu).Q_{i-1} \qquad 1 \leq i < c$$

$$\vdots \qquad \vdots$$

$$Q_j \stackrel{\text{def}}{=} (accept, \lambda).Q_{j+1} + (serve, c\mu).Q_{j-1} \qquad c \leq j < N - 1$$

$$\vdots \qquad \vdots$$

$$Q_N \stackrel{\text{def}}{=} (loss, \lambda).Q_N + (serve, c\mu).Q_{N-1}$$

Single Server Queue as Two Cooperating Components

Consider an $M/M/1/N/N$ queue, a single server queue with buffer capacity N, and customer population N. As in the previous example we assume that customers arrive at a rate λ. However the arrival process will be suspended when the queue is full as all the customers will already be present in the queue. We represent the queue as two interacting components: a *Server* and a *Line*. The behaviour of the *Server* is very simple. Whenever it is able it will engage in a *serve* activity at rate μ.

$$Server \overset{\text{def}}{=} (serve, \mu).Server$$

The *Line* models the buffer. When the buffer is not full customers will arrive at rate λ so the *Line* will engage in an *accept* activity at rate λ. When the buffer is non-empty a customer will be available for service at a rate determined by the server, so the *Line* will engage in a *serve* activity at an unspecified rate. $Line_i$ will denote the behaviour of the *Line* when there are i customers in the buffer.

$$Line_0 \overset{\text{def}}{=} (accept, \lambda).Line_1$$
$$\vdots \qquad \vdots$$
$$Line_i \overset{\text{def}}{=} (accept, \lambda).Line_{i+1} + (serve, \top).Line_{i-1} \qquad 1 \le i \le N-1$$
$$\vdots \qquad \vdots$$
$$Line_N \overset{\text{def}}{=} (serve, \top).Line_{N-1}$$

The *Queue* is formed by the cooperation of the *Line* and the *Server* for the *serve* activity:

$$Queue_0 \overset{\text{def}}{=} Line_0 \underset{\{serve\}}{\bowtie} Server$$

Simple Resource Usage System as Cooperating Components

Consider a simple system in which a process repeatedly carries out some task. In order to complete its task the process needs access to a resource for part, but not all, of the time. Thus the task can be regarded as being in two stages: the first requiring access to the resource, the second involving only the process. The resource meanwhile is continuously available except for a short period after it has been used during which it is reset and therefore unavailable.

We model the process and the resource as two components: *Process* and *Resource* respectively. The process will undertake two activities consecutively: *use* with some rate r_1, in cooperation with the resource, and *task* at rate r_2, representing the remainder of its processing task. Similarly the resource will engage in two activities consecutively: *use*, at a rate r_3 and *update*, at rate r_4.

$$Process \overset{\text{def}}{=} (use, r_1).(task, r_2).Process$$
$$Resource \overset{\text{def}}{=} (use, r_3).(update, r_4).Resource$$

$$System \overset{\text{def}}{=} Process \underset{\{use\}}{\bowtie} Resource$$

In this case it would be straightforward to model this as a single component:

$$System' \overset{\text{def}}{=} (use, r_{13}).\,((task, r_2).(update, r_4).System' \,+\, (update, r_4).(task, r_2).System')$$

$$\text{where } r_{13} = \min(r_1, r_3)$$

However, note that this does not reflect what is happening in the system as clearly as the first representation. Moreover, representing the components of the system as separate components in the model means that we can easily extend the model to represent a system in which there are two processes, independent of each other but competing for the use of the resource.

$$System2 \stackrel{\text{def}}{=} (Process \parallel Process) \underset{\{use\}}{\bowtie} Resource$$

3.3.5   Passive Activities

When the cooperation between components is unequal, possibly representing *cooption* or *coercion*, one component may be *passive* with respect to an action type. This will mean that all activities of that type enabled by the component will have an unspecified activity rate. These activities must be shared with another component, the other component determining the rate of this shared activity. A model will be termed *incomplete* if it has a component which is passive with respect to an individual action type, i.e. a passive action type is not shared or restricted by a cooperation set.

If more than one activity of a given passive type can be simultaneously enabled by a component, each unspecified activity rate must also be assigned a weight. These weights are natural numbers used to determine the relative probabilities of the possible outcomes of the activities of that action type. For example, if a component is passive with respect to action type α and if, when α is completed, the component may, with probability $w_1/(w_1 + w_2)$, subsequently behave as P, or with probability $w_2/(w_1 + w_2)$, subsequently behave as Q, the component will be represented as

$$(\alpha, w_1\top).P + (\alpha, w_2\top).Q$$

We assume that $(\alpha, \top)$ is an abbreviation for $(\alpha, 1\top)$. Also, if no weights are assigned we assume that multiple instances have equal probabilities of occurring.

The following inequalities and equations define the comparison and manipulation of unspecified activity rates:

$$
\begin{aligned}
r &< w\top & &\text{for all } r \in \mathbb{R}^+ \text{ and for all } w \in \mathbb{N} \\
w_1\top &< w_2\top & &\text{if } w_1 < w_2 \text{ for all } w_1, w_2 \in \mathbb{N} \\
w_1\top + w_2\top &= (w_1 + w_2)\top & &\text{for all } w_1, w_2 \in \mathbb{N} \\
\frac{w_1\top}{w_2\top} &= \frac{w_1}{w_2} & &\text{for all } w_1, w_2 \in \mathbb{N}
\end{aligned}
\tag{3.2}
$$

3.3.6   Some Further Definitions

Apparent Rate

As explained in Section 3.3.3, it may be convenient within a model to represent a single action of the system by more than one activity in the model. However to an external observer of the system or the model the *apparent rate* of activities of that type will be the same, since in the model the race condition ensures that the rate at which *an* α activity is done is the sum of the rates of all the enabled type α activities.

Alternatively a system may have multiple capacity to perform an action, as in the case of a queue with multiple servers and n customers waiting ($n > 1$). This would have the same apparent rate for the *serve* action type as a PEPA component enabling a single type *serve* activity which has a rate n times the actual service rate, as in the first example presented above. Thus we can see that the *apparent rate* at which an action type occurs will be of importance when comparing models with systems, and models with models.

Definition 3.3.1 *The apparent rate of action of type α in a component P, denoted $r_\alpha(P)$, is the sum of the rates of all activities of type α in $Act(P)$.*

1. $r_\alpha((\beta,r).P) = \begin{cases} r & \text{if } \beta = \alpha \\ 0 & \text{if } \beta \neq \alpha \end{cases}$

2. $r_\alpha(P + Q) = r_\alpha(P) + r_\alpha(Q)$

3. $r_\alpha(P/L) = \begin{cases} r_\alpha(P) & \text{if } \alpha \notin L \\ 0 & \text{if } \alpha \in L \end{cases}$

4. $r_\alpha(P \bowtie_L Q) = \begin{cases} \min(r_\alpha(P), r_\alpha(Q)) & \text{if } \alpha \in L \\ r_\alpha(P) + r_\alpha(Q) & \text{if } \alpha \notin L \end{cases}$

Note that an apparent rate may be unspecified: if P is defined as,

$$P \stackrel{\text{def}}{=} (\alpha, w_1\top).P_1 + (\alpha, w_2\top).P_2$$

then, by Definition 3.3.1 and Equation 3.2 the apparent rate of α in P is $r_\alpha(P) = (w_1 + w_2)\top$.

In contrast the apparent rate will be *undefined* for component expressions containing *unguarded* variables, i.e. variables which are not prefixed by an activity. Consequently we do not allow a component to be defined by such an expression.

Current Action Types

It will be convenient to refer to the set of action types enabled by a component P, denoted $\mathcal{A}(P)$. When the system is behaving as component P these are the action types which may be observed when an activity next completes. The following definition shows how the set may be constructed for any PEPA component.

Definition 3.3.2 (Set of Current Action Types)

1. $\mathcal{A}((\alpha,r).P) = \{\alpha\}$

2. $\mathcal{A}(P + Q) = \mathcal{A}(P) \cup \mathcal{A}(Q)$

3. $\mathcal{A}(P/L) = \begin{cases} \mathcal{A}(P) & \text{if } \mathcal{A}(P) \cap L = \emptyset \\ (\mathcal{A}(P) \setminus L) \cup \{\tau\} & \text{if } \mathcal{A}(P) \cap L \neq \emptyset \end{cases}$

4. $\mathcal{A}(P \bowtie_L Q) = \left(\mathcal{A}(P) \setminus L\right) \cup \left(\mathcal{A}(Q) \setminus L\right) \cup \left(\mathcal{A}(P) \cap \mathcal{A}(Q) \cap L\right)$

Current Activities

The multiset of current activities of P, denoted $\mathcal{A}ct(P)$, will also play an important part in the analysis of a component P. When the system is behaving as component P these are the activities which are enabled. The following definition defines how this multiset may be constructed. We adopt the following abbreviations:

$$\mathcal{A}ct_{\setminus L}(P) = \{\!| \, (\beta, r) \in \mathcal{A}ct(P) \mid \beta \notin L \, |\!\}$$

$$\mathcal{A}ct_{\cap L}(P) = \{\!| \, (\beta, r) \in \mathcal{A}ct(P) \mid \beta \in L \, |\!\}.$$

Definition 3.3.3 (Activity Multiset)

1. $\mathcal{A}ct((\alpha, r).P) = \{\!| \, (\alpha, r) \, |\!\}$

2. $\mathcal{A}ct(P + Q) = \mathcal{A}ct(P) \uplus \mathcal{A}ct(Q)$

3. $\mathcal{A}ct(P/L) = \mathcal{A}ct_{\setminus L}(P) \uplus \{\!| \, (\tau, r) \mid (\alpha, r) \in \mathcal{A}ct_{\cap L}(P) \, |\!\}$

4. $\mathcal{A}ct(P \bowtie_{L} Q) = \mathcal{A}ct_{\setminus L}(P) \uplus \mathcal{A}ct_{\setminus L}(Q) \uplus$
   $$\{\!| \, (\alpha, r) \mid \alpha \in L, \, \exists \, (\alpha, r_1) \in \mathcal{A}ct_{\cap L}(P), \, \exists \, (\alpha, r_2) \in \mathcal{A}ct_{\cap L}(Q),$$
   $$r = \frac{r_1}{r_\alpha(P)} \frac{r_2}{r_\alpha(Q)} \min(r_\alpha(P), r_\alpha(Q)) \, |\!\}$$

3.3.7   Formal Definition: Operational Semantics

The semantics of PEPA, presented in the structured operational semantics style of [32], are shown in Figure 3.1. The operational rules are to be read as follows: if the transition(s) above the inference line can be inferred, then we can infer the transition below the line. The rules outline the activities which a component can witness—each activity completion brings about a transition in the system. Time is not represented explicitly in the rules but it is assumed for each one that an activity takes some time to complete and consequently each transition represents some advance of time. All activities are assumed to be *(time) homogeneous* meaning that the rate and type of an activity are independent of the time at which it occurs. Also the activity set of a component is assumed to be independent of time, i.e. $\mathcal{A}ct(P)$ does not depend upon the time at which it is considered.

The rules are straightforward and are presented without comment except for the third rule for cooperation, the rule defining shared activities. The apparent rate of a shared action type (i.e. $\alpha \in L$) in the component $E \bowtie_{L} F$ is taken to be the slower of the apparent rates of that action type in E and F. It is assumed that in general both components of a cooperation will need to complete some work, as reflected by their own version of the activity, for the shared activity to be completed. In the case where the apparent rate is unspecified in one component the apparent rate will be completely determined by the other component.

Recall that multiple instances of the same action type within a component may be used to represent different possible outcomes. We assume independence between the choice of outcome made by each of the cooperating components and choose the rate of each shared activity to maintain the same probability of outcome in each of the components. For example, for an instance of action type α in $\mathcal{A}ct(E)$, say (α, r_1), the probability, given that an α type activity occurs, that this is the activity that completes, is $r_1/r_\alpha(E)$. Similarly for an instance of action type α in $\mathcal{A}ct(F)$, say (α, r_2), the probability, given that an α type activity occurs, that this is the activity that completes, is $r_2/r_\alpha(F)$. Given that a shared α type activity has occurred in $E \bowtie_{L} F$ then, assuming independence of choice in E and F, the probability these two instances combined to form the shared activity is: $r_1/r_\alpha(E) \times r_2/r_\alpha(F)$.

Prefix

$$(\alpha,r).E \xrightarrow{(\alpha,r)} E$$

Choice

$$\frac{E \xrightarrow{(\alpha,r)} E'}{E + F \xrightarrow{(\alpha,r)} E'} \qquad\qquad \frac{F \xrightarrow{(\alpha,r)} F'}{E + F \xrightarrow{(\alpha,r)} F'}$$

Cooperation

$$\frac{E \xrightarrow{(\alpha,r)} E'}{E \underset{L}{\bowtie} F \xrightarrow{(\alpha,r)} E' \underset{L}{\bowtie} F} (\alpha \notin L) \qquad \frac{F \xrightarrow{(\alpha,r)} F'}{E \underset{L}{\bowtie} F \xrightarrow{(\alpha,r)} E \underset{L}{\bowtie} F'} (\alpha \notin L)$$

$$\frac{E \xrightarrow{(\alpha,r_1)} E' \quad F \xrightarrow{(\alpha,r_2)} F'}{E \underset{L}{\bowtie} F \xrightarrow{(\alpha,R)} E' \underset{L}{\bowtie} F'} (\alpha \in L) \quad \text{where } R = \frac{r_1}{r_\alpha(E)} \frac{r_2}{r_\alpha(F)} \min(r_\alpha(E), r_\alpha(F))$$

Hiding

$$\frac{E \xrightarrow{(\alpha,r)} E'}{E/L \xrightarrow{(\alpha,r)} E'/L} (\alpha \notin L) \qquad\qquad \frac{E \xrightarrow{(\alpha,r)} E'}{E/L \xrightarrow{(\tau,r)} E'/L} (\alpha \in L)$$

Constant

$$\frac{E \xrightarrow{(\alpha,r)} E'}{A \xrightarrow{(\alpha,r)} E'} (A \overset{\text{def}}{=} E)$$

Figure 3.1: Operational Semantics of PEPA

For any activity instance its activity rate is the product of the apparent rate of the action type in this component and the probability, given that an activity of this type occurs, that it is this instance that completes. This leads to the following rule:

$$\frac{E \xrightarrow{(\alpha,r_1)} E' \quad F \xrightarrow{(\alpha,r_2)} F'}{E \underset{L}{\bowtie} F \xrightarrow{(\alpha,R)} E' \underset{L}{\bowtie} F'} (\alpha \in L) \qquad \text{where } R = \frac{r_1}{r_\alpha(E)} \frac{r_2}{r_\alpha(F)} \min(r_\alpha(E), r_\alpha(F))$$

On the basis of the semantic rules PEPA can be defined as a labelled multi-transition system. In general a *labelled transition system* $(S, T, \{\xrightarrow{t} \mid t \in T\})$ is a system defined by a set of states S, a set of transition labels T and a transition relation $\xrightarrow{t} \subseteq S \times S$ for each $t \in T$. In a multi-transition system the relation is replaced by a multi-relation in which the number of instances of a transition between states is recognised. Thus PEPA may be regarded as a labelled multi-transition system $(\mathcal{C}, \mathcal{A}ct, \{\xrightarrow{(\alpha, r)} \mid (\alpha, r) \in \mathcal{A}ct\})$ where $\mathcal{C}$ is the set of components, $\mathcal{A}ct$ is the set of activities and the multi-relation $\xrightarrow{(\alpha, r)}$ is given by the rules in Figure 3.1.

3.3.8   Examples

Following these rules we can construct transition diagrams representing the possible behaviours of a component. The transitions are labelled by the activities which they represent. This is often a useful representation of a component, initially more illuminating than the defining equations. We consider each of the examples presented in Section 3.3.4 to illustrate.

Example 1 - $M/M/c/N$ queue

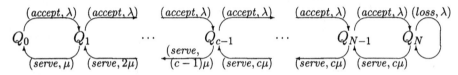

Example 2 - $M/M/1/N/N$ queue

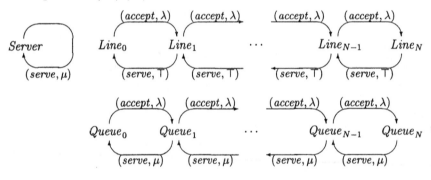

Example 3 - Processor/Resource System

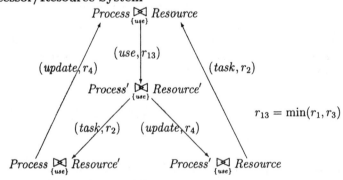

where $Process'$ and $Resource'$ are defined as follows:

$$Process' \stackrel{\text{def}}{=} (task, r_2).Process \qquad Resource' \stackrel{\text{def}}{=} (update, r_4).Resource$$

3.4 Basic Properties

If we envisage a graph in which language terms form the nodes and where arcs represent the possible transitions between them, then the operational rules define the form of this graph. We have already remarked that we distinguish between different instances of the same activity. As a result, the graph we consider is a multigraph—if there is more than one instance of an arc between terms we distinguish between them. This underlying graph, the *derivation graph*, describing the possible behaviour of any PEPA component, provides a useful way to reason about the behaviour of a model. First we make precise the notion of a *derivative* informally introduced in Section 3.3.1.

Definition 3.4.1 *If* $P \xrightarrow{(\alpha,r)} P'$, *then* P' *is a (one-step) derivative of* P. *More generally, if* $P \xrightarrow{(\alpha_1,r_1)} \cdots \xrightarrow{(\alpha_n,r_n)} P'$, *then* P' *is a derivative of* P.

These derivatives are the states of the labelled multi-transition system. We will often find it convenient to expand the definition of a component and name all the derivatives individually. For any PEPA component the set of derivatives (behaviours) which can evolve from the component can be defined recursively.

Definition 3.4.2 *The* derivative set *of a PEPA component* C *is denoted* $ds(C)$ *and defined as the smallest set of components such that*

- *if* $C \stackrel{\text{def}}{=} C_0$ *then* $C_0 \in ds(C)$;
- *if* $C_i \in ds(C)$ *and there exists* $a \in Act(C_i)$ *such that* $C_i \xrightarrow{a} C_j$ *then* $C_j \in ds(C)$.

Thus the derivative set is the set of components which capture all the reachable states of the system. We have already seen that the transition graph of a system can be a useful tool for visualising the possible states of the system and the relationships among them. This can be defined in terms of the derivative set of a system as the *derivation graph*.

Definition 3.4.3 *Given a PEPA component* C *and its derivative set* $ds(C)$, *the* derivation graph $\mathcal{D}(C)$ *is the labelled directed multigraph whose set of nodes is* $ds(C)$ *and whose multiset of arcs* A *is defined as follows:*

- *The elements of* A *are taken from the set* $ds(C) \times ds(C) \times Act$;
- $\langle C_i, C_j, a \rangle$ *occurs in* A *with the same multiplicity as the number of distinct inference trees which infer* $C_i \xrightarrow{a} C_j$.

The initial component C_0, *where* $C \stackrel{\text{def}}{=} C_0$, *is taken to be the initial node of the graph.*

The derivative set and derivation graph of a component expression, E, $ds(E)$ and $\mathcal{D}(E)$ respectively, can be defined in the intuitive way. Note that variables in the expression will form *leaves* of the derivation graph, and when the variable is instantiated the appropriate derivation graph is attached at that point.

It is occasionally necessary to refer to the complete set of action types which are used within the derivation graph of a system, i.e. all the possible action types which may be witnessed as a component evolves. This set will be denoted $\vec{A}(C)$.

Definition 3.4.4 *The* complete action type set *of a component* C *is*

$$\vec{A}(C) = \bigcup_{C_i \in ds(C)} A(C_i).$$

3.5   The Underlying Stochastic Model

In this section we explain how the derivation graph of a PEPA model may be used to generate a representation of the system as a stochastic process. Moreover we show that when the activity durations are assumed to be exponentially distributed random variables the resulting stochastic model is a continuous time Markov process.

The relationship between the structure of the PEPA model and the ergodicity of the Markov process is discussed, and assuming that a steady state solution exists, a method for solving the process is presented. In Section 3.5.6 we show how performance measures can be derived from a PEPA model. This is illustrated by an example in Section 3.5.7. In the following section, Section 3.6, we discuss the relationship between PEPA and other paradigms for specifying Markov models used for performance modelling.

3.5.1   Generating the Markov Process

For any finite PEPA model we take a naïve approach to generating the underlying stochastic process based on the derivation graph of the model. Recall that the derivation graph is a multigraph which has the component defining the model as its initial node. Each subsequent component, or derivative, is a node in the graph and there is an arc between nodes, labelled by the action type and the activity rate, for each possible transition between the corresponding components. To form the stochastic process a state is associated with each node of the graph, and the transitions between states are defined by the arcs of the graph. We assume that the model is finite so that the number of nodes in the derivation graph is finite.

Since all activity durations are exponentially distributed, the total transition rate between two states will be the sum of the activity rates labelling arcs connecting the corresponding nodes in the derivation graph, as shown in the following theorem. This use of the derivation graph is analogous to the use of the reachability graph in stochastic extensions of Petri nets such as GSPNs [17].

Theorem 3.5.1 *For any finite PEPA model $C \stackrel{\text{def}}{=} C_0$, if we define the stochastic process $X(t)$, such that $X(t) = C_i$ indicates that the system behaves as component C_i at time t, then $X(t)$ is a Markov process.*

Proof   By definition, $X(t)$ is a Markov process, if and only if, for $t_0 < t_1 < \cdots < t_n < t_{n+1}$, the joint distribution of $(X(t_1), X(t_2), \ldots, X(t_n), X(t_{n+1}))$ is such that

$$\Pr(X(t_{n+1}) = C_{j_{n+1}} \mid X(t_0) = C_{j_0}, \ldots, X(t_n) = C_{j_n}) =$$
$$\Pr(X(t_{n+1}) = C_{j_{n+1}} \mid X(t_n) = C_{j_n})$$

In other words, the past behaviour, and the future behaviour, conditional on the present behaviour, are independent. This can also be stated as follows:

> *The distribution of time until the next state change is independent of the time that has elapsed since the last state change.* $(*)$

For an arbitrary, finite PEPA model C, with underlying stochastic process $X(t)$, consider the *sojourn time* in an arbitrary state $X(t_i) = C_{j_i}$, that is the duration of a period spent behaving as component C_{j_i}. Let $S_i(t)$ denote the sojourn time distribution. Then $S_i(t)$ is the probability that a sojourn in the state corresponding to C_{j_i} has duration less than or equal to t. Recall that for each component C_{j_i}, $\mathcal{A}ct(C_{j_i})$ is the multiset of activities which are enabled when the system is behaving as component C_{j_i}. For each $a \in \mathcal{A}ct(C_{j_i})$, we define $S_{ia}(t)$ to be the *conditional sojourn time* distribution. $S_{ia}(t)$ is the probability that a sojourn in the state corresponding to C_{j_i} has duration less than or equal to t and ends by the completion of activity a. Note that the unconditional sojourn distribution is the sum of conditional sojourn time distributions:

$$S_i(t) = \sum_{a \in \mathcal{A}ct(C_{j_i})} S_{ia}(t)$$

We assume that the duration of each activity a is exponentially distributed with some parameter r_a, i.e. the distribution function for the duration of a is $F_a(t) = 1 - e^{-r_a t}$, which has density function $f_a(t) = r_a e^{-r_a t}$.

The enabled activities of component C_{j_i} are $\mathcal{A}ct(C_{j_i}) = \{ a_1, a_2, \ldots a_n \}$. Without loss of generality we assume that each activity in $\mathcal{A}ct(C_{j_i})$ is uniquely named, i.e. the multiplicity of each a_k in $\mathcal{A}ct(C_{j_i})$ is one. Then,

$$S_{ia_k}(t) = \int_0^t \left(\prod_{\substack{1 \le \ell \le n \\ \ell \ne k}} (1 - F_{a_\ell}(x)) \right) dF_{a_k} = \int_0^t \left(\prod_{\substack{1 \le \ell \le n \\ \ell \ne k}} (1 - F_{a_\ell}(x)) \right) f_{a_k}(x)\, dx$$

$$= \int_0^t \left(\prod_{\substack{1 \le \ell \le n \\ \ell \ne k}} (e^{-r_{a_\ell} x}) \right) r_{a_k} e^{-r_{a_k} x}\, dx = r_{a_k} \int_0^t e^{-\Sigma x} dx = \frac{r_{a_k}}{\Sigma} (1 - e^{-\Sigma t})$$

where $\Sigma = \displaystyle\sum_{\ell=1}^n r_{a_\ell}$. Hence,

$$S_i(t) = \sum_{a_j \in \mathcal{A}ct(C_i)} S_{ia_j}(t) = \frac{1 - e^{-\Sigma t}}{\Sigma} \sum_{\ell=1}^n r_{a_\ell} = 1 - e^{-\Sigma t}.$$

Therefore, the sojourn time in any state corresponding to a component C_{j_i} is exponentially distributed with mean $1/\Sigma$, where Σ is the sum of the rates of the current activities.

The memoryless property of the exponential distribution implies that the time until the system, behaving as component C_{j_i}, completes some activity, and starts to behave as some derivative C_{j_k}, is independent of the time that has elapsed since it started behaving as C_{j_i}. Thus the system satisfies condition $(*)$—the distribution of the time until the next state change is independent of the time that has elapsed since the last state change. Hence the stochastic process based on the derivation graph of a finite PEPA model is a Markov process.

□

3.5.2 Some Definitions

In this section we introduce the notation and terminology which will be used throughout the rest of the thesis to describe the Markov process underlying a PEPA model.

Exit Rates and Transition Rates

The *sojourn time* of a component C is an exponentially distributed random variable, whose parameter is the sum of the activity rates of the activities enabled by C. The mean, or expected, sojourn time will therefore be $\left(\sum\limits_{a \in Act(C)} r_a \right)^{-1}$.

We will generally find it more convenient to consider the related notion of the *exit rate* from C. This is the rate at which the system leaves the state corresponding to the component C. It is denoted, $q(C)$, and is defined as,

$$q(C) = \sum_{a \in Act(C)} r_a$$

This can be regarded as the rate at which the component C does *something*, or equivalently, the rate at which it completes an arbitrary activity.

The *transition rate* between two components C_i and C_j is denoted by $q(C_i, C_j)$. This is the rate at which the system changes from behaving as component C_i to behaving as C_j, or the rate at which transitions between the states corresponding to C_i and C_j occur. It will be the sum of the activity rates labelling arcs which connect the node corresponding to C_i to the node corresponding to C_j in the derivation graph, i.e.

$$q(C_i, C_j) = \sum_{a \in Act(C_i|C_j)} r_a$$

where $Act(C_i|C_j) = \{|a \in Act(C_i) \mid C_i \xrightarrow{a} C_j|\}$. Typically this multiset will only contain one element. Clearly if C_j is not a one-step derivative of C_i, $q(C_i, C_j) = 0$.

The $q(C_i, C_j)$, or q_{ij}, are the off-diagonal elements of the infinitesimal generator matrix of the Markov process, $\mathbf{Q}$.

$$Pr(X(t + \delta t) = C_j \mid X(t) = C_i) = q(C_i, C_j)\, \delta t + o(\delta t), \qquad i \neq j$$

Diagonal elements are formed as the negative sum of the non-diagonal elements of each row, i.e. $q_{ii} = -q(C_i)$. A steady state probability distribution for the system, $\Pi(\cdot)$, if it exists, can be computed by solving the matrix equation,

$$\Pi \mathbf{Q} = \mathbf{0}$$

subject to the normalisation condition, $\sum \Pi(C_i) = 1$.

The *conditional transition rate* from C_i to C_j via an action type α is denoted $q(C_i, C_j, \alpha)$. This is the sum of the activity rates labelling arcs connecting the corresponding nodes in the derivation graph which are also labelled by the action type α. It is the rate at which a system behaving as component C_i evolves to behaving as component C_j as the result of completing a type α activity.

The *conditional exit rate* will also sometimes be considered. This is the rate of leaving a component C via an activity of a given action type α. It is denoted $q(C, \alpha)$. It will be the sum of all activity rates for type α activities enabled in C. It is clear that the conditional exit rate of C via α is the same as the apparent rate of α in C, i.e. $q(C, \alpha) = r_\alpha(C)$.

Probabilities and the Embedded Markov Chain

The conditional probabilities of a component C ending a sojourn by completing a given activity a, or any activity of a given action type α, are denoted by $p(C, a)$ and $p(C, \alpha)$

respectively. These are defined in the natural way; for example, given that C completes an activity, $p(C, a)$ is the probability that the activity is an instance of activity a:

$$p(C, a) = \frac{r_a}{\sum\limits_{b \in Act(C)} r_b}$$

Transition probabilities may also be defined: $p(C_i, C_j)$ denotes the probability, given that C_i completes an activity, that the resulting derivative is C_j.

$$p(C_i, C_j) = \frac{q(C_i, C_j)}{q(C_i)} = \frac{\sum\limits_{a \in Act(C_i|C_j)} r_a}{\sum\limits_{b \in Act(C_i)} r_b}$$

If we disregard the period spent as component C_i and consider only those points in time when an activity completes we can define a (discrete time) Markov chain associated with the model. The $p(C_i, C_j)$, or simply p_{ij}, are the transition probabilities of this embedded Markov chain. Note that in general the equilibrium distribution of this Markov chain, if it exists, will differ from that of the Markov process from which it was derived, because the Markov chain disregards the amount of time the process remains in each state.

3.5.3 Stochastic Processes with an Equilibrium Distribution

Performance analysis is usually concerned with the behaviour of systems over an extended period of time. The system should have settled into some "normal" pattern of behaviour. The analogous statistical notion is the idea of *steady state* or *equilibrium*. This is expressed by the *global balance equations* $\Pi Q = 0$: the rate of flow out of any state is balanced by the rate of flow into the state.

To clarify when a PEPA model represents a system which has such a regular pattern of behaviour in the next section we establish the necessary condition which must be satisfied by the model if the underlying Markov process is to have an equilibrium distribution. First, some terminology is introduced.

A Markov process is *finite* if the number of states in the state space is finite. This does not restrict the behaviour of the process to be finite in the sense of operating for only a finite time. On the contrary the processes in which we will be interested exhibit infinite behaviour over a finite number of states. Similarly a PEPA model is *finite* if its derivative set contains a finite number of components.

A state in a Markov process, X_i, is called *persistent* or *recurrent* if the probability that the process will eventually return to X_i is one. Otherwise the state is called *transient*. In terms of a system, the recurrent states correspond to the behaviour which is repeatedly exhibited by the system whereas transient states correspond to a behaviour which will be no longer exhibited after a certain time. For example, in a queue in which arrivals occur more frequently than service, the empty state is transient as the queue length will grow unboundedly, never returning to this state after a certain time. A recurrent state X_j is termed *positive-recurrent*, or sometimes *ergodic*, if the expected number of steps until the process returns to X_j is less than infinity.

A Markov process is *time homogeneous* if the transition rates are independent of the time at which the transitions occur, i.e. $\Pr(X(t + \tau) = C_k \mid X(t) = C_j)$ does not depend on t. This implies that the behaviour of the system does not depend on when it is observed.

A Markov process is called *irreducible* if all states can be reached from all other states. If the process is not irreducible the state space may be split into separate classes of states; states within each class communicating with each other only. An initial choice by the process determines which class is entered and which set of behaviours will be exhibited. These classes of states, or sets of behaviours, can be studied separately as distinct processes. Further explanations of these terms, and the following theorem, can be found in Feller [63].

Theorem 3.5.2 (Feller) *A stationary or equilibrium probability distribution, $\Pi(\cdot)$, exists for every time homogeneous irreducible Markov chain whose states are all positive-recurrent. Moreover this distribution is the same as the limiting distribution*

$$\lim_{t \to \infty} \Pr(X(t) = C_k \mid X(0) = C_0) = \Pi(C_k).$$

3.5.4   PEPA Models with Equilibrium Behaviour

We assume that all PEPA models are time homogeneous since the rate and type of an activity are independent of time, as are the activities available within a component. Irreducibility is easily expressed in terms of the derivation graph of the PEPA model.

Definition 3.5.1 *A PEPA component is* cyclic, *or* irreducible, *if it is a derivative of all the components in its derivative set.*

$$C \in ds(C_i) \text{ for all } i \text{ such that } C_i \in ds(C)$$

A cyclic component is one in which behaviour may always be repeated—how ever the model evolves from this component it will always eventually return to this component and this set of behaviours. In particular this means that for every choice, whichever component is chosen the model must eventually return to the point where the choice can be made again, possibly with a different outcome. If we consider the layering imposed on a component by cooperation combinators, this implies that choice combinators may only be introduced at the lowest level of a cyclic component. In other words, a component which involves a choice combinator may subsequently be used in a cooperation, but a component involving a cooperation may not be subsequently used in a choice.

For example, consider the component $C \stackrel{def}{=} C_1 + C_2$ in which C_1 is $P_0 \bowtie_L Q_0$ and C_2 is $R_0 \bowtie_K S_0$. Whichever component C_i first completes an activity the component will then behave as C_i, C_1 say. All derivatives of C_1 must have the form $C_1' \equiv P_i \bowtie_L Q_j$ for some $P_i \in ds(P_0)$ and $Q_j \in ds(Q_0)$.

The component C is cyclic only if $C_1 + C_2 \in ds(C)$. This implies that there is some derivative of C_1 which is syntactically equivalent to $(P_0 \bowtie_L Q_0) + (R_0 \bowtie_K S_0)$, i.e. some P_i and Q_j such that $P_i \bowtie_L Q_j \equiv (P_0 \bowtie_L Q_0) + (R_0 \bowtie_K S_0)$. However this is not possible and it follows that C cannot be cyclic. Thus we deduce the following proposition.

Proposition 3.5.1 *If a PEPA component is irreducible then all choices must occur within cooperating components.*

This is as we would expect if we consider the implicit resources implied by the combinators.

A component $P+Q$ in which the choice cannot be revisited, i.e. $P+Q \notin (ds(P) \cap ds(Q))$, may be considered to generate two separate models corresponding to P and Q respectively.

Clearly there is a strong relationship between irreducibility in PEPA components and irreducibility in the underlying Markov processes. This is formalised in the following theorem.

Theorem 3.5.3 *The Markov process underlying a PEPA model is irreducible if, and only if, the initial component of the model is cyclic.*

Proof By the definitions whether the underlying Markov process is irreducible, and whether the initial component of a PEPA model is cyclic, both rely on the connectivity of the derivation graph of the model. Thus it follows that the Markov process will be irreducible if, and only if, the derivation graph is strongly connected, and this will be the case if, and only if, the initial component of the model is cyclic. □

If a Markov process that is irreducible has a finite state space all its states are positive-recurrent. Thus it follows from Theorem 3.5.3 that a finite irreducible PEPA model represents a system with steady state behaviour.

NB: Throughout the rest of the thesis we will only consider cyclic PEPA components unless otherwise stated.

3.5.5 Solving the Markov Process

As explained in Section 3.5.2, the component-to-component transition rates $q(C_i, C_j)$, or q_{ij}, are the off-diagonal elements of the infinitesimal generator matrix of the underlying Markov process, $\mathbf{Q}$. Assuming that the PEPA model is finite and irreducible, this process will have a steady state distribution $\Pi(\cdot)$, which may be found by using the normalisation condition and global balance equations:

$$\sum_{C_i \in ds(C_0)} \Pi(C_i) = 1 \qquad (5.5)$$

$$\Pi \mathbf{Q} = \mathbf{0} \qquad (5.6)$$

This distribution $\Pi(\cdot)$ is interpreted at the PEPA level as the equilibrium probability (or the long run relative frequency) of the model behaving as each of its derivatives. The probability that the model is behaving as derivative C_i is $\Pi(C_i)$.

The models presented in this thesis have been numerically solved using the computer algebra package Maple[2] [64]. The Equations 5.6 and 5.5 are combined by replacing a column of $\mathbf{Q}$ by a column of 1s and placing a 1 in the corresponding row of 0. Moreover, since Maple deals with row vectors instead of column vectors, this modified $\mathbf{Q}$ is transposed. The package solves this system of linear equations using algorithms based on Gaussian elimination. These algorithms are intended to cope with sparse systems, such as these Markov processes.

Since Maple allows symbols to be included in the matrix to be solved, it is easy to study the effect that varying the value of an activity rate has on performance characteristics. The use of computer algebra packages such as Maple and Mathematica for solving performance models has been advocated by several authors [65, 66, 67].

3.5.6 Derivation of Performance Measures: Reward Structures

We have shown in the previous sections how an underlying Markov process may be derived for any PEPA model, and how this process may be solved to find a steady state, or equilibrium, distribution $\Pi(\cdot)$. This distribution allows us to derive the probability, when the system has settled into a regular pattern of behaviour, that the system is behaving in the way characterised by some component of the PEPA model, C_i. We can regard this as the

---

[2]Maple is a registered trademark of Waterloo Maple Software.

probability that the system, observed at random when it has been running for some time, will be exhibiting the behaviour, or set of behaviours, characterised by C_i. Alternatively, this can be interpreted as the proportion of time that the system will spend behaving as component C_i.

Most performance studies are concerned with characteristics of the system which are not directly expressed in terms of the behaviour of a single component. However, performance measures such as throughput, average delay time and queue lengths can be derived from the steady state distribution, possibly considering a set of components or behaviours. In this thesis we will use the notion of *reward structures* to define the performance measures in which we are interested.

In the framework for reward structures introduced by Howard [68], rewards are associated with states of a Markov (or semi-Markov) process or with transitions between states. Rewards which accumulate continuously while a process is resident within a state are termed *yield functions*. The discrete rewards made when the process changes states are termed *bonuses*. We will adapt the reward structure based on yield functions to fit into the PEPA model world.

Reward structures are commonly used in the context of performability modelling, where reliability and performance aspects of a system are considered together [69]. However such structures may also be present, perhaps implicitly, in performance models. In queueing networks the extraction of performance measures is well-understood and can often be achieved without resorting to the underlying Markov process. In stochastic Petri nets several authors attribute a reward to certain markings in order to derive performance results from models, although this is not necessarily done explicitly. Examples of the explicit use of reward structures with stochastic Petri nets are stochastic Reward nets [70, 21], GSPN reward models [71] and stochastic activity networks (SANs) [72, 5].

As the emphasis of PEPA is on behaviour in terms of activities, rather than states, we associate rewards with certain activities within the system. The reward associated with a component, and the corresponding state, is then the sum of the rewards attached to the activities it enables. Performance measures are then derived from the total reward based on the steady state probability distribution. If ρ_i is the reward associated with component C_i $(\mathcal{A}ct(C_i))$, and $\Pi(\cdot)$ is the steady state distribution, then the total reward R is

$$R = \sum_i \rho_i \, \Pi(C_i). \tag{5.7}$$

In this way, the rewards can be defined at the level of the PEPA model, rather than at the level of the underlying Markov process.

Many performance measures of interest may be phrased in terms of some identifiable aspect of system behaviour. Therefore, since the behaviour of the system is associated with activities, many performance measures can be expressed by associating a reward with an activity or set of activities.

3.5.7 Example

To demonstrate the solution of a PEPA model and the derivation of performance results we consider one of the examples introduced earlier—the simple resource usage system.

$$Process \stackrel{\text{def}}{=} (use, r_1).(task, r_2).Process$$
$$Resource \stackrel{\text{def}}{=} (use, r_3).(update, r_4).Resource$$
$$System \stackrel{\text{def}}{=} Process \underset{\{use\}}{\bowtie} Resource$$

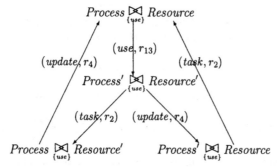

where $r_{13} = \min(r_1, r_3)$ and *Process'* and *Resource'* are the one-step derivatives of *Process* and *Resource* respectively.

Let the states of the underlying process be labelled $X_0, \ldots, X_3$, identified as follows:

$$X_0 \leftrightarrow Process \underset{\{use\}}{\bowtie} Resource$$

$$X_1 \leftrightarrow Process' \underset{\{use\}}{\bowtie} Resource'$$

$$X_2 \leftrightarrow Process \underset{\{use\}}{\bowtie} Resource'$$

$$X_3 \leftrightarrow Process' \underset{\{use\}}{\bowtie} Resource$$

The generator matrix, $\mathbf{Q}$, has the following form:

$$\mathbf{Q} = \begin{pmatrix} -r_{13} & r_{13} & 0 & 0 \\ 0 & -(r_2 + r_4) & r_2 & r_4 \\ r_4 & 0 & -r_4 & 0 \\ r_2 & 0 & 0 & -r_2 \end{pmatrix}$$

Solving the global balance equations, with the normalisation condition, using Gaussian elimination, we obtain:

$$\Pi(X_0) = \frac{r_2 r_4 (r_2 + r_4)}{(r_2 + r_4) r_2 r_4 + r_{13} r_2 r_4 + r_{13} r_2^2 + r_{13} r_4^2}$$

$$\Pi(X_1) = \frac{r_2 r_4 r_{13}}{(r_2 + r_4) r_2 r_4 + r_{13} r_2 r_4 + r_{13} r_2^2 + r_{13} r_4^2}$$

$$\Pi(X_2) = \frac{r_{13} r_2^2}{(r_2 + r_4) r_2 r_4 + r_{13} r_2 r_4 + r_{13} r_2^2 + r_{13} r_4^2}$$

$$\Pi(X_2) = \frac{r_{13} r_4^2}{(r_2 + r_4) r_2 r_4 + r_{13} r_2 r_4 + r_{13} r_2^2 + r_{13} r_4^2} \tag{5.8}$$

Suppose the activities have the following rates:

$$(use, r_1) : r_1 = 2 \qquad\qquad (task, r_2) : r_2 = 2$$
$$(use, r_3) : r_3 = 6 \qquad\qquad (update, r_4) : r_4 = 8$$
$$(use, r_{13}) : r_{13} = \min(2, 6) = 2$$

With these values substituted into the equations 5.8 we obtain:

$$\Pi(X_0) = \frac{20}{41} \qquad \Pi(X_1) = \frac{4}{41} \qquad \Pi(X_2) = \frac{1}{41} \qquad \Pi(X_3) = \frac{16}{41}$$

Suppose we wish to find the utilisation of the resource and the expected throughput of the process. The resource will be utilised whenever it is engaged in a *use* activity or an *update* activity. Therefore to derive the utilisation we associate a reward of 1 with each of these activities. Then, if ρ_i denotes the reward associated with state X_i, we see that

$$\rho_0 = 1 \qquad \rho_1 = 1 \qquad \rho_2 = 1 \qquad \rho_3 = 0$$

The utilisation, U, of the resource will be equal to the total reward:

$$U \;=\; \rho_0 \times \Pi(X_0) + \rho_1 \times \Pi(X_1) + \rho_2 \times \Pi(X_2) \;=\; \frac{25}{41} \;=\; 60.98\%$$

The throughput of the process will be the expected number of completed (*use*, *task*) pairs of activities to be completed per unit time. Since each activity is visited only once, this throughput will be the same as the throughput of either of the activities. The throughput for activity *use* is found by associating a reward equal to the activity rate with each instance of the activity. Thus, in this case, the rewards associated with states will be

$$\rho_0 = 2 \qquad \rho_1 = 0 \qquad \rho_2 = 0 \qquad \rho_3 = 0$$

Therefore the throughput, T, of the process is

$$T \;=\; \rho_0 \times \Pi(X_0) \;=\; \frac{40}{41} \;=\; 0.975$$

3.6 Comparison to other Modelling Paradigms

In this section we present a comparison of PEPA with the standard paradigms for specifying stochastic performance models. These paradigms, queueing networks and stochastic Petri nets, were reviewed in Section 2.2.1 and Section 2.2.2 respectively. More detail can be found in the literature: queueing networks are described in detail in [8, 9, 11, 12], while descriptions of stochastic extensions of Petri nets can be found in [22, 73] (SPNs), [17, 74] (GSPNs), and [19, 28] (SANs).

In order to compare the paradigms we will consider three aspects of the modelling capabilities which each offers: expressiveness and modelling power; techniques of model manipulation, transformation and comparison; and facilities for model solution and performance measure derivation. We will generally consider the whole class of stochastic Petri nets but in some of the following discussion it will be useful to distinguish between SPNs, GSPNs and SANs.

The most important difference between PEPA and both queueing networks and stochastic Petri nets is the notion of *flow*. In the standard paradigms the flow of entities within a system is represented explicitly as the flow of *customers* or *jobs* in queueing networks, and *tokens* in Petri nets. There is no corresponding notion of flow within PEPA models. Instead the focus is upon the activities of the system and the flow of jobs/information/control associated with these activities is implicit within the model. This difference pervades all aspects of the modelling process and is responsible for many of the differences outlined below.

3.6.1 Model Construction

Queueing networks are a compact notation in which many systems may be represented concisely. Models are described in terms of entities with embedded meaning. For example, *single server queue with preemptive restart priority queueing discipline, service rate μ*. Thus each modelling entity encodes a great deal of information. The variety of such entities is based on the six characteristics which define the behaviour of a queue: arrival rate, queueing discipline, service discipline, service rate, number of servers and buffer capacity. The sophistication of the notation has resulted in queueing network analysis, and consequently performance modelling, being regarded as a specialised topic.

The penalty for the compact notation is the limited expressiveness of the language. Most notably, queueing models cannot represent systems in which more than one resource must be simultaneously retained or in which there is internal concurrency. Work has been done to extend queueing networks to such systems [75, 76, 77], but the results have not been generally applicable.

In contrast Petri net notation and PEPA notation are much simpler, with only a few primitives in each case. These notations can be regarded as being at a lower level, closer to the Markov process they specify. As a result they are capable of representing a much larger class of systems.

In SPNs the entities of the notation are places, transitions and tokens. Markings and transitions correspond to the PEPA primitives, components and activities. In GSPNs there are additional language features—immediate transitions, and sometimes inhibitor arcs—but recent work has concluded that although these features offer a modelling convenience they do not increase the expressiveness of the language [27]. In SANs there are also *gates* and *cases* which modify the effect of transitions in state dependent ways. Such state dependent behaviour is modelled explicitly in PEPA activities.

The structure of a queueing network will often bear a close resemblance to the physical structure of the system being modelled. For example, the CPU and the disk subsystem will be modelled by separate servers, and the flow of jobs between them will be captured by the routing behaviour of jobs in the network. Thus the queueing network, although largely schematic in terms of the detailed execution of the model, provides a good representation of the structure and the dynamic behaviour of the system.

In contrast the graphical representation of Petri nets presents a clear image of the dynamic behaviour of the model but it provides little insight into the structure of the system. In the more complex notation of SAN, some of the intuitive appeal of the graphical notation is lost. PEPA does not provide a graphical notation but the component structure within the model will reflect the structure of the system being modelled.

A consequence of the lower level of model expression employed in Petri nets and PEPA compared to queueing networks, is that these notations are relatively verbose. This is particularly a problem in PEPA models where repeated components within a system and state dependent behaviour will be modelled explicitly. However the ability to define the components separately, compositional construction and abstraction mechanisms, help to alleviate this problem.

3.6.2 Model Manipulation

The facilities available for manipulating and reasoning about models vary widely. In queueing networks there is very little support for structuring models or developing them systematically. Some work has been carried out on hierarchical modelling based on queueing networks. However, this is largely intended to improve model tractability, rather than being a means of introducing structure into models (see Section 3.6.3). There is no well-established notion of when two models may be considered to be equivalent. Similarly, model validation, ensuring that the model is an accurate representation of the system, is often a problem.

Although the situation with stochastic Petri nets is slightly better, the support for reasoning about models is generally poor. There has been a great deal of interest in model decomposition, and hierarchical modelling but, as with queueing networks, this is largely motivated by tractability issues. Some work has been done on compositional model construction for SAN [5]. This approach is based on repeated structures within the system being modelled. Such subsystems are modelled as basic units which are subsequently combined to form complex models using the *replicate* and *join* operators. But in general, stochastic Petri nets do not support such a structured approach.

Recent work on *stochastic well-formed nets* (SWN) with symbolic markings has investigated the relationship between coloured Petri nets which have the same structure but different initial markings [78]. Otherwise there has been little work on when nets may be considered to be equivalent, except when the role of immediate transitions was under investigation [27].

In contrast PEPA, being based on a process algebra, is equipped with many facilities for manipulating, and reasoning about models. These facilities have been shown to allow models to be developed in a compositional way, complex models being systematically developed from smaller ones. Abstraction, as provided by the hiding operator, allows the internal details of components to be hidden and their interactions to be limited.

Comparing models is based on notions of equivalence defined in terms of the operational semantics. These formal rules also form the basis of model transformation techniques, based on term rewriting. The circumstances under which one component within a more complex component may be replaced by another without affecting the overall behaviour are established in this thesis. Since these model transformations are based on the operational semantics this suggests the possibility of tool support for model simplification.

3.6.3   Model Solution

As described in Section 2.2.1, a large class of queueing network models exhibit *product form* solutions. Based on this solution simple algorithms exist for computing most performance measures directly from the model parameters. Although this class is by no means comprehensive it provides the means for computationally efficient solution and is largely responsible for the popularity of queueing networks for performance modelling.

In contrast Petri net models are generally solved numerically at the level of the underlying Markov process. Some recent work has considered product form solution for SPNs [73, 23, 79, 80] and the direct derivation of performance measures such as throughput [81]. These results rely on restricting the synchronisations which can occur within the system. Under similar restrictions, PEPA models may exhibit a product form solution. However the modelling capabilities of such a restricted language are anticipated to be few.

The reliance on numerical solution means that stochastic Petri net models are prone to *state space explosion*—the large number of states needed to represent the underlying Markov process makes the model intractable. PEPA models may be expected to suffer from similar problems. However, we will show in Chapters 6, 7 and 8 that techniques exist to reduce the number of states required in the underlying Markov process to represent the model. Moreover these techniques do not require the generation of the original state space.

An alternative approach to the problem of state space explosion is the use of tensor algebra techniques for state space representation, as originally proposed by Plateau [82], and more recently by Buchholz [83].

Structure may be introduced in queueing networks using the technique of hierarchical decomposition. Here a structure is imposed after the model has been constructed to simplify model solution by solving subnetworks separately. This technique may be used to reduce a non-product form model to a product form one, by the use of a flow equivalent server, or other aggregation techniques. Similar techniques have been applied to GSPNs [24].

Unlike the situation in queueing networks, in stochastic Petri net models and PEPA models the performance measures are derived from the steady state solution of the underlying Markov chain. In GSPNs and SANs, as in PEPA, performance measures may be characterised by a reward structure [5, 27]. This reward structure relates possible behaviour of the process to specified performance measures. Typically this means associating a reward rate with each state. In a GSPN model these states will be the markings of the Petri net. In a SAN model the states are defined to be (*activity, marking*) pairs, where the *activity* is the last transition to have fired.

Queueing network models are only used for analysis of the performance related behaviour of systems. Stochastic Petri nets and PEPA are based on formal system description techniques: Petri nets and process algebra respectively. Consequently these models may also be analysed to investigate the functional, or qualitative, aspects of system behaviour.

Chapter 4

Modelling Study: Multi-Server Multi-Queue Systems

4.1 Introduction

In this chapter we present a modelling study demonstrating the use of PEPA for performance evaluation. Examples drawn from the modelling study will be used to exhibit the model simplification techniques developed later in the thesis. This study considers and compares various *multi-server multi-queue* systems. Such systems, an extension of the traditional polling system, have been used to model applications in which multiple resources are shared among several users, possibly with differing requirements. Examples include local area networks with multiple tokens, and multibus interconnection networks in distributed systems. Similar systems have been investigated in [26, 84, 85, 86, 87, 88].

A polling system consists of several queues and a single server which moves round the queues in cyclic order. These systems have been found to be good models of many systems which arise in computer network and communication scenarios, and consequently they have been extensively studied. A recent survey by Takagi [89] references over four hundred contributions.

A variety of extensions and modifications to the traditional polling system have been investigated [89], including non-cyclic polling, priority queues, and queues with feedback. One extension which is particularly suited to modelling innovative local area networks is the introduction of additional servers, each of which moves around the queues providing service where it is needed. These systems, sometimes known as *multi-server multi-queue* systems, are not readily amenable to queueing theory solution. Several suggested approximation techniques, based on queueing theory, and exact solutions based on GSPNs are reviewed in Section 4.3.1.

Multi-server multi-queue systems were chosen as the basis for the modelling study presented in this thesis because they are simply stated and easy to understand, although the extraction of performance measures is not a trivial problem. The subtlety of these systems lies in the dependencies that exist between queues—the congestion at each queue is dependent on the congestion at the other queues in the system—and between servers.

In the rest of the chapter we present the background of polling and multi-server multi-queue systems, and several models developed in PEPA illustrating some of their characteristics. Section 4.2 describes the major characteristics of polling systems and briefly reviews their solution. In Section 4.2.2, as an illustration, a PEPA model of a simple polling system is given, together with some numerical results. The additional characteristics of multi-server

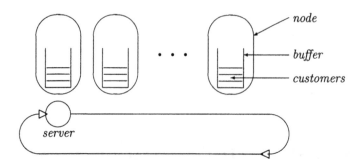

Figure 4.1: Schematic Representation of a Polling System

multi-queue systems are outlined in Section 4.3, which goes on to present an overview of the related literature. Finally in Section 4.4 various PEPA models of multi-server multi-queue systems exhibiting different characteristics are presented.

4.2   Polling Systems

The term *polling system* has evolved from the polling scheme used for data transfer between terminals and a central computer, using multi-drop lines. The central computer would approach each terminal in turn to ascertain whether it had any data to transmit. If so, the terminal would transmit the data and the computer would then interrogate the next terminal; if not, the computer would move on to the next terminal immediately. Subsequently polling systems have been used to model a wide range of applications characterised by scheduled, or demand-based, multiple access to a shared resource. In the example above each terminal has a scheduled opportunity to transmit data to the central computer.

In general, a polling system consists of a collection of *nodes* or *queues*, and a single *server* which circulates between them in cyclic order. Within each node *customers* requiring service are accumulated in a *buffer*. The server will visit each node in turn, providing service if the buffer is non-empty, but otherwise moving straight on to the next node. The time required by the server to move from one node to the next is known as the *walk* or *switchover* time.

It is important to make the distinction between polling systems and synchronous time division multiplexing (STDM) systems. In the latter the server will spend a predetermined amount of time at each node regardless of whether service is required, or completed, before moving on to the next node. As a result the congestion at each node in a STDM system is independent of the congestion at the other nodes, and each can be analysed separately as a single queue with server *vacations*. This is not the case in polling systems because the duration of a server's visit to a node will be dependent on the characteristics of the node, and the time until the server returns to the node will depend on the characteristics of the other nodes in the system.

The characteristics of a polling system fall into three categories: customer characteristics, polling characteristics and service characteristics.

Customer Characteristics

The behaviour of the customers is determined by the rate at which they arrive in the node, the *arrival rate*, and the amount of service that they require from the server when they are served, the *service demand*. These are standard characteristics of any queueing model. The interarrival time is usually taken to be exponentially distributed although other distributions have also been considered. Service demand has been variously assumed to be deterministic, exponentially distributed and generally distributed.

We also consider the number of customers who might be waiting for service at any time— this is determined by the *buffer capacity*. The two cases which have been treated extensively in the literature are infinite buffer and single buffer nodes, in which an unlimited number of customers may be waiting or only a single customer, respectively. However *K-capacity* buffers, in which K customers may wait, where K is some finite constant, have been studied. In the case of finite buffers, including single buffers, it is assumed that the arrival process is suspended when the buffer is full, or that any subsequent customers, who arrive before there is space in the buffer, are lost.

In some models it is assumed that a customer occupies a place in the buffer until service is complete, *restricted buffering*, while others consider a customer in service to have left the buffer, *relaxed buffering*. If the buffer is finite the distinction is important since the arrival process is suspended when the buffer is full.

Polling Characteristics

The characteristics of the polling are the amount of time that the server takes to move between nodes, the *walk* time, and the discipline that the server follows in deciding which node to visit next. Deterministic, exponentially distributed and generally distributed walk times have all been considered by various authors.

In general the polling discipline is assumed to be cyclic. However, several alternatives, motivated by applications, appear in the literature [89]. The polling discipline may be *deterministic, probabilistic* or *state-dependent*.

In deterministic polling disciplines each node has scheduled access to the server as in the cyclic discipline. However, how the schedule is formed may vary. For example the following have all been studied: systems in which the server alternates the direction in which it circulates between nodes after each visit to a fixed node; systems in which a base node is visited between each visit to the other nodes; and systems in which the server moves around the nodes according to some fixed order looked up in a polling table.

In probabilistic polling disciplines the route taken by the server is not pre-determined. Instead, when the server is leaving one node it will move according to some probability distribution. In the *random* discipline at each polling step the next node will be node i with probability p_i, where $\sum_{i=1}^{N} p_i = 1$, if N is the number of nodes. In the *Markovian polling* discipline routing probabilities between nodes are given in the form p_{ij}—this is the probability that when the server leaves node i the next node it will visit will be node j. The walk time between nodes may also be dependent on i and j.

In state-dependent polling the scheduling is in some sense *demand-based*—when the server moves from a node its decision of which node to visit will be based on the current state of the system. For example in the *greedy server* discipline a server will move to the closest node in which there is a customer waiting, and if the system is empty it will remain stationary. This is based on the *shortest-seek-time-first* discipline for moving arm disks. In the *threshold switching* discipline for two queue systems the server will stay at a queue until the number of messages waiting at the other queue passes a given threshold, or the difference in the queue lengths reaches a specified size.

A system is considered to be *symmetric* if all the nodes have the same customer characteristics (the nodes are statistically identical) and all walk times between nodes in the system are the same.

Service Characteristics

In all cases a server arriving at a node and finding an empty buffer will immediately walk on to the next node. If it finds a non-empty buffer it will immediately start serving the first customer in the buffer. The number of waiting customers which will be served during this visit to the node depends upon the *service discipline*. Possibilities which have been investigated in the literature are *exhaustive, gated, limited* and *decrementing* service.

In exhaustive service the server will remain at a node until there are no customers remaining to be served and the buffer is empty. In gated service the server will remain at the node until all the customers which were present at the instant when it arrived at the node have been served. Any customers which subsequently arrived will remain in the buffer until the next visit of the server. These are the more straightforward cases from a queueing theory point of view.

In k-limited service the server will remain at the node until k customers have been served, for some constant k, or until the buffer is empty, whichever occurs first. For example, in the case of 1-limited service, often termed simply *limited* service, the server will serve a single customer only before leaving the node. For k-limited, where $k > 1$, the discipline must be further qualified to be exhaustive or gated.

In the decrementing service discipline the server will remain at a node until the number of customers waiting in the buffer is one less than the number present when the server arrived at the node. A variation is the consideration of k-decrementing service, which must be further qualified, as above, to be either exhaustive or gated.

4.2.1   Solution of Polling System Models

The performance measure usually required from a polling system is the mean, or the distribution, of the *customer waiting time*. This is the time a customer spends in the system prior to starting service. If the system is asymmetric this measure will differ for different nodes and must be calculated separately for each node. Other measures of interest are the *mean polling time* (the average time it takes the server to complete a circuit of the system), the *mean customer sojourn time* (the mean time the customer spends in the system including time in service), the *system throughput* and the *mean queue length*.

Most of the work carried out on polling systems has involved queueing networks and direct manipulation of stochastic processes. There are many variations in the characteristics of polling systems and as a result many different techniques have been applied to their solution with varying degrees of success. In the last decade many complex and sophisticated techniques have been applied to the exact and approximate solution of these models.

Exact closed form solutions, solutions in which expressions for the performance measures are given in terms of the system parameters, have been found for symmetric infinite buffer systems with limited, exhaustive or gated service. Exact solutions based on the numerical solution of systems of linear equations have been given for single buffer systems (symmetric and asymmetric), and asymmetric infinite buffer systems with exhaustive or gated service.

Several approximation techniques have been proposed for systems which have not yielded to exact solution or for which exact solution is computationally expensive. These have generally been based on the independent analysis of each node as a queue with server vacations, the length of the vacations being found by analysis of the interaction between the queues. This interaction is estimated using the expected cycle time and the probability that the server finds each queue empty. Several authors have proposed iterative solution schemes based on these techniques.

There has been some work recently applying the GSPN modelling technique to polling systems [90, 91, 26]. In this approach a GSPN model of the polling system is used to generate a continuous time Markov process. This process is solved numerically to find the steady state solution, from which the performance measures are derived.

Limitations of this approach have been identified [91, 90, 89]—all buffers must be finite; all random variables used within the model must be exponentially distributed; and the state space of the underlying model grows very rapidly. The restriction to finite buffers, although in contrast to the established queueing theory approach, is often a more accurate depiction of the application being studied. Previously only approximate analysis of such systems had been carried out [91]. Using the method of stages it would be possible to use phase type distributions for walk times, interarrival times, and service demands within GSPN models. In contrast, the problem of state space explosion is a serious one and, without the application of simplification techniques, only moderately sized systems can be solved. The GSPN approach has the advantage that asymmetric systems are as readily handled as symmetric ones.

4.2.2   Example: A PEPA Model of a Polling System

In this section we present a PEPA model of a simple symmetric single-buffer polling system with relaxed buffering and limited service. The model is shown in Figure 4.2. The components of the model are the server and the nodes.

S_j denotes the server when it is present at the jth node in the system. On arriving at a node the server will query the node to see if there is a customer to be served. If so, it will remove the customer from the buffer in the node and service it before walking on to the next node; if not, it will walk on to the next node. Each node j has two distinct states depending on whether the buffer in the node is empty or full. These are represented by the two derivatives of the node component, $Node_{j0}$ and $Node_{j1}$. An arrival may occur only when the node is empty; in either state the node will respond appropriately to the server.

The activities represented in each node component are in, representing the arrival of a

$$Node_{j0} \stackrel{\text{def}}{=} (in, \lambda).Node_{j1} + (empty_j, \top).Node_{j0} \qquad\qquad 1 \le j \le N$$
$$Node_{j1} \stackrel{\text{def}}{=} (remove_j, r_N).Node_{j0}$$

$$S_j \stackrel{\text{def}}{=} (remove_j, r_S).(serve, \mu).(walk, w).S_{j\oplus 1} + (empty_j, e).(walk, w).S_{j\oplus 1}$$
$$\text{where } j \oplus 1 = 1 \text{ when } j = N$$

$$Polling \stackrel{\text{def}}{=} (Node_{10} \parallel Node_{20} \parallel Node_{30}) \underset{\{empty_j, remove_j\}}{\bowtie} S_1 \qquad\qquad \text{where } 1 \le j \le N$$

Figure 4.2: PEPA model of a symmetric polling system with relaxed buffering

in	*remove* (N)	*remove* (S)	*remove* (Polling)	*empty*	*serve*	*walk*
λ	r_N	r_S	$r = \min(r_N, r_S)$	e	μ	w
0.1–0.9	50	100	50	100	1	10, 15, 20

Table 4.1: Parameter values assigned to the PEPA polling model, *Polling*

customer to fill the buffer, *empty*, a response to a query from the server indicating that the buffer is empty, and *remove*, again in response to a query from the server but now occurring when there is a customer in the buffer and resulting in the removal of the customer by the server. The activities of the server include *walk* which moves it to the next node, and querying the node which is seen as an *empty* or a *remove* activity depending on whether there was a customer present at the node when the query takes place. If a customer is removed then the next activity is a *serve* activity—the server services the customer, before walking on to the next node.

The system we consider comprises three nodes, so that when the server leaves $Node_3$ it walks on to $Node_1$. The nodes are independent of each other, but each must cooperate with the server for any *empty* or *remove* activity. We assume that the rate of the *empty$_j$* activity at $Node_j$ is determined by the server, (the rate is unspecified in the node). In contrast the *remove$_j$* activity is assumed to require some work by both the server and $Node_j$, and its rate will be $r = \min(r_N, r_S)$.

The model has 72 states and 180 transitions. The values which were assigned to the parameters are shown in Table 4.1. The effect of varying the arrival rate of customers at the node on the mean customer waiting time, with three different rates for the *walk* activity, was investigated. The resulting graph is shown in Figure 4.3.

Since the system is symmetric we can use any one of the nodes to calculate the mean customer waiting time, W, as it will be the same in all the nodes. W is found by applying Little's Law to $Node_1$ to find the mean time to complete the activity *remove$_1$*. Little's Law states that the average number of entities in a system is equal to the product of the average rate at which entities arrive to the system and the average time an entity is resident in the system. This law holds for all systems in which these averages exist. The mean number of customers in the buffer, N, is found by attaching a reward of 1 to the activity *in* to calculate R_{in}. Then $N = 1 - R_{in}$: a customer is present whenever the *in* activity is not enabled. The throughput of the node is the throughput of the *remove$_1$* activity, X_{remove_1}, and this is found by attaching a reward r to the activity *remove$_1$*. In effect this associates a reward of r with all states in which the buffer in $Node_1$ is occupied and the server is present at the node. As the service takes place outside the node, unlike restricted buffering systems, the sojourn time of customers within the node is equal to the mean customer waiting time. Thus it follows from Little's Law that $W = N/X_{remove_1} = (1 - R_{in})/X_{remove_1}$.

4.3   Multi-server Multi-queue Systems

Polling systems in which there is more than one server concurrently active, *multi-server polling systems*, or *multi-server multi-queue* (MSMQ) systems, have been identified as a challenging area of further work on polling systems [92]. As yet there has been only limited work in this area [26, 84, 85, 86, 87, 88, 93].

A common application of these systems is to local area network architectures, based on ring

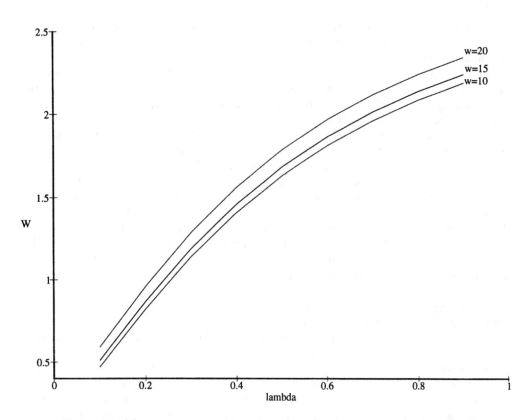

Figure 4.3: Mean customer waiting time plotted against customer arrival rate

topologies with scheduled access, in which more than one node may transmit simultaneously. These facilities are offered by slotted rings [86, 87], rings with multiple tokens [87] and insertion rings [86]. These models have also been used to study dynamic load sharing in distributed systems [85] and a multibus interconnection network in [84].

The additional features of the MSMQ system compared to a standard polling system provide additional service characteristics, relating to the interaction between servers within the system—the *service interaction characteristics*. We will assume that there are S servers present in the system.

Service Interaction Characteristics

The service interaction characteristics of a system are determined by the number of servers present in the system, how many of these may simultaneously attend a node, and whether overtaking is permitted.

Different policies have been considered in the literature for how many servers may be simultaneously occupied at a node, arising from the different system characteristics. In some cases only one server is allowed to be present at a queue at any given time, sometimes called the $Q \times 1$ policy. Alternatively there may be no restriction on the number of servers which may be occupied at a node, with any number, up to S, providing service to different customers at the node at the same time—the $Q \times S$ policy (in this case $K \geq S$ for buffer capacity K). Other policies, $Q \times m$, may also be considered where $1 < m < S, 1 < m \leq K$.

When a server arrives at a node there is the possibility that it will find another server already present and will not be able to provide service to the node: either due to the simultaneous service policy or because there are no customers in the buffer needing service. If overtaking is allowed the second server will immediately poll the next node, starting a fresh walk as soon as it realises that there is nothing for it to do at the current node. If overtaking is not allowed the second server will remain blocked at the node until the first has finished, at which time it will either provide service or walk on, depending on whether there is a customer present to be served.

The final feature which may be considered is the positional relationship between servers. Most authors have considered the movement of each server to be independent of other servers in the system except when blocked, if overtaking is not allowed. An alternative is suggested by Bunday and Khorran [94]. They consider a system of N machines served cyclically by two robot repairmen whose movement maintains constant, equal separation between them.

An MSMQ system is *symmetric with respect to nodes* if all the nodes have the same customer characteristics; it is *symmetric with respect to servers* if all the servers are statistically identical; and the system is *symmetric* if it is symmetric with respect to both nodes and servers.

Modified Kendall Notation for MSMQ Systems

Ajmone Marsan *et al.* [26] propose a compact notation for classifying MSMQ systems, derived from Kendall's notation for queueing systems. We will adopt this notation, with some minor variations, when describing the MSMQ systems considered in the rest of this chapter. Six short descriptors, $A/S/W/K/Q \times c/SD$, arranged in a set order are used to classify the system. These descriptors are:

1. The distribution of customer interarrival times. As in queueing systems the indicators M, D or G are used to signify exponential, deterministic or general distributions respectively. A subscript i is used to indicate that the rate is dependent on the node.

2. The service time distribution (M, D, or G). As with interarrival time this may vary between nodes and if so a subscript will be used.

3. The walk time distribution (M, D, or G). This also may differ between nodes, and this will be indicated in the usual way.

4. The capacity of the nodes, K. If the nodes have differing buffer capacities this will be a vector $\vec{K}$, the ith element of which indicates the capacity of the buffer in the ith node.

5. The simultaneous service policy, for example $Q \times 1$, or $Q \times S$.

6. The service discipline determining how many customers are serviced by each visit of each server to each node. We use L, E, and G to signify limited, exhaustive, and gated service respectively.

Thus, for example, $M_i/G/D/\vec{K}/Q \times 1/L$ identifies an MSMQ system with N nodes, with limited capacity depending on the node, Poisson arrival with node-dependent rates, S servers with general node-independent service times, constant walk times and a limited service discipline with the $Q \times 1$ simultaneous service policy. Other characteristics, such as whether overtaking is allowed, will be stated in words.

4.3.1 Solutions of Multi-Server Multi-Queue Systems

Models of MSMQ systems have proved difficult to analyse because, as well as the interaction noted between nodes in polling systems, interaction between servers must also be taken into account. The performance measures of interest for these systems are the same as in polling systems. The only exact results for the mean customer waiting time have been recently derived by Ajmone Marsan *et al.* [26] using a GSPN model. In that paper GSPN models of $M_i/M_i/M_i/\vec{K}/Q \times S/L$ systems with overtaking are discussed, but the models solved are of the form $M_i/M/M/\{1, 2, K\}/Q \times \{1, S\}/L$. The Markov process underlying the SPN is solved numerically to find the steady state probability distribution, from which the average throughput, and the average number of waiting customers, for each node are derived. Thus, applying Little's Law, the mean customer sojourn time, and the mean customer waiting time are calculated. The authors show that the number of states in the underlying Markov process grows very rapidly. For example, for a system with two servers and four nodes the number of states is 312, whereas doubling the number of nodes, while keeping just two servers, the number of states is increased to 19200.

Other authors have proposed various approximation techniques for finding the mean waiting time for customers in MSMQ models. However these models have all differed in their detailed operation and so it is difficult to compare the approaches. Most make some assumption of independence in the behaviour of the servers within the system. In each case the results are compared to the results obtained from a simulation of the same model. In general the results obtained by analysis are within 10–15% of the simulation results for low to medium loads. The notable exception is the technique suggested by Kamal and Hamacher [86] for which the results fall within the confidence interval of the simulation. The model they study is a $M/G/G/\infty/Q \times 1/L$ system which allows overtaking. It is intended to represent slotted ring or partial insertion ring local area networks.

The authors consider three distinct "cycles" within the system: the *server cycle*, the *node cycle* and the *server-node cycle*. Approximate expressions are derived, relating the server and node cycles to the server-node cycle and then an iterative procedure with these two expressions is used to find the node cycle time. This is then used in the solution of a $M/G/1$ system with vacations to find the mean waiting time at an arbitrary node.

Morris and Wang [85], also base their analysis of a $M_i/G/G/\infty/Q \times S/\{L, G\}$ system on expressions for the cycle times within the system. Their system, intended to model dynamic load sharing in a distributed system, has relaxed buffering. A server arriving at a node removes at once from the buffer all the customers that it will serve at this visit. These customers are kept together until all the service is completed, at which point they depart the system together. Conservation of work arguments and an assumption of server independence are used to derive an expression for the mean cycle time in terms of the mean walk time and the offered load. By a similar argument the mean inter-visit time is also derived. The average customer sojourn time in the system is then estimated, using an approximation based on the distribution of the inter-visit times. Both symmetric and asymmetric systems are considered.

The papers by Yang *et al.* [87], and Yuk and Palais [88], present similar approaches to the solution of MSMQ systems. In both cases assumptions about the independent movement of servers are made. The mean sojourn time of a customer is derived by consideration of the separate components of the time—latency until a server returns to the node; the service time of the customers ahead in the buffer; and the service of the customer. A gated $M/G/1$ queueing model is used. The system considered by Yang *et al.* is a $M/G/D/\infty/Q \times 1/L$ MSMQ system. It is used to represent multiple token ring and multiple slotted ring local area networks. The authors investigate the *single buffer/single transmission* protocol for these rings. In the paper by Yuk and Palais an $M/M/D/\infty/Q \times S/E$ MSMQ system is considered. This represents a token ring local area network with multichannel topology. The model is used to assess different strategies for token release within the ring. In the first case the token is released by the receiving station. In the second the token is released by the transmitting station when the transmitted message returns.

The system considered by Raith [84], falls within the $M_i/G/G/\vec{K}/Q \times 1/L$ classification but is unusual as each node contains an input and an output buffer. The system models the multibus interconnection network in a distributed system, the nodes representing the communicating units, the servers representing the buses and the customers representing the messages. A node may simultaneously transmit on one bus and receive on another but it is limited to only one interaction of each type at once. If the input buffer of the receiving node is full the transmission will be blocked and the model is used to investigate two possible strategies in this case. In the first strategy the transmission is abandoned; in the second the server remains occupied at the transmitting node until it is possible to complete the transmission. Assuming independent movement of servers around the system, the inter-visit time to an arbitrary node is approximated. This is then used to form an embedded Markov chain which is solved numerically.

Several authors note that the assumption of independent movement of servers, or equivalently uniform distribution of servers within the system, is a poor one [85, 87]. Observation of simulation models reveals that the servers tend to *coalesce* and progress around the system together. Morris and Wang show that if cyclic polling is replaced by *dispersive* scheduling the results of their model compares more favourably with simulation.

4.4   Examples: PEPA Models of MSMQ Systems

In the final section of this chapter we present PEPA models of several MSMQ systems exhibiting different characteristics. For ease of presentation the systems considered are relatively small, comprising of only three or four nodes and two servers in each case. However, it is straightforward to generalise these models to larger systems. In each case we consider the average waiting time (excluding service time) experienced by a customer in the system. The models all have several characteristics in common which are discussed in Section 4.4.1. The following subsections contain the detailed information about the operation of each model, the parameter values which were applied and one or more graphs showing how the mean waiting time varies as the conditions within the system are changed.

4.4.1 Introduction

Although the detailed characteristics of the systems considered differ, they all have the same components—nodes and servers. In addition in the model in Section 4.4.5 we introduce a component external to the node to represent the generation of customers.

In all the models the arrival process is represented by an *in* activity by the node, and it is assumed that the arrival process is suspended whenever the buffer is full. Buffering is assumed to be restricted in all the models, so customers continue to occupy a place in the buffer until service is completed. In most cases the nodes have only a single place buffer, but in Section 4.4.4 a two place buffer is considered.

All the node components have separate derivatives depicting the different states of the node, as characterised by the activities it may undertake. For example, a single buffer node may only perform an *in* activity when it is empty, and a *serve* activity when it is occupied, and a server is present. Three of the models are symmetric with respect to servers, and two of them are symmetric with respect to nodes.

For each of the models we calculate the mean waiting time of a customer at each node. As with the polling model presented in Section 4.2.2 this is found by applying Little's Law to the node. As the buffering is restricted the throughput of the node will be the throughput of the *serve* activity, calculated by attaching a reward equal to the activity rate to the *serve* activity. For a single buffer node the mean number present in the node, N, can be found by associating a reward of 1 with the *in* activity, as previously, to form R_{in}. Then $N = 1 - R_{in}$. For the two place buffer the mean number of customers is found by finding the probability that the node is empty, or only singly occupied in a similar way.

4.4.2 MSMQ System with Cyclic Polling, Without Overtaking

First we consider a symmetric MSMQ system in which polling is cyclic but where servers cannot overtake each other. Thus a server which arrives at a node to find the other server already serving a customer must wait until the service is complete before moving on to the next node. This system can be classified as an $M/M/M/1/Q \times 1/L$ system. The PEPA model is shown in Figure 4.4.

S_j denotes a server when it is ready to approach $Node_j$, S_{j1} denotes a server present at $Node_j$. When it arrives at the node the server will either *pass*, if the buffer is unoccupied, or *engage*, if there is a customer requiring service. Note that at most one of these activities will be enabled at any given time.

The system we consider has three nodes. The nodes are independent of each other but each must cooperate with a server for any $pass_j$, $engage_j$ or $serve_j$ activity. The two servers are independent of each other, in the sense that there is no cooperation between them.

The model has 444 states and 1446 transitions. The values which were assigned to the parameters are shown in Table 4.2. As for the polling model presented in Section 4.2.2, the

$$Node_{j0} \stackrel{\text{def}}{=} (in, \lambda).Node_{j1} + (pass_j, e).Node_{j0} \qquad\qquad 1 \leq j \leq N$$
$$Node_{j1} \stackrel{\text{def}}{=} (engage_j, e).(serve_j, \mu).Node_{j0}$$

$$S_j \stackrel{\text{def}}{=} (walk, \omega).S_{j1}$$
$$S_{j1} \stackrel{\text{def}}{=} (pass_j, \top).S_{j\oplus1} + (engage_j, e).(serve_j, \top).S_{j\oplus1}$$

$$\text{where } j \oplus 1 = 1 \text{ when } j = N$$

when $N = 3$:

$$MSMQ1 \stackrel{\text{def}}{=} (Node_{10} \parallel Node_{20} \parallel Node_{30}) \underset{\substack{\{engage_j, \\ pass_j, serve_j\}}}{\bowtie} (S_1 \parallel S_1) \qquad \text{where } 1 \leq j \leq N$$

Figure 4.4: PEPA model of a symmetric MSMQ system without overtaking

	in	$serve$	$walk$	$pass$	$engage$
	λ	μ	ω	e	e
0.1, 0.2, 0.3, 0.4, 0.5	1.0	10	50	50

Table 4.2: Parameter values assigned to the models, *MSMQ1* and *Poll*

effect of varying the arrival rate on the mean waiting time experienced by customers was investigated, and this was compared with the mean waiting time experienced in the related polling model:

$$Poll \stackrel{\text{def}}{=} (Node_{10} \parallel Node_{20} \parallel Node_{30}) \underset{\substack{\{engage_j, \\ pass_j, serve_j\}}}{\bowtie} S_1$$

Since the system is symmetric the performance characteristics of all the nodes will be the same. A graph showing how the mean waiting time increases as the arrival rate at each of the nodes is increased, for both the MSMQ model and the polling model, is given in Figure 4.5. We see that even when overtaking is not allowed, for a system of this size, the second server has the effect of reducing the mean waiting time of customers within the system.

4.4.3   Asymmetric MSMQ System with Cyclic Polling

In [26] the authors consider a system of N nodes in which one node has capacity K and arrival rate $K\lambda$ while all other nodes have capacity one and arrival rate λ. This represents a network in which one node has high traffic and the other nodes have light traffic, such as a LAN connecting several diskless workstations and one file server. It was shown that the presence of the heavily loaded node did not greatly affect the mean waiting time of customers at lightly loaded nodes.

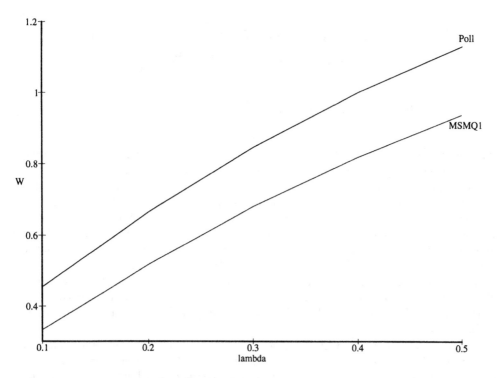

Figure 4.5: Mean customer waiting time, W, plotted against customer arrival rate, λ, for the models *MSMQ1* and *Poll*

$$Node_{j0} \stackrel{\text{def}}{=} (in, \lambda).Node_{j1} + (walk\_E_j, \top).Node_{j0} \qquad\qquad 1 \leq j \leq N$$
$$Node_{j1} \stackrel{\text{def}}{=} (walk\_F_j, \top).Node_{j2}$$
$$Node_{j2} \stackrel{\text{def}}{=} (serve_j, \mu_j).Node_{j0} + (walk\_E_j, \top).Node_{j2}$$

$$\text{where } \mu_j = \begin{cases} \mu & \text{if } j = 1 \\ m\mu & \text{if } 1 < j \leq N \end{cases}$$

$$S_j \stackrel{\text{def}}{=} (walk\_F_j, \omega).(serve_j, \top).S_{j\oplus 1} + (walk\_E_j, \omega).S_{j\oplus 1}$$

$$\text{where } j \oplus 1 = 1 \text{ when } j = N$$

when $N = 4$:

$$Asym \stackrel{\text{def}}{=} (Node_{10} \parallel Node_{20} \parallel Node_{30} \parallel Node_{40}) \underset{\substack{\{walk\_F_j, \\ walk\_E_j, serve_j\}}}{\bowtie} (S_1 \parallel S_1)$$

$$\text{where } 1 \leq j \leq N$$

Figure 4.6: PEPA model of an asymmetric MSMQ system

Here we consider a system of N nodes each with capacity 1 and arrival rate λ but with customers at one node placing a larger service requirement on the server. Polling is cyclic and overtaking is allowed. The system may be classified as $M/M_i/M/1/Q \times 1/L$. The PEPA model of this system is shown in Figure 4.6.

We investigate the effect of the larger service requirement at $Node_1$ on the average waiting time of customers at each of the nodes. We assume that the arrival process at each node

in	$serve_j$ $(j = 2, 3, 4)$	$serve_j$ $(j = 1)$	walk_E	walk_F
λ	μ	$m\mu$	ω	ω
0.1	1	$1 \leq 1/m \leq 5$	10	10

Table 4.3: Parameter values assigned to the model, *Asym*

is Poisson with parameter λ, and that normal service, heavy service and walk times in the system are exponentially distributed with rates μ, $m\mu$ and ω respectively.

As previously, S_j denotes a server ready to approach the jth node in the system. In this model there is no separate activity representing the interaction between the server and the node to determine whether there is a customer present in the buffer. This action is subsumed into the walk action, resulting in two activities, $walk\_E_j$ and $walk\_F_j$, representing a futile and a successful walk to $Node_j$ respectively. These activities cannot be simultaneously enabled.

Note that as overtaking is now permitted an occupied node which is currently being served will respond to the approach of a second server as if empty. The rate at which service occurs is determined by the node, and is dependent on the node. The rate of each walk activity is determined by the server.

The system we consider has four nodes, which do not interact with each other, and two servers which similarly do not directly interact. The cooperation of a node and a server is required for all $walk\_E$, $walk\_F$ and $serve$ activities. The values which were assigned to the parameters are shown in Table 4.3. The effect of varying the service rate of customers at $Node_1$ was investigated with respect to the mean customer waiting time at the other nodes.

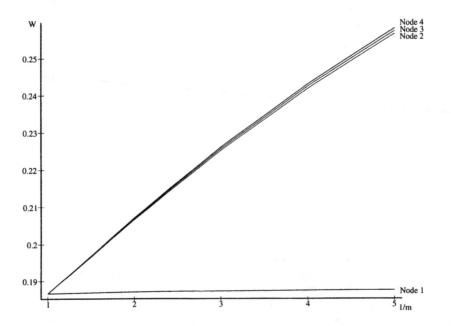

Figure 4.7: Expected customer waiting time plotted against service demand

The model has 560 states and 2064 transitions. The mean waiting time, W_j, is calculated for each node using Little's Law. These values, plotted against the service demand at $Node_1$, are shown in the graph in Figure 4.7.

The expected waiting time for customers at $Node_1$ increases slightly as the service demand at the node increases. At the other nodes the expected customer waiting time grows significantly as the service demand at the $Node_1$ increases. It is interesting to note that this rate of growth is slightly slower at the node immediately downstream from the distinguished node ($Node_2$) as it is able to take advantage of the second server overtaking the server occupied at $Node_1$.

4.4.4 Asymmetric MSMQ System with Random Polling

We now consider an asymmetric system in which the capacities of the nodes within the system differ. There are three nodes within the system, one with capacity two and two with capacity one. Polling in the system is random, which means that on leaving a node the server may then approach any node, even the same node again. Service is limited so that a server arriving at $Node_1$ when it is full may only serve one of the customers present before departing. However if the second server later arrives while the first service is still in progress it may simultaneously occupy the node. The system may be classified as $M_i/M_i/M/(2,1,1)/Q \times S/L$. "Overtaking" is allowed in the sense that a server arriving at a node and finding no customer to serve will just move on.

The PEPA model of this system is shown in Figure 4.8. We assume that $Node_1$ is a high performance node, distinguished not only by its larger capacity but also by a faster response to queries from servers. These queries are now represented separately by the activities $pass$ or $engage$. We also assume that there is a process generating customers for each place in the buffer in the node so that the arrival rate when the buffer is empty is twice the arrival rate when one place in the buffer is already occupied.

$$Node_{100} \stackrel{def}{=} (in, 2\lambda).Node_{110} + (pass_1, 2e).Node_{100}$$
$$Node_{110} \stackrel{def}{=} (in, \lambda).Node_{111} + (engage_1, 2e).Node_{120}$$
$$Node_{111} \stackrel{def}{=} (engage_1, 2e).Node_{121}$$
$$Node_{120} \stackrel{def}{=} (in, \lambda).Node_{121} + (pass_1, 2e).Node_{120} + (serve, \top).Node_{100}$$
$$Node_{121} \stackrel{def}{=} (engage_1, 2e).Node_{122} + (serve, \top).Node_{110}$$
$$Node_{122} \stackrel{def}{=} (pass_1, 2e).Node_{122} + (serve, \top).Node_{120}$$

$$Node_{j0} \stackrel{def}{=} (in, \lambda).Node_{j1} + (pass_j, e).Node_{j0} \qquad j = 2,3$$
$$Node_{j1} \stackrel{def}{=} (engage_j, e).Node_{j2}$$
$$Node_{j2} \stackrel{def}{=} (serve, \top).Node_{j0} + (pass_j, e).Node_{j2}$$

$$S \stackrel{def}{=} (walk, \omega/3).S_1 + (walk, \omega/3).S_2 + (walk, \omega/3).S_3$$
$$S_j \stackrel{def}{=} (pass_j, \top).S + (engage_j, \top).(serve, \mu).S \qquad 1 \le k \le 3$$

$$MSMQff \stackrel{def}{=} (Node_{100} \parallel Node_{20} \parallel Node_{30}) \underset{\substack{\{engage_j, \\ pass_j, serve\}}}{\bowtie} (S \parallel S)/\{pass_j, engage_j\}$$
$$\text{where } 1 \le j \le 3$$

Figure 4.8: Asymmetric MSMQ model with distinguished $Node_1$

$$Node'_{100} \overset{\text{def}}{=} (in, 2\lambda).Node'_{110} + (pass_1, 2e).Node'_{100}$$
$$Node'_{110} \overset{\text{def}}{=} (in, \lambda).Node'_{111} + (engage_1, e).Node'_{120} + (pass_1, e).Node'_{110}$$
$$Node'_{111} \overset{\text{def}}{=} (engage_1, 2e).Node'_{121}$$
$$Node'_{120} \overset{\text{def}}{=} (in, \lambda).Node'_{121} + (pass_1, 2e).Node'_{120} + (serve, \top).Node'_{100}$$
$$Node'_{121} \overset{\text{def}}{=} (engage_1, e).Node'_{122} + (pass_1, e).Node'_{121} + (serve, \top).Node'_{110}$$
$$Node'_{122} \overset{\text{def}}{=} (pass_1, 2e).Node'_{122} + (serve, \top).Node'_{120}$$

$$MSMQwf \overset{\text{def}}{=} (Node'_{100} \parallel Node_{20} \parallel Node_{30}) \underset{\substack{\{engage_j, \\ pass_j, serve\}}}{\bowtie} (S \parallel S)/\{pass_j, engage_j\}$$

$$\text{where } 1 \leq j \leq 3$$

Figure 4.9: A modified version of $Node_1$, with faulty interface

in	$pass_j$ or $engage_j$	$serve$	$walk$
λ or 2λ	e or $2e$	μ	ω
$\lambda = 0.1$	$e = 50$	1.0	$3, 6, 9, 12, 15$

Table 4.4: Parameter values assigned to $MSMQff$ and $MSMQwf$

In the server component S the $walk$ action is represented by three distinct activities, each with activity rate $\omega/3$, since there is a $1/3$ probability of each of the outcomes. S_j now denotes the server present at $Node_j$, when it might $engage$ or $pass$ depending on whether the node has a customer requiring service or not.

In Figure 4.9 a modified version of $Node_1$ is shown. In this second version we assume that there is a fault in $Node_1$ so that it is only guaranteed to respond correctly to a server when the buffer is completely empty or completely full. In the case when only one place in the buffer is occupied, with probability $1/2$ it will respond as if the buffer were empty. In the case when one customer is already in service but the other place in the buffer is also occupied it will similarly fail with probability $1/2$, allowing the second server to leave without providing service. We investigate the effect of this fault on the mean waiting time for customers at this node, and at the other nodes. In all the nodes, when a server is engaged the rate at which service occurs is determined by the server.

There is no cooperation between the three nodes in the system, nor between the two servers. However the activities $pass_j$, $engage_j$ and $serve$ are achieved by cooperation between a node and a server. The values which were assigned to the parameters are shown in Table 4.4.

The model of the fault free system has 368 states and 1570 transitions. The model of the faulty system has the same number of states but 1618 transitions. The mean waiting time at each node was calculated using Little's Law for each of the models as the average walk time was varied. These results, shown in Figures 4.10 and 4.11, were compared to assess the effect of the faulty connection. $Node_2$ and $Node_3$ exhibit the same characteristics, so only $Node_2$ is shown in the graphs.

In the fault free system $MSMQff$ we can see that although the expected waiting time is similar in all of the nodes, the customers in $Node_1$ experience slightly longer delays. For all the nodes the mean waiting time is reduced when the mean walking time of the servers is reduced, as we would expect. In the case of the faulty system $MSMQwf$ the expected

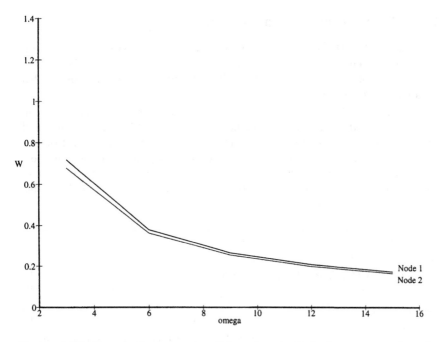

Figure 4.10: Expected customer waiting time in fault-free system plotted against *walk* rate (ω)

waiting time for customers at $Node_2$ or $Node_3$ is not greatly affected by the fault. However the expected waiting time for customers at $Node_1$ is drastically increased, especially when the rate of the *walk* activity is slow.

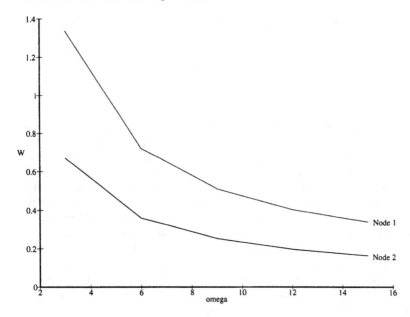

Figure 4.11: Expected customer waiting time in faulty system plotted against *walk* rate (ω)

4.4.5 MSMQ System with Detailed Nodes

The last model considered in this chapter recognises that a MSMQ system is usually embedded within a larger system, and gives an indication of how easily this is modelled within a PEPA model. In [89] Takagi highlights the embedding of a polling model within a global model as an area for future research.

We consider a symmetric MSMQ system, with capacity 1 nodes and limited service, in which overtaking is permitted. This could be classified as a $M/M/M/1/Q \times 1/L$ system, and is similar to the asymmetric model presented in Section 4.4.3 in the case $m = 1$. However we now also consider the components of the system responsible for generating the customers which arrive at the nodes. We assume that each customer is in fact a packet, and part of a message. Several packets may be necessary to transmit each message. The model of this enhanced system is shown in Figure 4.12.

$$Node_{j0} \stackrel{def}{=} (in, \top).Node_{j1} + (walk\_E_j, e).Node_{j0} \qquad\qquad 1 \le j \le N$$
$$Node_{j1} \stackrel{def}{=} (walk\_F_j, e).Node_{j2}$$
$$Node_{j2} \stackrel{def}{=} (serve_j, \top).Node_{j0} + (walk\_E_j, e).Node_{j2}$$

$$Gen_{j0} \stackrel{def}{=} (accept, \lambda).(pack, p).Gen_{j1}$$
$$Gen_{j1} \stackrel{def}{=} (in, d).((serve_j, w_1\top).Gen_{j1} + (serve_j, w_2\top).Gen_{j0})$$
$$\text{where } w_1 = M - 1, \ w_2 = 1 \quad (M \text{ is mean no. of packets/message})$$

$$Comp_j \stackrel{def}{=} Node_{j0} \underset{\{in, serve_j\}}{\bowtie} Gen_{j0}$$

$$S_j \stackrel{def}{=} (walk\_E_j, \omega).S_{j\oplus1} + (walk\_F_j, \omega).(serve_j, \mu).S_{j\oplus1}$$
$$\text{where } j \oplus 1 = 1 \text{ when } j = N$$

when $N = 3$:
$$System \stackrel{def}{=} (Comp_1 \ \| \ Comp_2 \ \| \ Comp_3) \underset{\substack{\{walk\_E_j, \\ walk\_F_j, serve_j\}}}{\bowtie} (S_1 \ \| \ S_1)/L \qquad \text{where } 1 \le j \le N$$
$$L = \{accept, pack, walk\_E_j, walk\_F_j\}$$

Figure 4.12: PEPA model of the enhanced MSMQ system, *System*

The MSMQ aspects of the system are similar to the models presented in the previous sections. However, note that the activity *in* now merely represents the delivery of a packet from the generator to the buffer. The rate of this activity is determined by the generator. We assume that there is a Poisson arrival process supplying messages to the generator when it is ready to accept them, with rate λ, and this is represented by the *accept* activity. Each accepted message is broken up into packets, as represented by the *pack* activity. We assume that the average message length is M packets. The packets are then delivered to the buffer, via the *in* activity, one at a time. When a packet has completed its service it will be replaced by another until the entire message has been sent. The arrival process is then resumed. Since the average number of packets in a message is M, when a packet has completed service, another packet is already available with probability $M - 1/M$, and so the passive *serve* activity with this outcome is given weight $M - 1$, whereas with probability $1/M$ a new message must be processed before another packet is available, so the weight of the *serve* activity which resumes the arrival process is 1.

mean no. packets M	accept λ	pack p	in d	walk_E and walk_F $\min(e, \omega)$	serve μ
$5 - 25$	0.05	0.1	20	$\min(50, 10) = 10$	1.0

Table 4.5: Parameter values assigned to *System*

The nodes of the system are now represented by composite components $Comp_j$, the co-operation of a generator, Gen_{j0} and a "node", $Node_{j0}$. These components must cooperate on the *in* and $serve_j$ activities. The composites are independent of each other, as are the servers. The activities $walk\_E_j$, $walk\_F_j$, $serve_j$ require the cooperation of a server and the appropriate composite. Note that this means that three components, Gen_j, $Node_j$ and S_j must cooperate in order to achieve a $serve_j$ activity.

The model has 888 states and 3858 transitions. The parameter values used to solve the model are shown in Table 4.5. As the system is symmetric the performance characteristics of all the nodes are the same. Instead of the mean waiting time for a customer, or packet, in the node, we calculate the mean transmission time for a message. As previously we use Little's Law, this time applied to the composite node-generator pair. We find the mean number of *messages* at a node, N_m, by noting that there is one message present whenever the *accept* activity is not enabled. Therefore we attach a reward of 1 to this activity, to find R_{accept}, and we deduce that $N_m = 1 - R_{accept}$. We find the message throughput, X_m, by attaching a reward of $1/M \times \mu$, to the activity $(serve, w_2\top)$, which will occur whenever all the packets within a message have been sent. The expected transmission time, T_m, for a message in the system is then $T_m = N_m/X_m$.

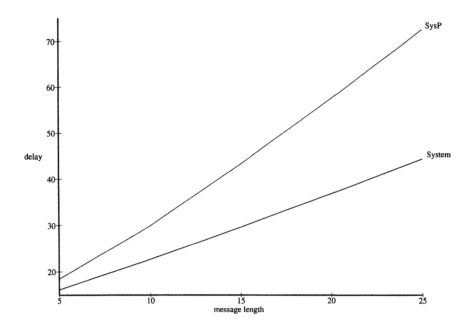

Figure 4.13: Mean message transmission time plotted against mean number of packets per message.

The value of the expected transmission time, when the mean number of packets in a message, M, varies between 5 and 25, is shown in Figure 4.13. This is compared with the expected transmission times for messages of the same length in the related polling model, $SysP$,

$$SysP \stackrel{\text{def}}{=} (Comp_1 \parallel Comp_2 \parallel Comp_3) \underset{\substack{\{walk\_E_j, \\ walk\_F_j, serve_j\}}}{\bowtie} (S_1)/\{accept, pack, walk\_E_j, walk\_F_j\}$$

Chapter 5

Notions of Equivalence

5.1 Introduction

In this chapter we develop a framework to analyse notions of equivalence between models. Within this framework we present several equivalences which have been applied to process algebra models and performance models. By *notions of equivalence* we mean criteria which may be applied to determine whether two entities can be considered to be, in some sense, the same. For example, a common concern for most modelling methodologies is *model verification*—the problem of ascertaining whether a model is the same as the system under study, in the sense of providing an adequate representation to meet the objectives of the study. For a performance model "adequate representation" is usually interpreted as the calculation of certain quantitative performance characteristics within acceptable error bounds. For a process algebra model it is interpreted as a condition on the observable behaviour of the model, as represented by its actions, compared with the observable or intended behaviour of the system.

The framework we consider identifies three different classes of entity-to-entity equivalence which may arise during a modelling study: system-to-model equivalence, model-to-model equivalence and state-to-state equivalence. We will see that for process algebra models these equivalences are all addressed by a single notion of equivalence, the *bisimulation*. Two agents are considered to be equivalent in this way when their externally observed behaviour appears to be the same. This is a formally defined notion of equivalence, based on the labelled transition system underlying the process algebra. Bisimulation can characterise all three classes of entity-to-entity equivalence since, in a process algebra, all the modelling entities—system, model and states—are represented as agents.

For performance modelling the three classes of equivalence are quite distinct, since the entities—system, model and state—are distinct. A representation of the system may not be available at all. If it is, it will generally be in a different notation, for example as a design. For a Markov process the behaviour of a model is characterised by the states it may visit and the time it will spend in them. Thus *models* and *states* are regarded as different types of entity. The states are not regarded as active entities. In contrast, in a process algebra the behaviour of a model is characterised by the actions it may engage in. At any particular time these will be embodied in the current derivative (state). However the ideas of *model* and *state* are interchangeable in a process algebra since, via the semantics of the language, each "state" also includes information about all possible future states which may be reached via the transitions of the language. Both model and state are represented as agents, or expressions in the language.

There has been little formal development of system-to-model, and model-to-model equivalences for performance models, although these have been of pragmatic concern. In contrast there has been much work on state-to-state equivalences. These equivalences form the basis of aggregation techniques for reducing the state space of the underlying Markov model, and thus provide a technique for making large models tractable.

In Section 5.2 we present the idea of bisimulation, which is widely used as a notion of equivalence for process algebras, and explain how it may be used to characterise system-to-model, model-to-model and state-to-state equivalences. We outline how the notion of bisimulation has been extended to apply to timed and probabilistic process algebras. In Section 5.3 we discuss the system-to-model and model-to-model equivalences which have been considered for performance models. In Section 5.4 we review aggregation techniques in model simplification and discuss the role of state-to-state equivalences. Finally in Section 5.5 we will discuss how the behaviour of a PEPA component may be captured by structural or bisimulation style equivalences. In Chapter 7 a strong bisimulation for PEPA is presented.

5.2 Process Algebras and Bisimulation

In this section the notion of bisimulation is defined in the context of a *pure* process algebra, such as CCS. Bisimulation is based on the idea of *observable behaviour*. Strong and weak forms of the equivalence are defined depending on whether internal actions are considered to be within the set of observable actions. How the notion of bisimulation has been extended to timed and probabilistic process algebras is described in Sections 5.2.2 and 5.2.3. In Section 5.2.4, how bisimulation may address the different classes of entity-to-entity equivalence for process algebra models is discussed.

5.2.1 Bisimulation for Pure Process Algebras

Bisimulation aims to capture the idea of equivalence as identical observed behaviour. If two agents are bisimilar it is not possible to distinguish between them by observation. However, we must specify which actions of the agents are considered visible to the observer and the context in which they are observed. In its strongest form bisimilarity means that two agents are capable of exactly the same transitions, and the derivatives which result from the same transitions in the agents are themselves bisimilar.

This notion of equivalence is based on the labelled transition system defined by the semantics of the language. Thus for a language whose labelled transition system is the triple $(\mathcal{P}, \mathcal{A}ct, \{\xrightarrow{\alpha} \mid \alpha \in \mathcal{A}ct\})$ the strong form of bisimulation is expressed as follows.

Definition 5.2.1 *Two agents, $P, Q \in \mathcal{P}$, are strongly bisimilar, denoted $P \sim Q$, if and only if, there is some relation $\mathcal{R}$ over $\mathcal{P} \times \mathcal{P}$ such that if $(P, Q) \in \mathcal{R}$ then for all $\alpha \in \mathcal{A}ct$:*

1. *Whenever $P \xrightarrow{\alpha} P'$, then for some Q', $Q \xrightarrow{\alpha} Q'$ and $(P', Q') \in \mathcal{R}$;*

2. *Whenever $Q \xrightarrow{\alpha} Q'$, then for some P', $P \xrightarrow{\alpha} P'$ and $(P', Q') \in \mathcal{R}$.*

Thus, if P and Q are strongly bisimilar agents, any action performed by one must be matched by the other. Moreover, any subsequent action must also be matched. It is important to note that this includes the internal, τ, actions. The definition of bisimulation may also be phrased in terms of sequences of actions rather than single actions i.e. two agents are strongly bisimilar if any transition, formed by a sequence of actions, which can be performed by one agent, can also be performed by the other agent and the resulting derivatives are themselves strongly bisimilar.

Weaker forms of bisimulation are defined by restricting the class of actions which may be observed to $Act \setminus \{\tau\}$. Thus the internal, τ, action is assumed to occur unobserved, reflecting its private nature within an agent. If α is a visible action, it will be indistinguishable to an external observer from the action sequence $\tau\alpha$, or even $\tau\tau\alpha\tau$. *Weakly bisimilar* agents can form the same sequences of visible actions, modulo the occurrence of a finite number of τ actions before or after any of the visible actions, and the resulting agents are themselves weakly bisimilar. In CCS an intermediate notion of equivalence is introduced, *observation congruence*. Two agents are observation congruent if any action by one of them (including a τ action) is matched by the other, up to the inclusion of additional τ actions, and the resulting derivatives are weakly bisimilar.

In order to show that two agents are equivalent in this sense it is necessary to find a relation $\mathcal{R}$ between the derivatives of each agent which satisfies the conditions of the Definition 5.2.1. A bisimulation forms equivalence classes over the set of process terms, $\mathcal{P}$. This partition will then induce a corresponding partition on the derivative set of any agent in a natural way. To show strong bisimulation between CCS agents it is sufficient to show that a relation satisfying the strong bisimulation conditions exists between the partitions in the derivative sets of the two agents [29]. This is the idea of *strong bisimulation up to* $\sim$.

5.2.2   Bisimulation for Timed Process Algebras

In [34], the notion of bisimulation is extended to temporal CCS. As discussed in Section 2.3.1, in TCCS time and actions are considered separately, the semantics of the language being given in terms of two distinct transition systems. Strong bisimulation for the language ensures that both types of transitions are matched by equivalent agents, and that the resulting agents are also strongly bisimilar. A weakened form of the bisimulation is also defined. Two agents are considered equivalent if they can witness the same sequence of delays or visible actions, up to the introduction of τ actions within either type of sequence, and the resulting agents are also equivalent.

5.2.3   Bisimulation for Probabilistic Process Algebras

For probabilistic process algebras the labelled transition system underlying the language may be extended to form a *probabilistic labelled transition system* [38, 36] (Section 2.3.2). In these systems a probability measure, μ, is defined over the transitions of a labelled transition system, $\mu : \mathcal{P} \times Act \times \mathcal{P} \longrightarrow [0, 1]$. If we consider all the transitions into a set of process terms, via a given action, this can be extended to the probability measure $\nu : \mathcal{P} \times Act \times 2^{\mathcal{P}} \longrightarrow [0, 1]$, such that

$$\nu(P \xrightarrow{\alpha} S) = \sum_{P' \in S} \mu(P \xrightarrow{\alpha} P').$$

The bisimulations already discussed, for CCS and TCCS, are equivalence relations. Thus they generate equivalence classes over the set of all process terms, $\mathcal{P}$. Exploiting this idea, a *probabilistic bisimulation* is defined to be an equivalence relation such that, for any two agents within an equivalence class, for any action $\alpha \in Act$ and any equivalence class S, the probability measure ν of each of the agents performing an α action and resulting in an agent within S, is the same.

Definition 5.2.2 *A probabilistic bisimulation* $\overset{p}{\sim}$ *is an equivalence relation over* $\mathcal{P}$ *such that whenever* $P \overset{p}{\sim} Q$, *then for all* $\alpha \in \mathcal{A}ct$, *and for all* $S \in \mathcal{P} / \overset{p}{\sim}$

$$\nu(P \overset{\alpha}{\longrightarrow} S) = \nu(Q \overset{\alpha}{\longrightarrow} S).$$

The definition of the probability measure μ, and consequently also ν, depends on whether the process algebra is reactive or generative. Larsen and Skou, [38], define $\mu(P \overset{\alpha}{\longrightarrow} P')$ for a reactive system, as the probability, given that P performs an action α, that P' is the derivative.

$$\sum_{P' \in \mathcal{P}} \mu(P \overset{\alpha}{\longrightarrow} P') = 1$$

In contrast, for a generative system, Jou and Smolka [36], define $\mu(P \overset{\alpha}{\longrightarrow} P')$ to be the probability that the transition $\overset{\alpha}{\longrightarrow} P'$ is the one that P performs.

$$\sum_{\substack{\alpha \in \mathcal{A}ct \\ P' \in \mathcal{P}}} \mu(P \overset{\alpha}{\longrightarrow} P') = 1$$

5.2.4 Bisimulation and Entity-to-Entity Equivalence

During a modelling study we may be concerned with different equivalences relating to a model. In order to establish confidence in the model as the representation of the system being investigated, system-to-model equivalence is considered. This is *model verification* and it is used to ensure that the model is a suitable tool for studying the behaviour of the system. Subsequently, it may be necessary to manipulate or compare models, in order to develop further knowledge about the system, or find alternative representations of the system. The modeller must be certain that such manipulation does not change the behaviour of the model, and jeopardise its relationship with the system. This leads to the analysis of model-to-model equivalences. When models are large and complex, model simplification strategies may be required to reduce the complexity of the model. One approach to model simplification is a search for state-to-state equivalences, which allow one *macro-state* [7] to replace a set of equivalent states.

As explained in Section 5.1, for process algebra models the concepts of *state* and *model* are interchangeable, both being represented as expressions in the language. The system, in the form of a design or specification, is also often expressed as an agent. Thus it is clear that the bisimulation notion of equivalence provides the apparatus for studying each form of entity-to-entity equivalence outlined above. State-to-state equivalences, bisimulation between agents within a derivative set, are found by considering the partition of the derivative set induced by the bisimulation relation. There has been little consideration in the literature of this as a model simplification technique but it is used extensively to reduce the complexity of finding the bisimulation relation between agents, via the approach of *bisimulation up to* $\sim$.

Due to its formal nature, based on the labelled transition system for the language, the bisimulation relation may be characterised by equational laws. These abstract laws may then be applied to any model, resulting in modifications which are guaranteed to preserve the observable behaviour of the model. Moreover, the formal nature of these laws makes it possible to provide machine-assistance for such model manipulation [95].

A relation is a congruence with respect to an algebra if it is preserved by all algebraic contexts. Bisimulation relations which are also congruence relations fully complement the compositional nature of the process algebra. For example, if we replace an agent within any language expression by any bisimilar agent then the resulting expression is bisimilar to the original expression. This property has distinct advantages. For example, model verification may be approached by showing bisimilarity between the components of the system and the model component by component.

5.3 Performance Modelling and Equivalences

In performance modelling studies, using queueing networks or stochastic Petri nets, the modelling entities—system, model and state—will generally all have distinct representations. This means that the three classes of entity-to-entity equivalence, outlined in the previous section, give rise to distinct notions of equivalence for performance models. In this section we will consider system-to-model and model-to-model equivalences. The notion of state-to-state equivalence is much more developed. Together with the resulting aggregation techniques, it will be considered separately in Section 5.4.

5.3.1 Performance Model Verification

Model verification, or establishing system-to-model equivalence, is important to ensure that the performance characteristics obtained from the model will be close to the performance characteristics of the system under study. When the system exists, model verification may be carried out by comparing data collected from the system and the model in identical circumstances. Such an approach is often costly in terms of intrusive system monitoring, extensive model executions and the amount of data which must be collected and analysed. In some circumstances a simulation model is used as an intermediate representation of the system, as seen in Section 4.3.1. In this case the results of the analytical model are tested against the results of the simulation when the context of operation is assumed to be the same for both. Obviously this relies on the assumption that the simulation is an accurate representation of the system.

When the system does not exist, as in the case of a projected system, the model must be verified against a design. Unfortunately, as explained in Section 2.4, the system design, even if formally developed, will generally use a different notation from the performance model. Thus comparison of the behaviour of the two is often necessarily informal, or experimental. The recent work on the use of system description formalisms as the basis for performance modelling has clear implications for model verification. Using a formal language, such as PEPA, it is intended that the *design* of the system will be annotated to form the performance model. Thus the *system*, i.e. the design, is by definition the same as the performance model, and so problems of model verification disappear.

There has been some formal work on the area of system-to-model equivalence, but this has been principally aimed at simulation models. For example, in early work based on Systems Theory [96], Zeigler develops the idea of equivalence within limited contexts of observation. These contexts are called *experimental frames*. It is assumed that behaviour is characterised by input-output pairs capturing the system's response to its environment. Equivalence is defined as generating the same set of input-output pairs. The experimental frame limits the inputs which may be considered and the outputs which may be observed.

Zeigler's work also considers experimental frames as a basis for model-to-model equivalence and model simplification. From a full representation of the input-output behaviour of the system, termed the *base model*, an equivalent *lumped model* is formed which will have identical behaviour in a given experimental frame. The lumped model is formed by combining components within the base model, and simplifying the interactions between them.

5.3.2   Model-to-Model Equivalence

For performance models based on queueing networks and Petri nets each model has two representations—one within its model construction paradigm, and the other as the underlying Markov process. There has been little work on notions of model-to-model equivalence at the level of the modelling paradigm. Most notions of equivalence arise solely from consideration of the underlying Markov process. A notable exception is Sanders and Meyer's work for SAN, based on Zeigler's experimental frame approach [5].

Sanders and Meyer use the reward structure incorporated into SAN models to define an experimental frame for a model. Using a constructive technique, a SAN model is developed representing the system—this is the base model. The reward structure is then defined to calculate the performance measures of interest for the current study. This reward structure defines an experimental frame in terms of which aspects of the model may not be modified if the integrity of the performance measures is to be ensured. The authors propose simplification techniques to reduce the state space, forming a lumped model which is still Markovian, within the context of this experimental frame. These techniques are applied at the level of the SAN, rather than directly manipulating the Markov process. As with Zeigler's experimental frames it is envisaged that different performance measures may lead to different lumped models.

A similar approach to model simplification for PEPA, resulting in the amalgamation of derivatives (states), is presented in Chapter 8.

In [27], Chiola *et al.* define a notion of equivalence between GSPN models, and between GSPN and SPN models. This equivalence implies equivalence of the underlying Markov processes but it is a stronger condition. Since performance indices are often defined at the net level, the authors argue that additional conditions are necessary to ensure that the same performance measures can be derived from the models. These conditions compensate for any information that is lost in going from the *marking* sequence of the GSPN to the *transition* sequence in the Markov process—if there is more than one transition between a pair of markings they appear as a single transition in the Markov process. This equivalence was developed with a clear objective. It is used to prove that for any GSPN, an equivalent SPN can be constructed, thus showing that immediate transitions are not necessary.

Equivalences Between Markov Processes

The usual notion of equivalence between Markov processes is the intuitive one—two Markov processes are equivalent if they have the same number of states and the same transition rates between those states. This implies an isomorphism between the states of the two processes and that they have the same infinitesimal generator matrix $\mathbf{Q}$ (up to a permutation of rows and columns). It follows that they will have the same transient and steady state probability distributions.

This notion of equivalence is quite different from the bisimulation style equivalence used in process algebras. Both notions are concerned with processes which exhibit the same behaviour: processes which when observed will display the same history. However, how these histories are defined differs in the Markov process and the process algebra worlds. In the Markov process the history of the process is regarded as the sequence of states in which the process spends time. In the process algebra the history of the process is regarded as the sequence of activities the process engages in.

The Markov process equivalence is very strict and of little practical use in terms of model manipulations or transformations. Several more relaxed forms of equivalence, perhaps more appropriately termed *near-equivalences*, have been considered. These equivalences have been used to identify Markov processes which, although outside a particular class of processes amenable to efficient solution, may be safely replaced by an appropriate process of that class.

The classes of processes which have been considered in these equivalences are characterised by a generator matrix which has a particular structure. For example, a *completely decomposable* matrix consists of stochastic blocks down the principal diagonal and zeroes everywhere else. A *nearly completely decomposable* matrix is one in which the blocks down the leading diagonal have elements which are at least an order of magnitude larger than any element outside these blocks [97]. Completely decomposable and nearly completely decomposable Markov processes are defined in the obvious way. Thus if a process is found to be nearly completely decomposable it may be replaced by its *equivalent* completely decomposable process, which may be solved by considering the submodels corresponding to the diagonal blocks separately. Decomposability has been used extensively in queueing networks. A similar notion, *near-independence*, has been recently developed for GSPNs [74].

In the recent paper [98], Buchholz develops the notion of *near-lumpability* which can be applied to any Markovian based model, and provides a technique for state space reduction. Lumpability is discussed in more detail in Section 5.4.2.

5.4 State-to-State Equivalence

In order to tackle the problem of state space explosion, model simplification techniques have been considered for performance models, at both the paradigm and the Markov process level. One such technique, *aggregation*, can be formalised in terms of state-to-state equivalences within the state space of the model. When an equivalence is found, sets of equivalent states may be formed into one *macro-state* thus reducing the overall state space of the model. In the following section we will briefly outline the aggregation procedure.

5.4.1 Aggregation of Markov Processes

An equivalence relation defined over the state space of a model will induce a partition on the state space. Aggregation is achieved by constructing such a partition and forming the corresponding *aggregated* process. In the aggregated process each partition of states in the original process forms one state. In some cases, this partition will be based on a defined equivalence relation over the states of the original process. In other cases, the partition will be abstract or artificial, but it will define an equivalence relation over the state space in the natural way. Thus we can always assume that there is an equivalence relation underlying the partition. If the original state space is $\{X_1, X_2, \ldots, X_n\}$ then the aggregated state space is some $\{X_{[1]}, \ldots, X_{[N]}\}$, where $N < n$, ideally $N \ll n$.

The infinitesimal generator matrix of the aggregated process is formed in the intuitive way. If the transition rates of the original process are denoted $q(X_i, X_k)$ then the transition rate into any partition from a given state is

$$q(X_i, X_{[j]}) = \sum_{k \in [j]} q(X_i, X_k).$$

The transitions between aggregated states are then formed as a weighted sum of the transition rates of the states in the first partition to the second partition, weighted by the conditional steady state probabilities of being in each state in the partition, $\bar{\Pi}_j(\cdot)$,

$$q(X_{[j]}, X_{[i]}) = \sum_{k \in [j]} \bar{\Pi}_j(X_k)\, q(X_k, X_{[i]}).$$

Exact calculation of the steady state probabilities, $\bar{\Pi}_j(X_k)$ will normally entail finding the steady state distribution of the original process. However, aggregation procedures include a plethora of iterative procedures based on the approximation of these values. Alternatively, if the partitions are based on a structural property of the model it may be possible to calculate these values by a separate analysis of the corresponding submodel. A comprehensive survey of aggregation techniques is presented in [7].

In general it will not be the case that the Markov property is preserved in the aggregated process. However it is assumed that the aggregated process is Markovian and this allows the steady state probability of being in each partition to be calculated correctly. The case when the aggregated process is a Markov process relies on a condition known as *lumpability*. The case of aggregation in which the aggregated model is treated as a Markov process although the Markov property is not conserved is sometimes called *pseudo-aggregation* [99].

5.4.2 Lumpability

The characteristics of the aggregated process will depend on the equivalence relation used to form the partitions on which the aggregation is based. When the partition is such that the Markov property is conserved in the aggregated process the process is said to be *ordinarily* or *strongly lumpable* with respect to the partition [100]. Such partitions are formed on the basis of a strong notion of equivalence between states. In the case of a lumpable partition the steady state solution of the aggregated process can be found without the conditional steady state probabilities of states within each partition. Moreover this steady state distribution may be used to derive an exact solution of the original model.

Definition 5.4.1 *A Markov process is* (strongly or ordinarily) lumpable *with respect to a partition* $\chi = \{X_{[i]}\}$ *if for every initial distribution the aggregated process is a Markov process.*

Theorem 5.4.1 (Kemeny and Snell 1960 [100, p. 124]) *A Markov process is lumpable with respect to a partition* $\chi = \{X_{[i]}\}$ *if, and only if, for any* $X_{[k]}, X_{[l]} \in \chi$, $X_i, X_j \in X_{[k]}$

$$q(X_i, X_{[l]}) = q(X_j, X_{[l]})$$

A strongly lumpable partition exists if there is an equivalence relation such that for any two states within a partition induced by the equivalence relation their aggregated transition rates to any other partition are the same. The related notions of *exactly lumpable* and *strictly lumpable* partitions [101], are defined as follows.

Definition 5.4.2 χ *is an* exactly lumpable *partition if, and only if, for all* $X_{[l]}, X_{[k]} \in \chi$, *and for all* $X_i, X_j \in X_{[k]}$

$$q(X_{[l]}, X_i) = q(X_{[l]}, X_j)$$

Thus an exactly lumpable partition exists if there is an equivalence relation such that for any two states within a partition, induced by the equivalence relation, the aggregated transition rates *into* the states from any other partition are the same. Here, the aggregated transition rate into a state is defined in the obvious way. For a strictly lumpable partition there must be the same aggregated flow both into, and out of, the equivalent states.

Definition 5.4.3 χ *is* strictly lumpable *if, and only if, it is ordinarily lumpable and exactly lumpable.*

Aggregation techniques in general, and lumpability in particular, are usually applied across the state space of a model considered as a whole. Recent work by Buchholz has shown that the lumpability equivalence is a congruence over a class of Markov processes expressed in terms of tensor algebra [44].

5.4.3 Folding in GSPNs

Another approach to model simplification based on state-to-state equivalences is the technique of *folding* in GSPNs [25]. This technique can greatly reduce the state space of a complex GSPN, but it may result in some loss of detail. Using an equivalence relation based on the enabled transitions a partition is formed over the markings of the GSPN. This identification of equivalent markings is used to construct a simpler, more compact model, from which a smaller Markov process is generated. Although very similar to aggregation using lumpable partitions, this approach has the advantage that it is not necessary to construct the Markovian generator matrix of the original model, which may be very large.

5.5 Notions of Equivalence for PEPA

In the following chapters we will develop four different notions of equivalence for PEPA, two of which are based on bisimulation. Unlike other performance modelling paradigms PEPA allows models and states to be regarded as equivalent entities—both are represented as components. Thus we may use the developed equivalence relations to analyse both model-to-model and state-to-state equivalences. For each equivalence we will consider its implications for the underlying Markov process and assess its potential for use as the basis for a model simplification technique.

In Chapter 6 we develop *isomorphism*, a structural equivalence similar to the equivalence between Markov processes described in Section 5.3. This relation is too strong to be used for model simplification but it does provide equational laws which may be used for model transformation. A weaker form of the relation, *weak isomorphism* is also presented. This introduces the consideration of how components appear to observers. Two components are considered equivalent in this way if they only differ in the detail of their internal activities. The relation is found to lead to a useful approach to model simplification which can, like Sanders and Meyer's approach for SAN, be varied according to the performance measures to be calculated.

The third notion of equivalence, developed in Chapter 7, is *strong bisimilarity* which is based on the labelled multi-transition system, presented in Chapter 3 as the semantics of PEPA. Although this relation is shown to be a congruence it is found that it is not sufficient to ensure equivalent behaviour. It illustrates the problems which can ensue because of the loss of information in going from the process algebra to the underlying Markov process. Nevertheless circumstances in which strongly bisimilar components will exhibit the same behaviour are identified, and this leads to the definition of a model simplification technique.

In Chapter 8 an alternative notion of equivalence is developed, called *strong equivalence*, in the style of the strong probabilistic bisimulation of Larsen and Skou. This equivalence uses the activity rates in a similar way to the probabilities used in probabilistic systems.

The equivalence relation is formed by consideration of total transition rates between partitions induced by the equivalence relation. The relationship between strong equivalence and lumpability in the underlying Markov process is demonstrated. Strong equivalence is also shown to be a congruence and its use for model simplification is illustrated by one of the MSMQ systems modelled in Chapter 4.

Chapter 6

Isomorphism and Weak Isomorphism

6.1 Introduction

In this chapter we develop a very strong notion of equivalence between PEPA components called *isomorphism*. This is a condition on the derivation graphs of components and it ensures that components are only considered equivalent if there is a one-to-one correspondence between their derivatives and they are capable of carrying out exactly the same activities. It is not an observation based notion of equivalence in the style of bisimulation which is usual for process algebras. It is structural, in the style of the equivalence between Markov processes introduced in Section 5.3. Isomorphism is defined in Section 6.2.

In Sections 6.3 to 6.5 we examine some properties of this notion of equivalence, from the perspectives of a process algebra, the modelled system components and the underlying Markov processes. As we might expect from such a strong notion of equivalence, we can derive strong properties for isomorphism. The relation is a congruence for PEPA. The relationship between isomorphism and the Markov processes underlying the PEPA components is found to be a close one—isomorphic components generate equivalent Markov processes.

In the remainder of the chapter we develop a weaker form of this equivalence called *weak isomorphism*. This equivalence reflects the *hidden* nature of τ type activities. We will consider two components equivalent in this way if they only differ in their capabilities to carry out such activities. A definition of this notion of equivalence is presented in Section 6.6.

The properties of weak isomorphism are examined from the process algebra perspective in Section 6.7 and from the system perspective in Section 6.8. Although it is not a congruence, it is found that weak isomorphism is preserved by some combinators of the language. In Section 6.9 we examine the relationship between weak isomorphism and the underlying Markov process. Weakly isomorphic components may generate Markov processes which are not equivalent. However it is shown that these processes will attract the same reward. Finally, in Section 6.10, an application of the weak isomorphism relation as a model-to-model equivalence for model simplification is explained and illustrated by an example taken from Chapter 4.

6.2 Definition of Isomorphism

If we consider the PEPA components $P \bowtie_L Q$ and $Q \bowtie_L P$ it is intuitive to regard them as equivalent. The semantic rules determining the behaviour of components of this form are symmetric, so the activities of the two components are exactly the same. It is this intuitive notion of equivalence, based on an exact match of behaviours, which we aim to capture within the definition of isomorphism. It is closely allied to the equivalence between Markov processes which ensures that the generator matrices of the two processes are the same up to a permutation of the rows and columns. PEPA components are isomorphic if there is a one-to-one correspondence between the derivatives of the components, equivalent derivatives enabling the same activities, which result in equivalent derivatives.

Definition 6.2.1 *A function,* $\mathcal{F} : ds(P) \longrightarrow ds(Q)$*, is a* component isomorphism *between* P *and* Q*, if* $\mathcal{F}$ *is an injective function, and for any component* P'*,* $\mathcal{A}ct(P') = \mathcal{A}ct(\mathcal{F}(P'))$*, and for all* $a \in \mathcal{A}ct$*, the set of* a*-derivatives of* $\mathcal{F}(P')$ *is the same as the set of* $\mathcal{F}$*-images of the* a*-derivatives of* P'*, i.e.*

$$\{Q' \mid \mathcal{F}(P') \xrightarrow{a} Q'\} = \{\mathcal{F}(P'') \mid P' \xrightarrow{a} P''\}.$$

Definition 6.2.2 *Two components,* P *and* Q*, are* isomorphic*, denoted* $P = Q$*, if there exists a component isomorphism* $\mathcal{F}$ *between them such that* $\mathcal{D}(\mathcal{F}(P)) = \mathcal{D}(Q)$*.*

Although the same notation is used, it should be noted that the isomorphism relation, $=$, is much stronger than observation congruence in CCS. In PEPA $P = Q$ signifies that P and Q are the same up to the naming of derivatives.

Isomorphism is an equivalence relation over the set of components: any component is trivially isomorphic to itself; as a component isomorphism is injective the relation is symmetric; and, since the composition of component isomorphisms is a component isomorphism, the relation is transitive.

In general, in order to show that two components are isomorphic we must exhibit a component isomorphism between their derivation graphs.

6.3 Properties of Isomorphism

In this section we investigate the properties of the isomorphism relation from a process algebra aspect. In particular we exhibit some straightforward equational laws which hold for the relation, and establish that isomorphism is a congruence for PEPA.

6.3.1 Equational Laws for Isomorphic Components

The following equational laws may be used to manipulate and transform PEPA components. Note that these laws alter the presentation or naming of derivatives: the structure of components remains the same. These equational laws can be proved by direct appeal to the definition of $=$ and the semantic rules in Figure 3.1.

Proposition 6.3.1 (Choice)

1. $P + Q = Q + P$

2. $P + (Q + R) = (P + Q) + R$

Proposition 6.3.2 (Hiding)

1. $(P + Q)/L = P/L + Q/L$

2. $((\alpha, r).P)/L = \begin{cases} (\tau, r).P/L & \alpha \in L \\ (\alpha, r).P/L & \alpha \notin L \end{cases}$

3. $(P/L)/K = P/(L \cup K)$

4. $P/L = P$ if $L \cap \vec{A}(P) = \emptyset$

Proposition 6.3.3 (Cooperation)

1. $P \underset{L}{\bowtie} Q = Q \underset{L}{\bowtie} P$

2. $P \underset{L}{\bowtie} (Q \underset{L}{\bowtie} R) = (P \underset{L}{\bowtie} Q) \underset{L}{\bowtie} R$

3. $(P \underset{L}{\bowtie} Q)/(K \cup M) = \left((P/K) \underset{L}{\bowtie} (Q/K) \right) / M$ *where* $K \cap M = K \cap L = \emptyset$

4. $P \underset{K}{\bowtie} Q = P \underset{L}{\bowtie} Q$ *if* $K \cap \left(\vec{A}(P) \cup \vec{A}(Q) \right) = L$

5. $(P \underset{L}{\bowtie} Q) \underset{K}{\bowtie} R = \begin{cases} P \underset{L}{\bowtie} (Q \underset{K}{\bowtie} R) & \textit{if } \vec{A}(R) \cap (L \setminus K) = \emptyset \wedge \vec{A}(P) \cap (K \setminus L) = \emptyset \\ Q \underset{L}{\bowtie} (P \underset{K}{\bowtie} R) & \textit{if } \vec{A}(R) \cap (L \setminus K) = \emptyset \wedge \vec{A}(Q) \cap (K \setminus L) = \emptyset \end{cases}$

Proposition 6.3.4 (Parallel)

1. $P \parallel Q = Q \parallel P$

2. $P \parallel (Q \parallel R) = P \parallel Q \parallel R = (P \parallel Q) \parallel R$

3. $(P \parallel Q)/K = P/K \parallel Q/K$

Proposition 6.3.5 (Constant)
If $A \overset{\text{def}}{=} P$ then $A = P$.

The laws presented in Proposition 6.3.4 are a reiteration of rules 1–3 of Proposition 6.3.3 for the special case $L = \emptyset$. They are stated here for clarity.

6.3.2 The Expansion Law

The Expansion Law, presented in Proposition 6.3.6, like the equational laws in the previous section, can be proved by direct appeal to the definition of isomorphism and the semantic rules for PEPA. It allows us to *unravel* the behaviour of a cooperation of components. Inherently this relies on the memoryless property of the exponential distributions used to determine the duration of activities. As explained in Section 3.3.3, this memoryless property allows us to treat the preemptive resume policy corresponding to the cooperation of components as equivalent to the preemptive restart policy corresponding to choice.

The law is presented in terms of two cooperating components—recall that the cooperation combinator is not associative. Thus we need only consider the cooperation between a pair of components, with the understanding that each of these components may itself be a cooperation of components at a lower level.

Proposition 6.3.6 (Expansion Law) *Let* $P \equiv (P_1 \bowtie_L P_2)/K$ *with* $L, K \subset \mathcal{A}$. *Then*

$$
\begin{aligned}
P \;=\; & \sum \{(\alpha, r).(P_1' \bowtie_L P_2)/K \mid P_1 \xrightarrow{(\alpha,r)} P_1' \;;\; \alpha \notin L \cup K\} \\
& + \sum \{(\alpha, r).(P_1 \bowtie_L P_2')/K \mid P_2 \xrightarrow{(\alpha,r)} P_2' \;;\; \alpha \notin L \cup K\} \\
& + \sum \{(\tau, r).(P_1' \bowtie_L P_2)/K \mid P_1 \xrightarrow{(\alpha,r)} P_1' \;;\; \alpha \in K \setminus L\} \\
& + \sum \{(\tau, r).(P_1 \bowtie_L P_2')/K \mid P_2 \xrightarrow{(\alpha,r)} P_2' \;;\; \alpha \in K \setminus L\} \\
& + \sum \{(\alpha, r).(P_1' \bowtie_L P_2')/K \mid P_1 \xrightarrow{(\alpha,r_1)} P_1' \;;\; P_2 \xrightarrow{(\alpha,r_2)} P_2' \;;\; \alpha \in L \setminus K \;; \\
& \qquad\qquad\qquad r = \frac{r_1}{r_\alpha(P_1)} \frac{r_2}{r_\alpha(P_2)} \min(r_\alpha(P_1), r_\alpha(P_2))\} \\
& + \sum \{(\tau, r).(P_1' \bowtie_L P_2')/K \mid P_1 \xrightarrow{(\alpha,r_1)} P_1' \;;\; P_2 \xrightarrow{(\alpha,r_2)} P_2' \;;\; \alpha \in L \cap K \;; \\
& \qquad\qquad\qquad r = \frac{r_1}{r_\alpha(P_1)} \frac{r_2}{r_\alpha(P_2)} \min(r_\alpha(P_1), r_\alpha(P_2))\}
\end{aligned}
$$

Associativity does apply in the case of parallel composition, as we see in Proposition 6.3.4, since the components proceed independently. An alternative form of the Expansion Law can be stated for parallel composition.

Proposition 6.3.7 (Expansion Law for Parallel Composition)
Let $P \equiv (P_1 \parallel P_2 \parallel \cdots \parallel P_n)/K$ *with* $n \geq 1$ *and* $K \subset \mathcal{A}$. *Then*

$$
\begin{aligned}
P = & \sum \{(\alpha, r).(P_1 \parallel \cdots \parallel P_i' \parallel \cdots \parallel P_n)/K \mid P_i \xrightarrow{(\alpha,r)} P_i' \;;\; \alpha \notin K\} \\
& + \sum \{(\tau, r).(P_1 \parallel \cdots \parallel P_i' \parallel \cdots \parallel P_n)/K \mid P_i \xrightarrow{(\alpha,r)} P_i' \;;\; \alpha \in K\}
\end{aligned}
$$

6.3.3 Isomorphism as a Congruence

A relation over PEPA components is a congruence if it is preserved by each of the combinators of the PEPA language and by recursive definition. It is straightforward to show that this is true for the isomorphism relation by constructing appropriate component isomorphisms.

Proposition 6.3.8 (Preservation by Combinators)
Let $P_1 = P_2$, *with component isomorphism* $\mathcal{F} : ds(P_1) \longrightarrow ds(P_2)$. *Then*

1. $a.P_1 = a.P_2$;
2. $P_1 + Q = P_2 + Q$;
3. $P_1 \bowtie_L Q = P_2 \bowtie_L Q$;
4. $P_1/L = P_2/L$.

Proof

1. Consider a function $\mathcal{G} : ds(a.P_1) \longrightarrow ds(a.P_2)$ defined as follows:

$$
\text{for any } P' \in ds(a.P_1), \quad \mathcal{G}(P') = \begin{cases} a.P_2 & \text{if } P' \equiv a.P_1 \\ \mathcal{F}(P') & \text{otherwise} \end{cases}
$$

Then, since $Act(a.P_1) = \{\!| a |\!\} = Act(a.P_2)$, $\mathcal{G}$ is a component isomorphism. Hence $a.P_1 = a.P_2$.

2. We remark that $ds(P_1 + Q) = ds(P_1) \cup ds(Q)$. Consider a function $\mathcal{G}$ such that, for any $P' \in ds(P_1 + Q)$,

$$\mathcal{G}(P') = \begin{cases} P_2 + Q & \text{if } P' \equiv P_1 + Q \\ \mathcal{F}(P') & \text{if } P' \in ds(P_1) \\ P' & \text{otherwise} \end{cases}$$

$Act(P_1 + Q) = Act(P_2 + Q)$ since $Act(P_1) = Act(P_2)$. For all $P' \in ds(P_1)$, by the definition of $\mathcal{F}$, $\mathcal{F}(P') \in ds(P_2)$. Moreover $P' \in ds(P_1 + Q) \setminus ds(P_1)$ and $P' \not\equiv P_1 + Q$ implies that $P' \in ds(Q)$. Thus $\mathcal{G}$ is a component isomorphism and $P_1 + Q = P_2 + Q$.

3. Any element of $ds(P_1 \underset{L}{\bowtie} Q)$ has the form $P' \underset{L}{\bowtie} Q'$, where $P' \in ds(P_1)$, $Q' \in ds(Q)$. Define $\mathcal{G} : ds(P_1 \underset{L}{\bowtie} Q) \longrightarrow ds(P_2 \underset{L}{\bowtie} Q)$ such that for any $P' \underset{L}{\bowtie} Q' \in ds(P_1 \underset{L}{\bowtie} Q)$,

$$\mathcal{G}(P' \underset{L}{\bowtie} Q') = \mathcal{F}(P') \underset{L}{\bowtie} Q'.$$

Since $\mathcal{F}$ is a component isomorphism, it follows that $\mathcal{G}$ is a component isomorphism. Hence $P_1 \underset{L}{\bowtie} Q = P_2 \underset{L}{\bowtie} Q$.

4. If $\mathcal{F}$ is a component isomorphism between P_1 and P_2 it follows immediately that a component isomorphism between P_1/L and P_2/L can be defined in terms of $\mathcal{F}$ in the natural way, and so $P_1/L = P_2/L$. □

As seen in Chapter 4, sets of recursive definitions are typically used to define the behaviour of PEPA components. Recall that if E is a component expression which contains an indexed set of variables $\tilde{X}$, then $E\{\tilde{P}/\tilde{X}\}$ denotes the component formed when every occurrence of each X in E is replaced by the component P from an indexed set of components $\tilde{P}$.

Definition 6.3.1 *Let E and F be component expressions, both containing the same indexed set of variables $\tilde{X}$. Then $\mathcal{F}_{\tilde{X}} : ds(E) \longrightarrow ds(F)$ is a component isomorphism between E and F if $\mathcal{F}_{\tilde{X}}$ is an injective function such that $X_i = \mathcal{F}_{\tilde{X}}(X_i)$ for all $X_i \in \tilde{X}$, for any derivative expression E', $Act(E') = Act(\mathcal{F}_{\tilde{X}}(E'))$, and for all $a \in Act$ the set of a-derivatives of $\mathcal{F}_{\tilde{X}}(E')$ is the same as the set of $\mathcal{F}_{\tilde{X}}$-images of a-derivatives of E'.*

Definition 6.3.2 *Two component expressions, E and F, containing variables $\tilde{X}$, are isomorphic, denoted $E = F$, if there exists a component isomorphism $\mathcal{F}_{\tilde{X}}$ between them such that $\mathcal{D}(\mathcal{F}_{\tilde{X}}(E)) = \mathcal{D}(F)$.*

Thus, by definition, $E = F$ implies that $\mathcal{D}(\mathcal{F}_{\tilde{X}}(E)) = \mathcal{D}(F)$, so if the variables $\tilde{X}$ are instantiated by an indexed set of components $\tilde{P}$ there exists a component isomorphism $\mathcal{F}_{\tilde{P}} : ds(E\{\tilde{P}/\tilde{X}\}) \longrightarrow ds(F\{\tilde{P}/\tilde{X}\})$, defined as $\mathcal{F}_{\tilde{P}}(E'\{\tilde{P}/\tilde{X}\}) = \mathcal{F}_{\tilde{X}}(E')\{\tilde{P}/\tilde{X}\}$. It follows that $E\{\tilde{P}/\tilde{X}\} = F\{\tilde{P}/\tilde{X}\}$ for all indexed sets of components $\tilde{P}$.

The following proposition shows that isomorphism is preserved by recursive definition. This means that if a subexpression is replaced by an isomorphic subexpression, then the resulting expression is isomorphic to the original expression.

Proposition 6.3.9 (Preservation by Recursive Definition) *Let $\tilde{E}$ and $\tilde{F}$ contain variables $\tilde{X}$ at most. Let $\tilde{A} \overset{\text{def}}{=} \tilde{E}\{\tilde{A}/\tilde{X}\}$, $\tilde{B} \overset{\text{def}}{=} \tilde{F}\{\tilde{B}/\tilde{X}\}$ and $\tilde{E} = \tilde{F}$. Then $\tilde{A} = \tilde{B}$.*

Proof It is sufficient to show the result for single recursion equations E and F such that $E = F$, $A \overset{\text{def}}{=} E\{A/X\}$, $B \overset{\text{def}}{=} F\{B/X\}$. By Proposition 6.3.5, it follows that $A = E\{A/X\}$ and $B = F\{B/X\}$. Moreover, $E = F$, implies that there is a component isomorphism $\mathcal{F}_X$ such that $\mathcal{D}(\mathcal{F}_X(E)) = \mathcal{D}(F)$. Therefore $E\{A/X\} = F\{B/X\}$ since the structure of the two expressions is identical. Hence, $A = B$ as required. □

This result, with Proposition 6.3.8, shows that $=$ is a congruence for PEPA.

6.4   Isomorphism between System Components

In this section we consider what we can deduce about the system components represented by the PEPA components P and Q in the case that $P = Q$. Let Sys_P and Sys_Q denote the system components modelled by P and Q respectively.

If $P = Q$ then there is a component isomorphism, $\mathcal{F}$, between the derivative sets, such that $\mathcal{D}(\mathcal{F}(P)) = \mathcal{D}(Q)$. In terms of the system components, Sys_P and Sys_Q this implies that they are capable of performing the same actions, at the same rates, resulting in states which also enable exactly the same actions. The exit rates from P and Q are the same, implying that the expected delay experienced by each system component before an action occurs will be the same. Actions in the two components progress at the same rate which implies that the implicit resources of the two system components are equivalent, i.e. equivalent underlying resources facilitating actions, which are not explicitly modelled, are available in Sys_P and Sys_Q. Moreover, since the activity multisets of the two components are identical, the probability that each system component undertakes a given action is the same. Also, if a particular action occurs, the probability of any given outcome will be the same in the two components.

In effect Sys_P and Sys_Q are the same component. They are capable of exactly the same sequences of activities, in the same order, with the same probabilities and transition rates. Thus if $P = Q$ then Sys_P and Sys_Q are indistinguishable in terms of behaviour and may be used interchangeably.

6.5   Isomorphism and the Markov Process

In this section we examine the relationship between isomorphism of PEPA components and the equivalence of Markov processes described in Section 5.3. Both these equivalences aim to capture the notion of models that exhibit exactly the same behaviour. In the PEPA components the behaviour is represented by derivatives and activities between them. In the Markov processes the behaviour is represented by states and transitions between them. It is clear that there is a strong correlation between these notions.

Proposition 6.5.1 *If P and Q are isomorphic PEPA components, i.e. $P = Q$, then P and Q generate Markov processes which are equivalent.*

Proof   By definition $P = Q$ implies that there is a component isomorphism $\mathcal{F}$ such that $\mathcal{D}(\mathcal{F}(P)) = \mathcal{D}(Q)$. Since the Markov process underlying a component is defined by the derivation graph the result follows immediately.   □

Isomorphism between components ensures that the underlying Markov processes must exhibit the same transient and steady state behaviours.

We can also consider whether equivalence of the underlying Markov processes implies isomorphism between the PEPA components. However, a PEPA component contains information about the type of an activity which is not recorded in the underlying Markov process. For example, consider the components,

$$T_1 \overset{\text{def}}{=} (task_1, r).T_1 \qquad\qquad T_2 \overset{\text{def}}{=} (task_2, r).T_2$$

T_1 and T_2 will generate the same Markov process although they are not isomorphic. Even if we consider an augmented Markov process in which transitions are annotated by the action types of the corresponding activities, equivalence at the level of the Markov process will not ensure that the components are isomorphic. Two or more activities in the PEPA component may be represented by a single transition in the Markov process. For example, consider the components X and Y shown in Figure 6.1. These components give rise to the same augmented Markov process although they are not isomorphic.

$$X_0 \stackrel{\text{def}}{=} (\alpha, r).X_1 + (\beta, s).X_1 \qquad Y_0 \stackrel{\text{def}}{=} (\alpha, s).Y_1 + (\beta, r).Y_1$$
$$X_1 \stackrel{\text{def}}{=} (\gamma, t).X_0 \qquad\qquad Y_1 \stackrel{\text{def}}{=} (\gamma, t).Y_0$$

Figure 6.1: Components which generate the same Markov process

A model-to-model equivalence between PEPA models should ensure that the same performance measures can be derived from the models. Since these measures are derived from reward structures, defined in terms of activities, the example in Figure 6.1 shows that equivalence of the underlying Markov processes, even if annotated, is not sufficient. Isomorphism does maintain performance measures but since it only relates models which generate Markov processes of the same size it is not useful for model simplification. In the rest of the chapter we develop a weaker notion of equivalence. We show that it guarantees the integrity of reward structures defined in terms of visible activities, whilst offering the possibility of model simplification in some circumstances.

6.6 Definition of Weak Isomorphism

Weak isomorphism aims to capture a notion of equivalence relating components which differ only in the details of their τ type activities. These activities are regarded as internal to the component enabling them, and as such their real type is hidden from external observation. No rewards may be attached to τ type activities. In particular we are interested in defining such a relation to find model simplifications which result in a smaller Markov process, whilst ensuring the integrity of the reward structure.

Weak isomorphism is based on the idea that for a component which carries out several consecutive τ type activities we may be able to find an equivalent *compact form*, which has the same visible behaviour but a single τ activity of longer duration. The relation is termed weak *isomorphism* because all other behaviours of the components are matched exactly. For components which do not enable such a sequence of τ activities there is a one-to-one correspondence with the compact form as in component isomorphism. Derivatives that are intermediate to, or start, such a sequence are mapped onto a single derivative in the compact form. As with isomorphism the equivalence is defined in terms of a structural relation between derivation graphs, the *weak component isomorphism*.

Thus, in effect, we eliminate nodes in the derivation graph whose only contribution is to introduce a τ type activity which is part of a sequence of τ type activities. For example, if a portion of the derivation graph is as shown on the left hand side below, we would like to replace it by the reduced graph shown on the right, where R is chosen appropriately.

Here, the node to be eliminated, P_j, can be identified as having only a single input arc and a single output arc, both of which correspond to τ type activities. However sequences of τ activities may also arise in more complex situations. For example, consider the component $P \stackrel{\text{def}}{=} Q_1 \bowtie_{\{\beta\}} Q_2$, where $b = (\beta, r_b)$ and

$$Q_1 \stackrel{\text{def}}{=} (\tau, r_1).(\tau, r_2).b.Q_1 \qquad\qquad Q_2 \stackrel{\text{def}}{=} a.c.b.Q_2$$

The derivation graph of P is shown below:

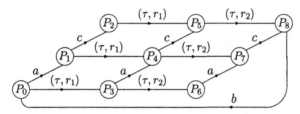

We would like the derivation graph shown below to be considered weakly isomorphic to this:

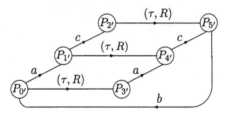

when R has the appropriate value.

In general, choosing this value, R, presents a problem. In each case we relate a sequence of τ activities to a single τ activity. We would like the duration of this single activity to be the same as the end-to-end delay incurred by the τ-sequence. However, the distribution of this end-to-end delay is found as the convolution of the appropriate distributions—for a sequence of exponential delays this will be a Coxian distribution. In the simplified PEPA model the distribution associated with the single τ type activity is assumed to be exponential. In Section 6.9 we will show when this assumption is justified by considering the PEPA model as a generalised semi-Markov process (GSMP) and applying insensitivity results.

Before we formalise the definition of weak isomorphism we introduce the notion of a *resource component*.

Resource Components

If we consider the enabled activities of any component we can find one or more collections of *competing* activities—these correspond to the implicit resources in the system. As explained in Section 3.3.3, in a choice of components, $P+Q$, it is assumed that P and Q are competing for the same implicit resource. Thus only one of the activities enabled by P and Q can have access to the resource at a time. It follows that the completion of an activity enabled by P will *abort* all the activities enabled by Q, as well as any other activities enabled by P. In contrast a cooperation, $P \bowtie_L Q$, represents an interaction between components, each of which has its own implicit resource. Thus, the completion of an individual activity of P will *interrupt*, but not abort, concurrently enabled individual activities of Q. It follows that, in general, each cooperation combinator in a component represents the introduction of another implicit resource.

We can identify a *resource component* within a component, C, with a multiset of activities within $Act(C)$ which are all dependent on the same implicit resource. Thus each cooperation combinator potentially introduces another resource component—this is not necessarily the case since the cooperation may inhibit some activities. Shared activities will belong to more than one resource component.

Definition 6.6.1 *A resource component within a multiset of enabled activities is a multiset of activities such that the completion of any one of them aborts all of them, and interrupts all other enabled activities.*

For example, if P and Q both enable a single resource component, then $P + Q$ has a single resource component corresponding to $Act(P + Q)$; on the other hand, $P \bowtie_L Q$ enables two resource components corresponding to $Act(P)$ and $Act(Q)$ respectively. Recall that for irreducible components, all choices must occur within cooperations, not between cooperations. It follows that in all the PEPA models we consider choices in the model will constitute single resource components.

If we consider the derivation graph fragment shown in Figure 6.2 it is clear that the τ activities, (τ, r_1), (τ, r_2) and (τ, r_3), correspond to the same implicit resource and the visible activities a and b correspond to a different one.

Definition 6.6.2 *A resource component is termed a* silent *resource component if it consists of a single hidden activity, i.e. $\{ (\tau, r) \}$.*

In the example shown in Figure 6.2 the activities (τ, r_1), (τ, r_2) and (τ, r_3) are silent resource components, occurring consecutively.

It is consecutive silent resource components which may be replaced by a single activity in a compact form. Replacing other sequences of τ activities would not leave the rest of the behaviour of the component unaffected. For example, if the first τ activity in the sequence was enabled in competition with visible activities, replacing the sequence by a single τ activity with a different duration will alter the probability of the visible activities occurring.

Definition 6.6.3 *A sequence of consecutive τ type activities in a derivation graph is termed a* reducible sequence *if the activities are all silent resource components corresponding to the same implicit resource.*

The activities (τ, r_1), (τ, r_2) and (τ, r_3) shown in Figure 6.2 form a reducible sequence.

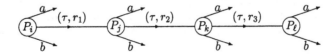

Figure 6.2: Derivation graph fragment for a PEPA model with a reducible sequence

Weak Component Isomorphism

We use reducible sequences to identify components which do not need to be maintained by the weak component isomorphism, the *hidden components*.

Definition 6.6.4 *A derivative P is a* hidden component *if it has a silent resource component, it is the derivative of a component with a silent resource component, via the completion of that activity, and all other resource components of the two derivatives are the same.*

If we consider the derivatives shown in Figure 6.2, the hidden components are P_j and P_k. The weak component isomorphism will map a hidden component onto the same derivative as its *silent precedent*, the previous derivative in the reducible sequence.

Definition 6.6.5 *For a hidden component P its* silent precedent *is the preceding derivative connected to it by an arc corresponding to the previous silent resource component in the reducible sequence.*

In Figure 6.2, P_i is the silent precedent of P_j and P_j is the silent precedent of P_k. The derivative that marks the end of a reducible sequence which starts with the activity (τ, r) will be called the *visible (τ, r)-derivative*. This derivative will not be a hidden component. Thus P_ℓ is the visible (τ, r_1)-derivative of P_i.

Definition 6.6.6 *Suppose component P has a reducible sequence with silent resource component $\{\!|\, (\tau, r)\, |\!\}$, such that $P \xrightarrow{(\tau,r)} P'$, then the* visible (τ, r)-derivative of P*, denoted $V_{(\tau,r)}(P)$ is defined as follows:*

$$
V_{(\tau,r)}(P) = \begin{cases} V_{(\tau,s)}(P') & \text{if (τ, s) is the next silent resource component in the} \\ & \text{reducible sequence.} \\ P' & \text{if P' is not a hidden component} \end{cases}
$$

We can now define a weak component isomorphism. The conditions imposed on it for components which are not hidden components and activities which do not form silent resource components are the same as the conditions for a component isomorphism.

Definition 6.6.7 *A function $\mathcal{F} : ds(P) \longrightarrow ds(C)$ is a* weak component isomorphism *from P to C if $\mathcal{F}$ is a surjective function such that if $P' \in ds(P)$, P' not a hidden component, all non-silent resource components of P' and $\mathcal{F}(P')$ are identical. For any $a \in \mathcal{A}ct(P')$, not part of a reducible sequence, the set of a-derivatives of $\mathcal{F}(P')$ is the same as the $\mathcal{F}$-image of the set of a-derivatives of P'. For any silent resource component of P', (τ, r), there is some silent resource component of $\mathcal{F}(P')$, (τ, R), such that $\mathcal{F}(V_{(\tau,r)}(P')) = V_{(\tau,R)}(\mathcal{F}(P'))$. Moreover the expected delay between P' and $V_{(\tau,r)}(P')$ is the same as the expected delay between $\mathcal{F}(P')$ and $V_{(\tau,R)}(\mathcal{F}(P'))$. On the other hand, if $P'' \in ds(P)$, P'' a hidden component, with silent precedent P', then $\mathcal{F}(P'') = \mathcal{F}(P')$.*

Definition 6.6.8 *If there is a weak component isomorphism $\mathcal{F}$ from P to C, then C is called a* compact form *of P, denoted $C \leq P$.*

If a component P has no hidden derivatives in its derivative set the identity function, or any component isomorphism, will be a weak component isomorphism on P. Moreover P, or any component isomorphic to it, will be a compact form of P, i.e. $P \leq P$, or if $P' = P$ then $P' \leq P$ and $P \leq P'$. The converse is also true, $P' \leq P$ and $P \leq P'$ only if $P' = P$.

If C is a compact form of P, and $Q = P$ then it follows that C is also a compact form of Q, i.e. $C \leq P$ and $Q = P$ implies $C \leq Q$. Similarly if C' is isomorphic to C, then C' is also a compact form of P, i.e. $C \leq P$ and $C' = C$ implies $C' \leq P$.

We can now define when we consider components to be weakly isomorphic. Clearly we would like to consider a component to be weakly isomorphic with its compact form. However we can make the relation more general than that—we consider a component to be weakly isomorphic with any component with which it shares a compact form.

Definition 6.6.9 *Two components P and Q are* weakly isomorphic, *denoted $P \approx Q$, if there is some component C which is a compact form of both P and Q,*

Thus a component may be weakly isomorphic to components which have more elaborate representations of internal activities as well as more compact ones.

If $P = Q$ then by the argument above, they must have a common compact form, and $P \approx Q$. If $P \approx Q$ and neither P nor Q has any hidden derivatives in its derivation graph, then P and Q are each their own, and each other's, compact form, so it follows that $P = Q$.

In general, in order to show that $P \approx Q$ we must find a compact form C and weak component isomorphisms, $\mathcal{F}_P$ and $\mathcal{F}_Q$, from P to C and Q to C respectively. However, in practice we will be interested in using weak isomorphism to guide model simplification, by finding a compact form of a component, which has a smaller derivative set, and so will generate a smaller Markov process.

6.7 Properties of Weak Isomorphism

In this section we consider the weak isomorphism relation, $\approx$, from a process algebra perspective. We see that weak isomorphism is not a congruence—it is not preserved by the choice combinator. For example, consider the components X, Y and Z shown in Figure 6.3. We assume that R has the appropriate value and that Y is a compact form of X, i.e. $Y \leq X$, with weak component isomorphism $\mathcal{F}$. It follows that $X \approx Y$ but $X + Z \not\approx Y + Z$.

$$X_0 \stackrel{\text{def}}{=} (\tau, r_1).X_1$$
$$X_1 \stackrel{\text{def}}{=} (\tau, r_2).X_2 \qquad Y_0 \stackrel{\text{def}}{=} (\tau, R).Y_1 \qquad Z_0 \stackrel{\text{def}}{=} (\alpha, s_a).Z_1$$
$$X_2 \stackrel{\text{def}}{=} (\beta, r_b).X_0 \qquad Y_1 \stackrel{\text{def}}{=} (\beta, r_b).Y_0 \qquad Z_1 \stackrel{\text{def}}{=} (\beta, s_b).Z_0$$

Figure 6.3: Components X, Y and Z such that $Y \leq X$

If we consider the derivation graphs of the components $X + Z$ and $Y + Z$ neither contains a hidden component. It follows that $X + Z \approx Y + Z$ only if $X + Z = Y + Z$. However this cannot be the case since the components do not even have the same number of derivatives.

The resource component of $X + Z$ is $\{\!| \, (\tau, r_1), (\alpha, s_a) \, |\!\}$ whereas the resource component of $Y + Z$ is $\{\!| \, (\tau, R), (\alpha, s_a) \, |\!\}$.

For the components $X \underset{\{\beta\}}{\bowtie} Z$ and $Y \underset{\{\beta\}}{\bowtie} Z$, we can form a weak component isomorphism $\mathcal{F}'$, from $X \underset{\{\beta\}}{\bowtie} Z$ to $Y \underset{\{\beta\}}{\bowtie} Z$, based on $\mathcal{F}$.

$$\mathcal{F}'(X_i \underset{\{\beta\}}{\bowtie} Z_j) \; = \; \mathcal{F}(X_i) \underset{\{\beta\}}{\bowtie} Z_j \qquad \text{for } i = 0, 1, 2 \text{ and } j = 0, 1$$

The resource components of $X \underset{\{\beta\}}{\bowtie} Z$ are $\{\!| \, (\tau, r_1) \, |\!\}$ and $\{\!| \, (\alpha, s_a) \, |\!\}$, and the resource components of $Y \underset{\{\beta\}}{\bowtie} Z$ are $\{\!| \, (\tau, R) \, |\!\}$ and $\{\!| \, (\alpha, s_a) \, |\!\}$. Thus we conclude that $X \underset{\{\beta\}}{\bowtie} Z \approx Y \underset{\{\beta\}}{\bowtie} Z$.

Note that $X + Z$ and $Y + Z$, unlike the rest of the examples used in the thesis, are not irreducible components. Indeed, we conjecture that if we considered only irreducible components weak isomorphism may be preserved by choice, and therefore be a congruence.

6.7.1   Preservation by Combinators

In the following proposition we show that weak isomorphism is in fact preserved by all the other combinators of PEPA except choice.

Proposition 6.7.1 (Preservation by Combinators)
If $P_1 \approx P_2$ then

1. $a.P_1 \approx a.P_2$;

2. $P_1 \underset{L}{\bowtie} Q \approx P_2 \underset{L}{\bowtie} Q$;

3. $P_1/L \approx P_2/L$

Proof   If $P_1 \approx P_2$ then they must have some common compact form, C say, such that there are weak component isomorphisms, $\mathcal{F}_1$ and $\mathcal{F}_2$, from P_1 and P_2 to C respectively.

1. We can extend $\mathcal{F}_1$ and $\mathcal{F}_2$ to $ds(a.P_1)$ and $ds(a.P_2)$ in the natural way:

$$\text{for all } \; P' \in ds(a.P_1) \qquad \mathcal{F}_1'(P') = \left\{ \begin{array}{ll} a.C & \text{if } P' \equiv a.P_1 \\ \mathcal{F}_1(P') & \text{otherwise} \end{array} \right.$$

   $\mathcal{F}_2'$ is defined analogously. $\mathcal{F}_1'$ and $\mathcal{F}_2'$ are weak component isomorphisms and $a.C$ is a compact form for both $a.P_1$ and $a.P_2$. Hence $a.P_1 \approx a.P_2$.

2. Let $\overline{Q}$ be a compact form of Q, with weak component isomorphism $\mathcal{F}_Q$, possibly the identity. We define a function $\mathcal{G}_1$ from $P_1 \underset{L}{\bowtie} Q$ to $C \underset{L}{\bowtie} \overline{Q}$:

$$\text{for any } P' \underset{L}{\bowtie} Q' \in ds(P_1 \underset{L}{\bowtie} Q), \qquad \mathcal{G}_1(P' \underset{L}{\bowtie} Q') = \mathcal{F}_1(P') \underset{L}{\bowtie} \mathcal{F}_Q(Q')$$

   $\mathcal{G}_1$ is surjective since $\mathcal{F}_1$ and $\mathcal{F}_Q$ are surjective. Since τ cannot belong to the cooperation set it follows that any reducible sequence in $P_1 \underset{L}{\bowtie} Q$ arises from a reducible sequence in P_1 or Q. Any activity a of $P' \underset{L}{\bowtie} Q'$ which is not a silent resource component will be an individual activity of P' or Q', or a shared activity arising from activities of P' and Q'. By the definition of weak component isomorphism these will be individual activities of $\mathcal{F}_1(P')$ or $\mathcal{F}_Q(Q')$, or a shared activity of $\mathcal{F}_1(P') \underset{L}{\bowtie} \mathcal{F}_Q(Q')$. It follows that $\mathcal{G}_1$ is a weak component isomorphism and $C \underset{L}{\bowtie} \overline{Q}$ is a compact form of $P_1 \underset{L}{\bowtie} Q$.

   We define $\mathcal{G}_2$ from $P_2 \underset{L}{\bowtie} Q$ to $C \underset{L}{\bowtie} \overline{Q}$ analogously, and thus it follows that it is a weak component isomorphism. Hence $C \underset{L}{\bowtie} \overline{Q}$ is a compact form of both $P_1 \underset{L}{\bowtie} Q$ and $P_2 \underset{L}{\bowtie} Q$. We conclude that $P_1 \underset{L}{\bowtie} Q \approx P_2 \underset{L}{\bowtie} Q$.

3. Let $\overline{C}$ be a compact form of C/L and let $\mathcal{F}_R$ be a weak component isomorphism from C/L to $\overline{C}$, possibly the identity. We can construct a weak component isomorphism $\mathcal{G}_1$ from P_1/L to $\overline{C}$ as follows:

$$\text{for all } P'/L \in ds(P_1/L) \qquad \mathcal{G}_1(P'/L) = \mathcal{F}_R(\mathcal{F}_1(P')/L)$$

We can define a weak component isomorphism, $\mathcal{G}_2$ from P_2/L to $\overline{C}$ analogously. It follows that $\overline{C}$ is a compact form of P_1/L and P_2/L, and we conclude that $P_1/L \approx P_2/L$.

$\square$

6.7.2 Equational Laws for Weak Isomorphism

Since isomorphism between components implies weak isomorphism, i.e. if $P = Q$ then $P \approx Q$, it follows that the equational laws stated in Section 6.3.1 can be restated for the weak isomorphism relation.

Proposition 6.7.2 (Choice)

1. $P + Q \approx Q + P$

2. $P + (Q + R) \approx (P + Q) + R$

Proposition 6.7.3 (Hiding)

1. $(P + Q)/L \approx P/L + Q/L$

2. $((\alpha, r).P)/L \approx \begin{cases} (\tau, r).P/L & \alpha \in L \\ (\alpha, r).P/L & \alpha \notin L \end{cases}$

3. $(P/L)/K \approx P/(L \cup K)$

4. $P/L \approx P$ if $L \cap \vec{A}(P) = \emptyset$

Proposition 6.7.4 (Cooperation)

1. $P \bowtie_L Q \approx Q \bowtie_L P$

2. $P \bowtie_L (Q \bowtie_L R) \approx (P \bowtie_L Q) \bowtie_L R$

3. $(P \bowtie_L Q)/(K \cup M) \approx \left((P/K) \bowtie_L (Q/K) \right) \big/ M$ *where* $K \cap M = K \cap L = \emptyset$

4. $P \bowtie_K Q \approx P \bowtie_L Q$ *if* $K \cap \left(\vec{A}(P) \cup \vec{A}(Q) \right) = L$

5. $(P \bowtie_L Q) \bowtie_K R \approx \begin{cases} P \bowtie_L (Q \bowtie_K R) & \text{if } \vec{A}(R) \cap (L \setminus K) = \emptyset \wedge \vec{A}(P) \cap (K \setminus L) = \emptyset \\ Q \bowtie_L (P \bowtie_K R) & \text{if } \vec{A}(R) \cap (L \setminus K) = \emptyset \wedge \vec{A}(Q) \cap (K \setminus L) = \emptyset \end{cases}$

Proposition 6.7.5 (Constant)

If $A \stackrel{\text{def}}{=} P$ *then* $A \approx P$.

Proposition 6.7.6 (Expansion Law) *Let* $P \equiv (P_1 \bowtie_L P_2)/K$ *with* $L, K \subset \mathcal{A}$. *Then*

$$
\begin{aligned}
P \approx \; & \sum \{(\alpha, r).(P_1' \bowtie_L P_2)/K \mid P_1 \xrightarrow{(\alpha, r)} P_1' \; ; \; \alpha \notin L \cup K\} \\
& + \sum \{(\alpha, r).(P_1 \bowtie_L P_2')/K \mid P_2 \xrightarrow{(\alpha, r)} P_2' \; ; \; \alpha \notin L \cup K\} \\
& + \sum \{(\tau, r).(P_1' \bowtie_L P_2)/K \mid P_1 \xrightarrow{(\alpha, r)} P_1' \; ; \; \alpha \in K \setminus L\} \\
& + \sum \{(\tau, r).(P_1 \bowtie_L P_2')/K \mid P_2 \xrightarrow{(\alpha, r)} P_2' \; ; \; \alpha \in K \setminus L\} \\
& + \sum \{(\alpha, r).(P_1' \bowtie_L P_2')/K \mid P_1 \xrightarrow{(\alpha, r_1)} P_1' \; ; \; P_2 \xrightarrow{(\alpha, r_2)} P_2' \; ; \; \alpha \in L \setminus K \; ; \\
& \qquad\qquad\qquad r = \frac{r_1}{r_\alpha(P_1)} \frac{r_2}{r_\alpha(P_2)} \min(r_\alpha(P_1), r_\alpha(P_2))\} \\
& + \sum \{(\tau, r).(P_1' \bowtie_L P_2')/K \mid P_1 \xrightarrow{(\alpha, r_1)} P_1' \; ; \; P_2 \xrightarrow{(\alpha, r_2)} P_2' \; ; \; \alpha \in L \cap K \; ; \\
& \qquad\qquad\qquad r = \frac{r_1}{r_\alpha(P_1)} \frac{r_2}{r_\alpha(P_2)} \min(r_\alpha(P_1), r_\alpha(P_2))\}
\end{aligned}
$$

6.8   Weak Isomorphism and System Components

In this section we consider the implications of the weak isomorphism relation, $P \approx Q$, for the system components being modelled by P and Q. As in Section 6.4, let Sys_P and Sys_Q denote the system components modelled by P and Q respectively. First, we consider what it means, from the aspect of system components, to hide some action types.

Hiding may be regarded as a representation of encapsulation of function by system components. We assume that if a system component is represented by $P/\{\alpha\}$ in the PEPA model, then implementations of the action α are internal to this component. No other components within the system may gain access to this instantiation of the action. In particular, even if the component is subsequently placed in a configuration in which cooperation is required to achieve actions of type α, the α action of P will not be available to the other component. Thus τ actions are not *visible* to the environment in this sense. Nevertheless, the component will still expend some effort to complete such actions and a delay will be incurred.

In terms of complete systems, hiding at the top level denotes those actions of the system which are not deemed visible to an external observer. This may place limitations on the performance measures which can be derived from the system. More often such top level hiding will be introduced in the model, without an interpretation in terms of the system, for the purposes of model simplification. Which action types are hidden may vary according to the required reward structure. In effect we may transform the model to suit the experimental frame in which it is placed.

$P \approx Q$ implies that there is some compact form C such that $C \leq P$ and $C \leq Q$. Note that we do not assume that C corresponds to any existing system component. It is the simplest representation of the components representing Sys_P and Sys_Q.

A reducible sequence in a PEPA component corresponds to a sequence of hidden actions in the system component which must be completed before it can engage in any other actions accessing the same implicit resource. $P \approx Q$ implies that for activities which are not part of a reducible sequence, P and Q have the same capabilities. This means that the system components Sys_P and Sys_Q are capable of performing the same visible actions, at the same rates, resulting in states which also enable the same visible actions. Moreover there is a

$$A \overset{\text{def}}{=} (task_1, r).(task_2, s).a.A \qquad B \overset{\text{def}}{=} (task_3, s).(task_2, r).a.B$$

$$A/L \equiv (\tau, r).(\tau, s).a.A/L \qquad B/L \equiv (\tau, s).(\tau, r).a.B/L$$

$$L = \{task_1, task_2, task_3\}$$

Figure 6.4: Weakly isomorphic components with different internal actions

one-to-one correspondence between the reducible sequences of the two components. Thus Sys_P and Sys_Q engage in internal activity, of the same mean duration, at corresponding points in their life cycles.

However the weak isomorphism relation does not tell us anything more about these internal tasks which occupy Sys_P and Sys_Q. They may be engaged in exactly the same actions ($P = Q$), the same actions in a different order, or completely different actions. For example, consider the components A/L and B/L shown in Figure 6.4. $A/L \approx B/L$ although A and B are differently occupied during the reducible sequence.

We cannot conclude, as we did when $P = Q$, that Sys_P and Sys_Q are the same component in effect. The tasks undertaken by the two components may differ. However, they are indistinguishable in terms of visible behaviour—they are capable of the same sequences of visible activities, in the same order, with the same transition rates. Since the interactions between components are defined only in terms of their visible behaviours it follows that Sys_P and Sys_Q may be used interchangeably within any configuration.

6.9 Weak Isomorphism and the Markov Process

In this section we examine the relationship between the Markov processes underlying a PEPA model with a reducible sequence and a compact form of its initial component respectively. It is clear that these Markov processes cannot be equivalent as they do not have the same number of states. However we will show that in some cases the steady state distributions of the two processes are such that the same reward may be derived from each of them. Therefore, it follows that the same rewards and performance measures may be derived from weakly isomorphic components when certain syntactic conditions are satisfied. As a preliminary we define a generalised semi-Markov process and discuss how a PEPA model may be used to generate such a process.

Generalised Semi-Markov Processes

A generalised semi-Markov process (GSMP) is a process in which each state is characterised by a set of *active elements*, each with an associated *lifetime*. A state change occurs when an active element completes a lifetime and all interrupted elements record their residual lifetimes. Whenever the element is again active it resumes its remaining lifetime. If the lifetimes are exponential we may disregard the residual lifetimes, restarting each element with a new lifetime whenever it is active.

Definition 6.9.1 *A generalised semi-Markov process (GSMP) is defined on a set of states $\{x \mid x \in X\}$. For each x there are active elements s, from the set S, which decay at the rate $r(s, x)$, $s \in S$. When the active element s dies, the process moves to state $x' \in X$ with probability $p(x, s, x')$. The set of active elements S may be partitioned into two sets S' and S^*, where $s \in S'$ if the element s has an exponentially distributed lifetime, and $s \in S^*$ if its lifetime has an arbitrary general distribution.*

As when generating the Markov process underlying a PEPA model, we associate a state in the GSMP with each node in the derivation graph of the model. The active elements of the state are the resource components of the corresponding derivative. The rate of decay of the resource component is the sum of the rates of the activities enabled by the component. The transition probabilities are determined by the relative probability of each activity within the resource component. Thus in a PEPA model all the active elements will have exponentially distributed lifetimes, i.e. $s \in S'$ for all $s \in S$. However we will consider an intermediate system between the GSMP underlying a model and the GSMP underlying its compact form, in which generally distributed lifetimes are introduced.

Example

Let P be a PEPA component with a single reducible sequence of length n. For convenience we assume that this is between derivatives P_{N-n} and P_N, where $|ds(P)| = N+1$, renumbering derivatives if necessary. Then there are silent resource components $\{| (\tau, r_1) |\}, \dots, \{| (\tau, r_n) |\}$ such that $P_{N-n} \xrightarrow{(\tau, r_1)} P_{N-n+1} \xrightarrow{(\tau, r_2)} \dots \xrightarrow{(\tau, r_n)} P_N$. Since there is only one reducible sequence, $\{| (\tau, r_1) |\}$ must be the only resource component of P_{N-n}. In general, if P_{N-n} has m other resource components there will be m or more reducible sequences started by the activity (τ, r_1) (cf. $P \stackrel{\text{def}}{=} Q_1 \bowtie_{\{\beta\}} Q_2$ illustrated in Section 6.6).

Let C be a compact form of P, via weak component isomorphism $\mathcal{F}$, with a single silent resource component $\{| (\tau, R) |\}$ corresponding to the reducible sequence of P, $C_{N-n} \xrightarrow{(\tau, R)} C_{N-n+1}$, $|ds(C)| = N - n + 2$. We assume that for $0 \le i \le N - n$, $\mathcal{F}(P_i) = C_i$ and $\mathcal{F}(P_N) = C_{N-n+1}$.

Let X_P and X_C denote the (exponential) GSMPs generated by P and C respectively. We can construct a reduced form of X_P, $\overline{X}_P$, if we amalgamate the states $x_{N-n-1}, \dots, x_{N-1}$, corresponding to the hidden derivatives $P_{N-n+1}, \dots P_{N-1}$, with x_{N-n}. Each silent resource component $\{| (\tau, r_1) |\}, \dots, \{| (\tau, r_n) |\}$, corresponds to an active element. We concatenate the lifetimes of these active elements to form a single active element, denoted s. The lifetime of s is a n-stage Coxian distribution and the conditional transition probability is $p(x_{N-n+1}, s, x_{N-1}) = 1$. Note that given $\overline{X}_P$, X_P would be the process formed to solve the model by the method of stages.

Insensitivity in Generalised Semi-Markov Processes

It has been established that for some GSMPs, elements with lifetimes governed by a general distribution, such as s in $\overline{X}_P$, may be replaced by an element, such as $\{| (\tau, R) |\}$ in X_C, with an exponential lifetime of the same mean, without affecting the steady state behaviour. A GSMP is said to be *insensitive* if its steady state distribution depends only on the *mean* of distributions governing the behaviour of its elements, not their *form*. Therefore any process which is identical except that the lifetime of an *insensitive element* is governed by a different distribution function, but with the same mean, will exhibit the same steady state behaviour. Thus, for the example above, if we can show that $\overline{X}_P$ is insensitive in the element s, it follows that $\overline{X}_P$ and X_C exhibit the same steady state behaviour.

Conditions for insensitivity were investigated by Matthes [102], and may be expressed in the following theorem:

Theorem 6.9.1 (Matthes) *For a generalised semi-Markov process it can be shown that the following two statements are equivalent:*

1. *The process is insensitive with respect to the active elements of S^*. That is, the general distributions of the lifetimes of the elements of S^* can be replaced by any other distributions with the same mean, and yet the process still retains the same steady state distribution.*

2. *(the insensitivity balance equations)*
   When all active elements of S^* are assumed to be exponentially distributed, the flux out of each state due to the death of an element of S^* is equivalent to the flux into that state which causes the birth of that element.

The death of an element is interpreted as the element completing its lifetime and causing a state change. In terms of the PEPA component this corresponds to one of the activities in the resource component completing. The birth of an element occurs when there is a transition into a state where the element is active from a state where it was inactive and had no residual lifetime, or from a state where it completed a lifetime. In terms of the PEPA component this corresponds to the completion of an activity by the resource component based on the same implicit resource in a previous derivative.

In the case of $\overline{X}_P$ in the example above, the insensitivity balance equation is exactly the global balance equation for x_{N-n} in X_C. It follows that $\overline{X}_P$ and X_C exhibit the same steady state behaviour. However, the steady state behaviour of $\overline{X}_P$ is the same as the steady state behaviour of X_P except that residence in any of the states $x_{N-n+1}, \ldots, x_{N-1}$ in X_P is regarded as prolonged residence time in x_{N-n} in $\overline{X}_P$,

$$\overline{\Pi}_P(x_{N-n}) = \Pi_P(x_{N-n}) + \Pi_P(x_{N-n+1}) + \cdots + \Pi_P(x_{N-1})$$

We can deduce that, for all $0 \le i \le N - n$,

$$\Pi_P(x_i) = \Pi_C(\mathcal{F}(x_i)) \qquad \text{and} \qquad \Pi_P(x_N) = \Pi_C(\mathcal{F}(x_N))$$

where the weak component isomorphism, $\mathcal{F}$, is defined for the underlying state spaces in the obvious way. Since rewards are attached to visible activities and no visible activities are active when P is engaged in the reducible sequence, or C is engaged in the activity (τ, R), it follows that the rewards derived from P and C will be the same.

In the following section we establish when the insensitivity balance equations are satisfied by an arbitrary PEPA model with more than one reducible sequence in its derivation graph. As in the simple example above, we will introduce an intermediate GSMP with an active element with a Coxian lifetime for each reducible sequence. We will show that the reward derived from the model and its compact form will be the same provided the insensitivity balance equations are satisfied by the GSMP corresponding to the compact form.

6.9.1   Insensitivity of Reducible Sequences

Let S be a PEPA model with N reducible sequences within its derivation graph. We assume that T is a compact form of S, via the weak component isomorphism $\mathcal{G}$. Let X_S and X_T

denote the (exponential) GSMPs generated by S and T respectively. As previously, we construct a reduced form of X_S, $\overline{X}_S$, in which each state corresponding to a hidden derivative in the derivation graph of S is amalgamated with its silent precedent. The lifetime of the silent resource component starting the sequence, denoted s_j, $1 \leq j \leq N$, becomes the concatenation of the lifetimes of each of the silent resource components within the sequence. Note that all other active elements associated with a state corresponding to a hidden derivative are also active in the state corresponding to its silent precedent, by definition.

In [45], Henderson and Lucic state that in order to ensure insensitivity of a GSMP it is sufficient if a state change cannot activate or kill two generally distributed active elements simultaneously, and interrupted generally distributed active elements carry over their residual lifetimes to the next state.

Since we assume a preemptive resume execution strategy for cooperating components, and therefore resource components, it follows that interrupted generally distributed active elements, s_j, carry over their residual lifetimes to the next state (different resource components must arise in different cooperating components). Two such elements, s_k and s_j say, cannot die simultaneously. If they are simultaneously active they must belong to different resource components and as such can only interrupt each other. Moreover, there will be a race condition between them and the continuous nature of the distributions ensures that the probability of their simultaneous completion is zero.

The requirement that two active elements with generally distributed lifetimes cannot be simultaneously activated is not necessarily satisfied by a PEPA model. For example, consider a component $P \bowtie_L Q$ in which both P and Q enable reducible sequences immediately after a shared activity. In the reduced GSMP representing $P \bowtie_L Q$, in which hidden derivatives have been removed, the state change brought about by the completion of the shared activity will activate both s_P and s_Q, active elements with generally distributed lifetimes. However this is the only way in which two such active elements may be simultaneously activated, since to be simultaneously active they must belong to different resource components. Such instances can be easily identified, and excluded.

Theorem 6.9.2 *If PEPA model S has compact form T, and S is such that reducible sequences are enabled by the same resource component, by resource components in parallel components, or by resource components in cooperating components but preceded by individual activities, then the reward derived from S will be the same as the reward derived from T.*

Proof Let X_S and X_T be the GSMPs generated by S and T respectively, and construct the reduced form of X_S, $\overline{X}_S$, as previously. We assume that there are N reducible sequences in the derivation graph of S and that for each $1 \leq j \leq N$, the sequence has length n_j and runs between derivatives S_{j_1} and $S_{j_{n_j}}$. We denote the set of derivatives of S_0 which do not belong to any reducible sequence by $ds_{NR}(S_0)$, i.e. $S_i \in ds_{NR}(S_0)$ implies that $i \neq j_k$ for all k, $1 \leq k \leq n_j - 1$ and for all j, $1 \leq j \leq N$. Let x_i denote the state of X_S corresponding to $S_i \in ds(S_0)$, and $x_{\mathcal{G}(i)}$ denote the state of X_T corresponding to $\mathcal{G}(S_i) = T_{\mathcal{G}(i)} \in ds(T_0)$.

Since no reducible sequences of S are enabled by resource components in cooperating components immediately following a shared activity, it follows that no active elements with generally distributed lifetimes in $\overline{X}_S$ can be simultaneously activated. Thus we see that $\overline{X}_S$ is insensitive to all its active elements with generally distributed lifetimes, and that $\overline{X}_S$ and X_T exhibit the same steady state behaviour, i.e. for all $S_i \in ds_{NR}(S_0)$,

$$\overline{\Pi}_S(x_i) = \Pi_T(x_{\mathcal{G}(i)}) \tag{9.2}$$

Moreover, if x_{j_1} is the start of a reducible sequence between x_{j_1} and $x_{j_{n_j}}$, by definition,

$$\overline{\Pi}_S(x_{j_1}) = \sum_{k=1}^{n_j-1} \Pi_S(x_{j_k}) \tag{9.3}$$

Recall that the reward associated with a derivative is the sum of the rewards attached to activities which the derivative enables. If we consider all the hidden derivatives in the jth reducible sequence, $S_{j_2}, \ldots, S_{j_{n_j}-1}$, by definition they all enable the same activities as the starting derivative S_{j_1}. Thus, the reward associated with each of them is the same, ρ_j say. Moreover, the same reward will be associated with the corresponding derivative of T, $\mathcal{G}(S_{j_1}) = T_{\mathcal{G}(j_1)} \in ds(T_0)$. By definition the total reward associated with T, R_T, is

$$R_T = \sum_{T_{\mathcal{G}(i)} \in ds(T_0)} \rho_{\mathcal{G}(i)} \, \Pi_T(x_{\mathcal{G}(i)})$$

Similarly, the total reward associated with S, R_S, is

$$R_S = \sum_{S_i \in ds(S_0)} \rho_i \, \Pi_S(x_i) = \sum_{S_i \in ds_{NR}(S_0)} \rho_i \, \Pi_S(x_i) + \sum_{j=1}^{N} \sum_{k=1}^{n_j-1} \rho_{j_k} \, \Pi_S(x_{j_k})$$

$$= \sum_{S_i \in ds_{NR}(S_0)} \rho_i \, \Pi_S(x_i) + \sum_{j=1}^{N} \rho_j \sum_{k}^{n_j-1} \Pi_S(x_{j_k})$$

$$= \sum_{S_i \in ds_{NR}(S_0)} \rho_i \, \Pi_T(x_{\mathcal{G}(i)}) + \sum_{j=1}^{N} \rho_j \, \Pi_T(x_{\mathcal{G}(j_1)}) \tag{9.4}$$

It follows, by equations 9.2 and 9.3, that $R_S = R_T$. That is, the total rewards derived from the model, S, and its compact form, T, are the same. $\square$

Corollary 6.9.1 *If $P \approx Q$ and the reducible sequences of P and Q satisfy the conditions of Theorem 6.9.2, then any performance measures derived from P and Q via a reward structure are the same.*

Proof It follows immediately from the definition of $\approx$ and Theorem 6.9.2 that the rewards derived from P and Q will be identical and the result follows. $\square$

6.10 Weak Isomorphism for Model Simplification

In the previous section it was shown that given a reward structure expressed in terms of activities, weakly isomorphic components will generate the same reward. In particular the same performance measures may be derived from a model and its compact form. The size of the derivative set of a compact form is never larger than the size of the derivative set of the model it reduces, i.e. $C \leq P$ implies that $|ds(C)| \leq |ds(P)|$. This suggests the use of weak component isomorphisms for model simplification, resulting in state space reduction.

6.10.1   An Approach to Model Simplification

In this section we outline how weak isomorphism and the identification of a compact form for model components may be used as a model simplification technique. The approach which we propose involves the identification of reducible sequences within components of a complete model. A component will be replaced by a compact form as long as the conditions of Theorem 6.9.2 are satisfied. Since weak isomorphism is preserved by cooperation, the modified model will be weakly isomorphic to the original model, although it is not necessarily a compact form of the original model as there may be other reducible sequences which have not been reduced.

As remarked in Section 6.8, hiding at the top level of a PEPA model may be introduced to reflect the experimental frame in which the model is currently viewed. Thus any activities to which rewards are not attached may be hidden. Using the equational laws of Propositions 6.3.2 and 6.3.3, the PEPA component representing the model may be manipulated into a form in which the reducible sequences are apparent. In particular hiding operators are moved inside cooperation combinators whenever possible.

As different performance measures are derived from rewards attached to different activities it may be possible to produce different simplified models according to the performance measure currently under consideration. For very large models, producing separate models to calculate each performance measure may be more efficient than solving a single large model suitable for calculating all the performance measures at once.

6.10.2   Simplifying an MSMQ Model using Weak Isomorphism

In this section we illustrate the technique outlined in the previous section with one of the case studies introduced in Chapter 4. Consider again the embedded MSMQ system shown in Figure 4.12:

$$
System \stackrel{def}{=} \left((Comp_1 \parallel Comp_2 \parallel Comp_3) \underset{\substack{\{walk\_E_j, \\ walk\_F_j, serve_j\}}}{\bowtie} (S_1 \parallel S_1) \right) / L \qquad (1 \leq j \leq N)
$$

where $L = \{accept_2, accept_3, pack_2, pack_3, walk\_E_j, walk\_F_j\}$. By Proposition 6.3.3 we know that this is isomorphic to

$$
\left(((Comp_1 \parallel Comp_2 \parallel Comp_3)/L_1) \underset{\substack{\{walk\_E_j, \\ walk\_F_j, serve_j\}}}{\bowtie} ((S_1 \parallel S_1)/L_1) \right) / L_2
$$

where $L_1 = \{accept_2, accept_3, pack_2, pack_3\}$ and $L_2 = \{walk\_E_j, walk\_F_j\}$. Continuing in this way, applying Proposition 6.3.3 and 6.3.2, we can see that this is isomorphic to

$$
\left((Comp_1 \parallel (Comp_2/L_{12}) \parallel (Comp_3/L_{13})) \underset{\substack{\{walk\_E_j, \\ walk\_F_j, serve_j\}}}{\bowtie} (S_1 \parallel S_1) \right) / L_2
$$

where $L_{12} = \{accept_2, pack_2\}$ and $L_{13} = \{accept_3, pack_3\}$. Then

$$
Comp_2/L_{12} = (Node_{20}/L_{12}) \underset{\{in, serve_2\}}{\bowtie} (Gen_{20}/L_{12})
$$

$$
= Node_{20} \underset{\{in, serve_2\}}{\bowtie} (Gen_{20}/\{accept_2, pack_2\})
$$

$$Node_{j0} \stackrel{def}{=} (in, \top).Node_{j1} + (walk\_E_j, e).Node_{j0} \qquad\qquad 1 \le j \le N$$
$$Node_{j1} \stackrel{def}{=} (walk\_F_j, e).Node_{j2}$$
$$Node_{j2} \stackrel{def}{=} (serve_j, \top).Node_{j0} + (walk\_E_j, e).Node_{j2}$$

$$Gen_{10} \stackrel{def}{=} (accept_1, \lambda).(pack_1, p).Gen_{11}$$
$$Gen_{11} \stackrel{def}{=} (in, d). ((serve_1, w_1\top).Gen_{11} + (serve_1, w_2\top).Gen_{10})$$

$$Gen'_{j0} \stackrel{def}{=} (\tau, \lambda_p).Gen'_{j1} \qquad\qquad \lambda_p = (\lambda\, p)/(\lambda + p) \qquad j = 2,3$$
$$Gen'_{j1} \stackrel{def}{=} (in, d). ((serve_j, w_1\top).Gen'_{j1} + (serve_j, w_2\top).Gen'_{j0})$$

$$\text{where } w_1 = M - 1, \ w_2 = 1 \ (M \text{ is mean no. of packets/message})$$

$$Comp_1 \stackrel{def}{=} Node_{10} \underset{\{in, serve_1\}}{\bowtie} Gen_{10}$$
$$Comp'_2 \stackrel{def}{=} Node_{20} \underset{\{in, serve_2\}}{\bowtie} Gen'_{20}$$
$$Comp'_3 \stackrel{def}{=} Node_{30} \underset{\{in, serve_3\}}{\bowtie} Gen'_{30}$$

$$S_j \stackrel{def}{=} (walk\_E_j, \omega).S_{j\oplus1} + (walk\_F_j, \omega).(serve_j, \mu).S_{j\oplus1}$$
$$\text{where } j \oplus 1 = 1 \text{ when } j = N$$

when $N = 3$:
$$System' \stackrel{def}{=} (Comp_1 \parallel Comp'_2 \parallel Comp'_3) \underset{\substack{\{walk\_E_j, \\ walk\_F_j, serve_j\}}}{\bowtie} (S_1 \parallel S_1)/\{walk\_E_j, walk\_F_j\}$$
$$\text{for } 1 \le j \le N$$

Figure 6.5: Modified PEPA model of the enhanced MSMQ system, *System'*

and by Proposition 6.3.2,

$$Gen_{20}/\{accept_2, pack_2\} = (\tau, \lambda).(\tau, p).(Gen_{21}/\{accept_2, pack_2\}).$$

Thus there is a reducible sequence within the component Gen_{20}/L_{12}. Similarly there will be a reducible sequence in the component Gen_{30}/L_{13}:

$$Gen_{30}/\{accept_3, pack_3\} = (\tau, \lambda).(\tau, p).(Gen_{21}/\{accept_3, pack_3\}).$$

We can construct the compact form of Gen_{20}/L_{12} as follows:

$$Gen'_{20} \stackrel{def}{=} (\tau, \lambda_p).Gen'_{21}$$
$$Gen'_{21} \stackrel{def}{=} (in, d). ((serve_j, w_1\top).Gen'_{21} + (serve_j, w_2\top).Gen'_{20})$$

where $\lambda_p = (\lambda p)/(\lambda + p)$, and we construct Gen'_{30}, the compact form corresponding to Gen_{30}/L_{13} similarly.

Since these components are in parallel composition with each other the conditions of Theorem 6.9.2 are satisfied if we replace Gen_{20} and Gen_{30} by their respective compact forms and consider the modified model, *System'*, shown in Figure 6.5.

mean no. packets M	accept λ	pack p	τ λ_p	in d	walk_E and walk_F min(e, ω)	serve μ
$5 - 25$	$1/20$	$1/10$	$1/30$	20	$10, 25$	1.0

Table 6.1: Parameter values assigned to *System′*

Recall that in Section 4.4.5 we saw that the Markov process underlying the model *System* had 888 states. In contrast the weakly isomorphic model *System′* has only 542 states. The same performance measures were calculated for the model using the parameter values shown in Table 6.1. The difference in values derived from this model and the original model, *System*, were found to be less than 0.001%. This error is attributed to the numerical technique used to solve the model in each case. The mean transmission time as message length varies as before is shown in Figure 6.6, for walk rates 10 and 25.

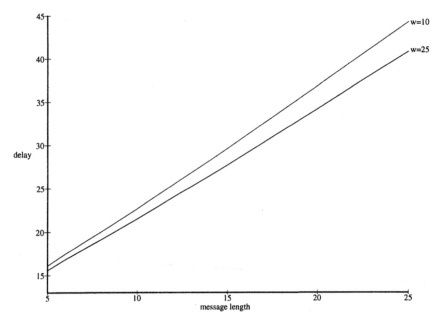

Figure 6.6: Mean message transmission time plotted against mean number of packets per message and walk rates

Chapter 7

Strong Bisimilarity

7.1 Introduction

In this chapter we develop a strong bisimulation, based on the labelled multi-transition system for PEPA developed in Chapter 3, and examine some of its properties. The strong bisimulation relation aims to capture the idea that strongly bisimilar components are able to perform the same activities, resulting in derivatives that are themselves strongly bisimilar. In Section 7.2 we show how this property may be expressed in the definition of a strong bisimulation relation. Strong bisimilarity is then defined as the largest relation satisfying the conditions of a strong bisimulation relation.

The rest of the chapter is concerned with the properties exhibited by the strong bisimilarity relation, $\sim$. In Section 7.3 the relation is investigated from a process algebra perspective. In particular it is shown that strong bisimilarity is a congruence relation for PEPA. The implications of strong bisimilarity for the system components being modelled are discussed in Section 7.4. The relationship between strong bisimilarity and the underlying Markov process is examined in Section 7.5, as we investigate whether the partition induced by the relation forms a suitable basis for exact aggregation. This is found not to be the case.

Finally in Section 7.6 we suggest how strong bisimilarity may be used as a model simplification technique. The relation is used to find components which exhibit the same activities. These may then be subjected to a simple further test to ensure that the behaviours of the components are indeed the same. Then if one component has a smaller derivative set it may replace the other component in a PEPA model and reduce the state space of the underlying Markov process. We demonstrate this use of strong bisimilarity for state space reduction on one of the MSMQ models developed in Chapter 4.

7.2 Definition of Strong Bisimilarity

As explained in Section 5.2, a bisimulation is intended to capture the idea of identical observed behaviour. Of course we must clarify which aspects of behaviour may be witnessed by the observer and the context in which the observation takes place. In terms of PEPA we have several choices of how "observant" we allow the observer to be. For example, can the observer record the rate of each activity or only the apparent rate of each action type? Can the observer remember the relative frequency with which alternative activities, or possible derivatives, occur in a race condition from a given component? Does the observer record the sojourn time in each component?

An alternative way to think about the strong bisimulation relation is in terms of the labelled multi-transition system used to give an operational semantics to the language. From this perspective, two components are strongly bisimilar if they are capable of exactly the same activities, and the resulting derivatives are also strongly bisimilar. When, as in PEPA, the labelled transition system generates a multigraph, the multiplicity of each activity should also be considered.

The definition of strong bisimulation we present in this chapter aims to be a simple extension of the strong bisimulation of CCS to PEPA. Recall that in CCS two agents are strongly bisimilar if any α action of one can be matched by an α action of the other; moreover every α-derivative of one is strongly bisimilar to some α-derivative of the other. Thus for PEPA we replace actions by activities and place the same requirement on derivatives. However, note that this does not impose any condition on the multiplicities of activities in components. For example this would lead to an equivalence in which $P + P$ is considered equivalent to P, although the first component, $P + P$, would appear to act twice as fast as P. The simplest way to avoid this problem is to place an additional condition on the strong bisimulation ensuring that the apparent rate of all action types is the same in the two components. Thus, in keeping with both CCS and Markov processes, we imagine an observer who bases his comparison on the current behaviour and has no memory of the previous behaviour of the components. In particular there is no consideration of the relative frequency, or probability, of transitions or derivatives.

Definition 7.2.1 *A binary relation, $\mathcal{R} \subseteq \mathcal{C} \times \mathcal{C}$, over components is a* strong bisimulation *if $(P, Q) \in \mathcal{R}$ implies, for all $\alpha \in \mathcal{A}$,*

   i) $r_\alpha(P) = r_\alpha(Q)$;

and for all $a \in \mathcal{A}ct$,

   ii) Whenever $P \xrightarrow{a} P'$ then, for some Q', $Q \xrightarrow{a} Q'$, and $(P', Q') \in \mathcal{R}$;

   iii) Whenever $Q \xrightarrow{a} Q'$ then, for some P', $P \xrightarrow{a} P'$, and $(P', Q') \in \mathcal{R}$.

Any component is trivially a member of a strong bisimulation since the identity relation satisfies all the conditions of the Definition 7.2.1. Similarly, we can see that, since the conditions are all symmetric, if $\mathcal{R}$ is a strong bisimulation then $\mathcal{R}^{-1}$ is also a strong bisimulation. The conditions are also transitive and preserved by union. Thus we can state the following proposition:

Proposition 7.2.1 *Assume that each $\mathcal{R}_i$ ($i = 1, 2, \ldots$) is a strong bisimulation. Then the following relations are all strong bisimulations:*

$$\begin{array}{ll} (1) \;\; Id_\mathcal{C} & (3) \;\; \mathcal{R}_1\mathcal{R}_2 \\ (2) \;\; \mathcal{R}_i^{-1} & (4) \;\; \bigcup_{i \in I} \mathcal{R}_i \end{array}$$

Proof   The proof follows trivially from the Definition 7.2.1.   □

We may now define the strong bisimilarity relation $\sim$.

Definition 7.2.2 *P and Q are* strongly bisimilar, *written $P \sim Q$, if $(P, Q) \in \mathcal{R}$ for some strong bisimulation $\mathcal{R}$.*

$$\sim \; = \; \bigcup \{ \mathcal{R} : \mathcal{R} \text{ is a strong bisimulation} \}$$

It follows immediately from the definition and the Proposition 7.2.1 that $\sim$ is itself a strong bisimulation, that it is the largest such relation and that it is an equivalence relation.

In general, in order to show that $P \sim Q$ we must find a strong bisimulation relation $\mathcal{R}$ such that $(P, Q) \in \mathcal{R}$. As this involves considering all the derivatives of P and Q and their possible activities this may be a non-trivial task. However we can define a weaker relation, *strong bisimulation up to* $\sim$, which takes advantage of equivalence classes induced on the derivative set of each component by the $\sim$ relation. Then two components satisfy the relation $\mathcal{R}$ if the activities and apparent rates of action types are matched, and each a-derivative belongs to an equivalence class which has an element which is in $\mathcal{R}$ with some element of an equivalence class, containing an a-derivative, in the other component's derivative set.

Definition 7.2.3 $\mathcal{R}$ *is a* strong bisimulation up to $\sim$ *if* $P \mathcal{R} Q$ *implies for all* $\alpha \in \mathcal{A}$,

i) $r_\alpha(P) = r_\alpha(Q)$;

and for all $a \in \mathcal{A}ct$,

ii) *Whenever* $P \xrightarrow{a} P'$ *then, for some* Q', $Q \xrightarrow{a} Q'$, *and* $P' \sim \mathcal{R} \sim Q'$;

iii) *Whenever* $Q \xrightarrow{a} Q'$ *then, for some* P', $P \xrightarrow{a} P'$, *and* $P' \sim \mathcal{R} \sim Q'$.

Proposition 7.2.2 shows that in order to exhibit strong bisimilarity between components it is sufficient to find a strong bisimulation up to $\sim$ between them. First, the following Lemma is needed.

Lemma 7.2.1 *If* $\mathcal{R}$ *is a strong bisimulation up to* $\sim$, *then the relation* $\sim \mathcal{R} \sim$ *is a strong bisimulation.*

Proof Let $P \sim \mathcal{R} \sim Q$. Then there are derivatives $P_1 \in ds(P)$ and $Q_1 \in ds(Q)$ such that $P \sim P_1 \mathcal{R} Q_1 \sim Q$. Considering the activities of P and Q the diagrams below can be inferred:

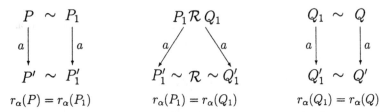

Recall that $\sim$, as an equivalence relation, is transitive, and compose these diagrams to obtain:

$$P \sim \mathcal{R} \sim Q$$
$$a \downarrow \qquad \qquad \downarrow a$$
$$P' \sim \mathcal{R} \sim Q'$$
$$r_\alpha(P) = r_\alpha(Q)$$

as required. □

Proposition 7.2.2 *If* $\mathcal{R}$ *is a strong bisimulation up to* $\sim$ *then* $\mathcal{R} \subseteq \sim$.

Proof   Since, by Lemma 7.2.1, $\sim \mathcal{R} \sim$ is a strong bisimulation, it follows that $\sim \mathcal{R} \sim \subseteq \sim$. But recall that $Id_\mathcal{C} \subseteq \sim$, so $\mathcal{R} \subseteq \sim \mathcal{R} \sim$. Consequently, we conclude that $\mathcal{R} \subseteq \sim$.   □

We will make use of this result when we prove that $\sim$ is a congruence relation.

7.3   Properties of the Strong Bisimilarity Relation

In this section we investigate the properties of the strong bisimilarity relation in a process algebra context. We prove that strong bisimilarity is a congruence relation by showing that it is preserved by the combinators of the language and by recursive definitions. We also show that any isomorphic components are strongly bisimilar.

7.3.1   Strong Bisimilarity as a Congruence

In order to show that strong bisimilarity is a congruence for PEPA we must show that the relation is preserved by each of the combinators of the language. For example, this means that if P_1 is strongly bisimilar to P_2, we may replace P_1 in a component $P_1 \bowtie_L Q$ by P_2 and be confident that the activities of the component remain the same.

Proposition 7.3.1 (Preservation by Combinators)
Let $P_1 \sim P_2$, then

1. $a.P_1 \sim a.P_2$;

2. $P_1 + Q \sim P_2 + Q$;

3. $P_1 \bowtie_L Q \sim P_2 \bowtie_L Q$;

4. $P_1/L \sim P_2/L$.

Proof

1. The only possible activity of $a.P_1$ or $a.P_2$ is a, where $a = (\alpha, r)$ for some action type α and rate r. Thus it is clear that for all $\beta \in \mathcal{A}$,

$$r_\beta(a.P_1) = \left\{ \begin{array}{ll} r & \text{if } \beta = \alpha \\ 0 & \text{if } \beta \neq \alpha \end{array} \right\} = r_\beta(a.P_2)$$

   Moreover, these derivatives, P_1 and P_2, are themselves bisimilar, $P_1 \sim P_2$, by the hypothesis. Consequently $a.P_1 \sim a.P_2$.

2. Consider $P_1 + Q$ and $P_2 + Q$. Recall that for any P and Q, and for all $\alpha \in \mathcal{A}$, $r_\alpha(P + Q) = r_\alpha(P) + r_\alpha(Q)$. Thus, since by the hypothesis $r_\alpha(P_1) = r_\alpha(P_2)$ for all $\alpha \in \mathcal{A}$, we conclude that $r_\alpha(P_1 + Q) = r_\alpha(P_2 + Q)$ as required.
   Now suppose $P_1 + Q \xrightarrow{a} P'$. Then

   Case 1 $P_1 \xrightarrow{a} P'$; since $P_1 \sim P_2$ then, for some P'', $P_2 \xrightarrow{a} P''$, and $P' \sim P''$. It follows that $P_2 + Q \xrightarrow{a} P''$, and $P' \sim P''$.

   Case 2 $Q \xrightarrow{a} P'$. Then $P_2 + Q \xrightarrow{a} P'$ and $P' \sim P'$.

   The result follows by symmetry.

3. Consider $P_1 \bowtie_L Q$ and $P_2 \bowtie_L Q$ and define a relation $\mathcal{R}$ as follows

$$\mathcal{R} = \{(Q_1 \bowtie_L Q, Q_2 \bowtie_L Q) \mid Q_1 \sim Q_2\}.$$

Recall that for any P and Q, and for all $\alpha \in \mathcal{A}$,

$$r_\alpha(P \bowtie_L Q) = \begin{cases} \min(r_\alpha(P), r_\alpha(Q)) & \text{if } \alpha \in L \\ r_\alpha(P) + r_\alpha(Q) & \text{if } \alpha \notin L \end{cases}$$

By definition $(P_1 \bowtie_L Q, P_2 \bowtie_L Q) \in \mathcal{R}$. Moreover, since for all $\alpha \in \mathcal{A}$, $r_\alpha(P_1) = r_\alpha(P_2)$, it follows that $r_\alpha(P_1 \bowtie_L Q) = r_\alpha(P_2 \bowtie_L Q)$, for all $\alpha \in \mathcal{A}$.

Consider $P_1 \bowtie_L Q \xrightarrow{a} R$, where $a = (\alpha, r)$.

Case 1 $P_1 \xrightarrow{a} P_1'$ and $R \equiv P_1' \bowtie_L Q$, $\alpha \notin L$.
Since $P_1 \sim P_2$ there is a P_2' such that $P_2 \xrightarrow{a} P_2'$, and $P_1' \sim P_2'$. Thus, if $R' \equiv P_2' \bowtie_L Q$, $P_2 \bowtie_L Q \xrightarrow{a} R'$ and by the definition of $\mathcal{R}$, $(R, R') \in \mathcal{R}$.

Case 2 $Q \xrightarrow{a} Q'$ and $R \equiv P_1 \bowtie_L Q'$, $\alpha \notin L$. Similar to Case 1.

Case 3 $\alpha \in L$ and $P_1 \xrightarrow{(\alpha, r_1)} P_1'$, $Q \xrightarrow{(\alpha, r_2)} Q'$, $R \equiv P_1' \bowtie_L Q'$.
Then $r = \frac{r_1}{r_\alpha(P_1)} \frac{r_2}{r_\alpha(Q)} \min(r_\alpha(P_1), r_\alpha(Q))$.

Since $P_1 \sim P_2$ there is a P_2' such that $P_2 \xrightarrow{(\alpha, r_1)} P_2'$, and $P_1' \sim P_2'$. Therefore there is $R' \equiv P_2' \bowtie_L Q'$ such that $P_2 \bowtie_L Q \xrightarrow{a} R'$.
Then, by definition, $(R, R') = (P_1' \bowtie_L Q', P_2' \bowtie_L Q') \in \mathcal{R}$.

It follows by symmetry that $\mathcal{R}$ is a strong bisimulation.
Hence, $P_1 \bowtie_L Q \sim P_2 \bowtie_L Q$ as required.

4. To show that $P_1/L \sim P_2/L$, we define a relation $\mathcal{R}$ as follows:

$$\mathcal{R} = \{(Q_1/L, Q_2/L) \mid Q_1 \sim Q_2\}$$

and show that it is a strong bisimulation, analogously to above.

$\square$

In the following proposition we show that sets of recursive definitions also preserve the strong bisimilarity relation. The definition of strong bisimilarity is extended to component expressions as follows:

Definition 7.3.1 *Let E and F be component expressions, containing variables $\tilde{X}$ at most. Then $E \sim F$ if, for all indexed sets of components $\tilde{P}$, $E\{\tilde{P}/\tilde{X}\} \sim F\{\tilde{P}/\tilde{X}\}$.*

This proposition, together with Proposition 7.3.1, shows that $\sim$ is a congruence.

Proposition 7.3.2 (Preservation by Recursive Definition)
Let $\tilde{E}$ and $\tilde{F}$ contain variables $\tilde{X}$ at most. Let $\tilde{A} \overset{\text{def}}{=} \tilde{E}\{\tilde{A}/\tilde{X}\}$, $\tilde{B} \overset{\text{def}}{=} \tilde{F}\{\tilde{B}/\tilde{X}\}$ and $\tilde{E} \sim \tilde{F}$. Then $\tilde{A} \sim \tilde{B}$.

Proof   It is sufficient to show the result for single recursion equations E and F such that $E \sim F$, where $A \stackrel{\text{def}}{=} E\{A/X\}$ and $B \stackrel{\text{def}}{=} F\{B/X\}$. We construct a relation $\mathcal{R}$ as follows,

$$\mathcal{R} = \{(G\{A/X\}, G\{B/X\}) \mid G \text{ contains at most variable } X\}$$

and show that $\mathcal{R}$ is a strong bisimulation up to $\sim$. First we show by induction on the maximal depth of inference that, for an arbitrary activity type α, the apparent rate of activities of type α in $G\{A/X\}$ and $G\{B/X\}$ are the same, i.e. $r_\alpha(G\{A/X\}) = r_\alpha(G\{B/X\})$. The possible forms of G are considered separately; the case $G \equiv X$ is omitted since the apparent rate is not defined for unguarded variables.

Case 1 (Base Case): $G \equiv (\beta, r).G'$

Then $G\{A/X\} \equiv (\beta, r).G'\{A/X\}$ and $r_\alpha(G\{A/X\}) = \begin{cases} r & \text{if } \alpha = \beta \\ 0 & \text{otherwise.} \end{cases}$

Similarly we can see that $r_\alpha(G\{B/X\}) = \begin{cases} r & \text{if } \alpha = \beta \\ 0 & \text{otherwise.} \end{cases}$

Thus it follows immediately that $r_\alpha(G\{A/X\}) = r_\alpha(G\{B/X\})$.

Case 2: $G \equiv G_1 + G_2$

Then, applying the induction hypothesis and the definition of $r_\alpha(\cdot)$, we see that

$$\begin{aligned} r_\alpha(G\{A/X\}) &= r_\alpha(G_1\{A/X\}) + r_\alpha(G_2\{A/X\}) \\ &= r_\alpha(G_1\{B/X\}) + r_\alpha(G_2\{B/X\}) = r_\alpha(G\{B/X\}). \end{aligned}$$

Case 3: $G \equiv G_1 \underset{L}{\bowtie} G_2$

By definition,

$$r_\alpha(G\{A/X\}) = \begin{cases} r_\alpha(G_1\{A/X\}) + r_\alpha(G_2\{A/X\}) & \text{if } \alpha \notin L \\ \min(r_\alpha(G_1\{A/X\}), r_\alpha(G_2\{A/X\})) & \text{if } \alpha \in L. \end{cases}$$

Thus, by the induction hypothesis, since G_1 and G_2 must have a shorter maximal depth of inference $r_\alpha(G\{A/X\}) = r_\alpha(G\{B/X\})$ as required.

Case 4: $G \equiv G'/L$

If $\alpha \in L$ then clearly, $r_\alpha(G\{A/X\}) = 0 = r_\alpha(G\{B/X\})$.
Otherwise $r_\alpha(G\{A/X\}) = r_\alpha(G'\{A/X\})$ and the result follows by induction.

Case 5: $G \equiv C$ where C is constant.

Then C is associated with some component definition, $C \stackrel{\text{def}}{=} S$. Therefore, it follows that $r_\alpha(G\{A/X\}) = r_\alpha(S) = r_\alpha(G\{B/X\})$.

Since α was arbitrary, we have shown that $(G\{A/X\}, G\{B/X\}) \in \mathcal{R}$ implies that for all $\alpha \in \mathcal{A}$, $r_\alpha(G\{A/X\}) = r_\alpha(G\{B/X\})$.

Now we show that any activity of $G\{A/X\}$ can be matched by an activity of $G\{B/X\}$. Consider an arbitrary activity, $a \in Act(G\{A/X\})$, such that $G\{A/X\} \xrightarrow{a} P'$. We will use transition induction on the depth of inference by which the activity a is inferred to show that there exist Q'' and Q' such that $G\{B/X\} \xrightarrow{a} Q'' \sim Q'$ and $(P', Q') \in \mathcal{R}$.

The possible forms of G are considered separately.

Case 1: $G \equiv a.G'$

Then $G\{A/X\} \equiv a.G'\{A/X\}$ and $P' \equiv G'\{A/X\}$.
Similarly $G\{B/X\} \equiv a.G'\{B/X\} \xrightarrow{a} G'\{B/X\}$ where, $(G'\{A/X\}, G'\{B/X\}) \in \mathcal{R}$, by definition.

Case 2: $G \equiv X$

Then $G\{A/X\} \equiv A$, and $A \xrightarrow{a} P'$. It follows that $E\{A/X\} \xrightarrow{a} P'$, by a shorter depth of inference. By the induction hypothesis, we can assume that there exist Q'' and Q', such that $E\{B/X\} \xrightarrow{a} Q'' \sim Q'$ with $(P', Q') \in \mathcal{R}$.

Since $E \sim F$, there exists Q''' such that $F\{B/X\} \xrightarrow{a} Q''' \sim Q'$.

However $B \stackrel{\text{def}}{=} F\{B/X\}$ and $G\{B/X\} \equiv B$ which means that the activities of $G\{B/X\}$ are exactly the activities of $F\{B/X\}$, so $G\{B/X\} \xrightarrow{a} Q''' \sim Q'$ with $(P', Q') \in \mathcal{R}$ as required.

Case 3: $G \equiv G_1 + G_2$

Then $G\{A/X\} \equiv G_1\{A/X\} + G_2\{A/X\}$, and the activity $G\{A/X\} \xrightarrow{a} P'$ may be due to either component. These cases, $G_1\{A/X\} \xrightarrow{a} P'$ and $G_2\{A/X\} \xrightarrow{a} P'$, are considered separately. Since each of these transitions has a shorter depth of inference the proof is a straightforward application of the induction hypothesis, which is omitted here.

Case 4: $G \equiv G_1 \underset{L}{\bowtie} G_2$

Then $G\{A/X\} \equiv G_1\{A/X\} \underset{L}{\bowtie} G_2\{A/X\}$. Let us consider some activity $a = (\alpha, r)$, such that $G\{A/X\} \xrightarrow{a} P'$. It may arise in three distinct ways: $\alpha \notin L$, a an individual activity of $G_1\{A/X\}$; $\alpha \notin L$, a an individual activity of $G_2\{A/X\}$; and $\alpha \in L$, a a shared activity of $G_1\{A/X\}$ and $G_2\{A/X\}$. Here we present only the third case, the other two are similar.

Case 4.3 $\alpha \in L$: $G_1\{A/X\} \xrightarrow{(\alpha, r_1)} P'_1$, $G_2\{A/X\} \xrightarrow{(\alpha, r_2)} P'_2$, $P' \equiv P'_1 \underset{L}{\bowtie} P'_2$.

$$r = \frac{r_1}{r_\alpha(G_1\{A/X\})} \frac{r_2}{r_\alpha(G_2\{A/X\})} \min(r_\alpha(G_1\{A/X\}), r_\alpha(G_2\{A/X\}))$$

As the transitions of G_1 and G_2 have a shorter depth of inference, by induction there exist Q''_1 and Q'_1, and Q''_2 and Q'_2 such that,

$$G_1\{B/X\} \xrightarrow{(\alpha, r_1)} Q''_1 \sim Q'_1, \qquad G_2\{B/X\} \xrightarrow{(\alpha, r_2)} Q''_2 \sim Q'_2$$

such that $(P'_1, Q'_1) \in \mathcal{R}$, and $(P'_2, Q'_2) \in \mathcal{R}$. Thus, setting $Q'' \equiv Q''_1 \underset{L}{\bowtie} Q''_2$ and $Q' \equiv Q'_1 \underset{L}{\bowtie} Q'_2$ we obtain $G\{B/X\} \xrightarrow{a'} Q'' \sim Q'$ where $a' = (\alpha, r_B)$. But $r_\alpha(G_1\{A/X\}) = r_\alpha(G_1\{B/X\})$ and $r_\alpha(G_2\{A/X\}) = r_\alpha(G_2\{B/X\})$ so it follows that

$$r_B = \frac{r_1}{r_\alpha(G_1\{B/X\})} \frac{r_2}{r_\alpha(G_2\{B/X\})} \min(r_\alpha(G_1\{B/X\}), r_\alpha(G_2\{B/X\})) = r$$

Since $(P'_1, Q'_1) \in \mathcal{R}$ we can find H_1 such that $P'_1 \equiv H_1\{A/X\}$, and $Q'_1 \equiv H_1\{B/X\}$. Similarly we can find H_2 such that $P'_2 \equiv H_2\{A/X\}$ and $Q'_2 \equiv H_2\{B/X\}$.

Consequently, setting $H \equiv H_1 \underset{L}{\bowtie} H_2$, we see that

$$(P', Q') \equiv (H\{A/X\}, H\{B/X\}) \in \mathcal{R}$$

Case 5: $G \equiv G'/L$

We consider the cases for transitions of G' being hidden or not, separately. Since all transitions of G are derived from transitions of G' which have a shorter depth of inference, the proof is a straightforward application of the induction hypothesis and is omitted here.

Case 6: $G \equiv C$ where C is a constant

Suppose that C is associated with some definition $C \stackrel{\text{def}}{=} S$. Since X does not appear in G, $G\{A/X\}$ and $G\{B/X\}$ are both identical to C. Consequently, both will have the same a-derivative P', where $(P', P') \equiv (P'\{A/X\}, P'\{B/X\}) \in \mathcal{R}$ as required.

Thus we have shown that every activity of $G\{A/X\}$ is matched by $G\{B/X\}$, and by a symmetric argument we can see that every activity of $G\{B/X\}$ is similarly matched by $G\{A/X\}$. It follows that the relation

$$\mathcal{R} = \{(G\{A/X\}, G\{B/X\}) \mid G \text{ contains at most variable } X\}$$

is a strong bisimulation up to $\sim$. Consequently, if we take $G \equiv X$, it follows that $A \sim B$ as required.   □

7.3.2   Isomorphism and Strong Bisimilarity

In Section 6.2 the concept of isomorphic components was introduced. Two components are isomorphic if they generate derivation graphs which have the same structure. Such components differ only in the naming of derivatives. In the following proposition we establish that isomorphism between components is a stronger relation between components than strong bisimilarity, i.e.,

$$= \subset \sim . \tag{3.1}$$

Lemma 7.3.1 *If $\mathcal{F}$ is a component isomorphism then for any P, $P \sim \mathcal{F}(P)$.*

Proof   Since $\mathcal{F}$ is a component isomorphism we know that it is an injective function with $Act(P) = Act(\mathcal{F}(P))$, and for all $a \in Act$ the a-derivatives of $\mathcal{F}(P)$ are the same as the $\mathcal{F}$-images of a-derivatives of P. Thus it is clear that P and $\mathcal{F}(P)$ enable the same activities, in the same multiplicities , so all activities of P and $\mathcal{F}(P)$ are matched and the apparent rates of all action types are the same in the two components. It follows by structural induction on the structure of P, and Proposition 7.3.1 that every a-derivative of P is strongly bisimilar to an a-derivative of $\mathcal{F}(P)$.   □

Proposition 7.3.3 *If P and Q are isomorphic components then $P \sim Q$.*

Proof   This follows immediately from the Lemma.   □

From this we can deduce that the equational laws stated for isomorphic components in Section 6.3 can be restated with "=" replaced by "$\sim$".

Corollary 7.3.1 (Choice)

   1. $P + Q \sim Q + P$

   2. $P + (Q + R) \sim (P + Q) + R$

Corollary 7.3.2 (Hiding)

   1. $(P + Q)/L \sim P/L + Q/L$

   2. $((\alpha, r).P)/L \sim \begin{cases} (\tau, r).P/L & \alpha \in L \\ (\alpha, r).P/L & \alpha \notin L \end{cases}$

   3. $(P/L)/K \sim P/(L \cup K)$

   4. $P/L \sim P$ *if $L \cap \vec{A}(P) = \emptyset$*

Corollary 7.3.3 (Cooperation)

1. $P \bowtie_L Q \sim Q \bowtie_L P$

2. $P \bowtie_L (Q \bowtie_L R) \sim (P \bowtie_L Q) \bowtie_L R$

3. $(P \bowtie_L Q)/(K \cup M) \sim \big((P/K) \bowtie_L (Q/K)\big)/M$ $\quad$ *where* $K \cap M = K \cap L = \emptyset$

4. $P \bowtie_K Q \sim P \bowtie_L Q$ $\quad$ *if* $K \cap (\vec{A}(P) \cup \vec{A}(Q)) = L$

5. $(P \bowtie_L Q) \bowtie_K R \sim \begin{cases} P \bowtie_L (Q \bowtie_K R) & \text{if } \vec{A}(R) \cap L \setminus K = \emptyset \wedge \vec{A}(P) \cap K \setminus L = \emptyset \\ Q \bowtie_L (P \bowtie_K R) & \text{if } \vec{A}(R) \cap L \setminus K = \emptyset \wedge \vec{A}(Q) \cap M \setminus L = \emptyset \end{cases}$

Corollary 7.3.4 (Constant)
If $A \overset{\text{def}}{=} P$ then $A \sim P$.

Corollary 7.3.5 (The Expansion Law)
Let $P \equiv (P_1 \bowtie_L P_2)/K$ with $L, K \subset A$. Then

$$
\begin{aligned}
P \sim \ & \sum \{(\alpha, r).(P_1' \bowtie_L P_2)/K \mid P_1 \xrightarrow{(\alpha, r)} P_1' \; ; \; \alpha \notin L \cup K\} \\
& + \sum \{(\alpha, r).(P_1 \bowtie_L P_2')/K \mid P_2 \xrightarrow{(\alpha, r)} P_2' \; ; \; \alpha \notin L \cup K\} \\
& + \sum \{(\tau, r).(P_1' \bowtie_L P_2)/K \mid P_1 \xrightarrow{(\alpha, r)} P_1' \; ; \; \alpha \in K \setminus L\} \\
& + \sum \{(\tau, r).(P_1 \bowtie_L P_2')/K \mid P_2 \xrightarrow{(\alpha, r)} P_2' \; ; \; \alpha \in K \setminus L\} \\
& + \sum \{(\alpha, r).(P_1' \bowtie_L P_2')/K \mid P_1 \xrightarrow{(\alpha, r_1)} P_1' \; ; \; P_2 \xrightarrow{(\alpha, r_2)} P_2' \; ; \; \alpha \in L \setminus K \; ; \\
& \hspace{4cm} r = \frac{r_1}{r_\alpha(P_1)} \frac{r_2}{r_\alpha(P_2)} \min(r_\alpha(P_1), r_\alpha(P_2))\} \\
& + \sum \{(\tau, r).(P_1' \bowtie_L P_2')/K \mid P_1 \xrightarrow{(\alpha, r_1)} P_1' \; ; \; P_2 \xrightarrow{(\alpha, r_2)} P_2' \; ; \; \alpha \in L \cap K \; ; \\
& \hspace{4cm} r = \frac{r_1}{r_\alpha(P_1)} \frac{r_2}{r_\alpha(P_2)} \min(r_\alpha(P_1), r_\alpha(P_2))\}.
\end{aligned}
$$

Note that it is easy to construct components which are strongly bisimilar but not isomorphic, showing that the relation in equation 3.1 is "$\subset$" and not "$\subseteq$". For example, it is straightforward to verify that the relation,

$$
\mathcal{R} = \{(A_0, B_0), (A_1, B_1), (A_0, B_2), (A_1, B_3)\}, \tag{3.2}
$$

is a strong bisimulation for the components A and B shown in Figure 7.1. However, there can be no isomorphism between the derivative sets of A and B since they do not have the same number of elements. Thus $A \sim B$ but $A \neq B$.

	$B_0 \overset{\text{def}}{=} a.B_1$
$A_0 \overset{\text{def}}{=} a.A_1$	$B_1 \overset{\text{def}}{=} b.B_2$
$A_1 \overset{\text{def}}{=} b.A_0$	$B_2 \overset{\text{def}}{=} a.B_3$
	$B_3 \overset{\text{def}}{=} b.B_0$

Figure 7.1: An example to show $A \sim B$ does not imply $A = B$

7.4   Strong Bisimilarity and System Components

In this section we consider what the relation $P \sim Q$ tells us about the system components modelled by the PEPA components P and Q. Let Sys_P and Sys_Q denote the system components modelled by P and Q respectively and assume that $P \sim Q$. It is clear from the definition of strong bisimulation that the action sets, the activity multisets and the exit rates of the two components are equal.

$$\mathcal{A}(P) = \mathcal{A}(Q) \qquad \mathcal{A}ct(P) = \mathcal{A}ct(Q) \qquad q(P) = q(Q) \qquad (4.3)$$

In terms of the system components Sys_P and Sys_Q this means that under observation they appear to carry out the same actions, at the same rates and that their average delay before performing some action will be the same. Moreover we can deduce from equation 4.3 that the probability (or relative frequency) that the action performed will have a given type will be the same in the two components, Sys_P and Sys_Q.

The strong bisimulation relation between P and Q ensures that the same relation must exist between matching derivatives, i.e. if $P \xrightarrow{a} P'$ there must be some Q' such that $Q \xrightarrow{a} Q'$ and $P' \sim Q'$. This implies that any sequence of activities which can be performed by P can also be performed by Q. Thus if we consider the system components Sys_P and Sys_Q the possible sequences of actions that they can perform are the same. However we cannot draw conclusions about the relative frequencies of these sequences of actions. When the same activity in a PEPA component may result in different derivatives the strong bisimilarity relation does not necessarily tell us anything about the relative frequency of these different outcomes of the activity, or even the transition rates between derivatives. For example consider the simple components in Figure 7.2. It is straightforward to verify that the relation $\mathcal{R} = \{(P, Q), (P', Q')\}$ is a strong bisimulation since, assuming $a = (\alpha, r_a)$ and $b = (\beta, r_b)$,

$$r_\gamma(P) = \left\{ \begin{array}{ll} 3r_a & \gamma = \alpha \\ 0 & \gamma \neq \alpha \end{array} \right\} = r_\gamma(Q) \qquad r_\gamma(P') = \left\{ \begin{array}{ll} r_b & \gamma = \beta \\ 0 & \gamma \neq \beta \end{array} \right\} = r_\gamma(Q')$$

and the activities can be matched in the pairs:

$$\left\{ \begin{array}{l} P \xrightarrow{a} P \\ Q \xrightarrow{a} Q \end{array} \right\} \qquad \left\{ \begin{array}{l} P \xrightarrow{a} P' \\ Q \xrightarrow{a} Q' \end{array} \right\} \qquad \left\{ \begin{array}{l} P' \xrightarrow{b} P \\ Q' \xrightarrow{b} Q \end{array} \right\}$$

However if we consider the transition rates between the derivatives of P and Q respectively,

$$q(P, P) = 2r_a \qquad\qquad q(P, P') = r_a \qquad\qquad q(P', P) = r_b$$
$$q(Q, Q) = r_a \qquad\qquad q(Q, Q') = 2r_a \qquad\qquad q(Q', Q) = r_b.$$

$$P \stackrel{\text{def}}{=} a.P + a.P + a.P' \qquad\qquad Q \stackrel{\text{def}}{=} a.Q + a.Q' + a.Q'$$

$$P' \stackrel{\text{def}}{=} b.P \qquad\qquad\qquad\qquad Q' \stackrel{\text{def}}{=} b.Q$$

Figure 7.2: Strongly bisimilar components with different transition rates

In terms of the system components Sys_P and Sys_Q this implies that continued observation of the two systems would distinguish between them since β actions will occur less frequently in Sys_P.

Multiple instances of activities with the same action type may arise in PEPA components in two ways. Firstly, the system component being modelled might have multiple capacity to carry out the corresponding action. For example, if the component is a cooperation of two identical components and the action type is not in the cooperation set then there are two different ways in which the action may occur, represented as two separate activities. Secondly, an action in the system component may have more than one possible outcome. In this case the PEPA component represents the single action in the system by several activities, each with the appropriate action type and suitably adjusted activity rates to reflect the probability of the outcome they lead to. Note that in this second case it is only when the outcomes have equal probability that the multiple representations of the same action will appear as multiple instances of the same activity in the PEPA component, and so potentially cause problems. Of course, in any PEPA model combinations of these circumstances may occur.

Since in strongly bisimilar components all activities occur with the same multiplicity, a mismatch of transition rates can only occur when there is more than one derivative resulting from a given activity and at least one of those derivatives may be reached by more than one instance of the activity. In the two strongly bisimilar components this "extra" capacity to carry out the activity leads to different derivatives, resulting in the differing transition rates.

Thus it is apparent that this naïve definition of strong bisimilarity is not strong enough to ensure that components are indistinguishable under experimentation. On the other hand if we can ensure that the problem discussed above does not occur, the relation is enough to guarantee the same behaviour between components. A model simplification technique aiming to take advantage of such circumstances is outlined in Section 7.6.

7.5 Strong Bisimilarity and the Markov Process

In this section we investigate the strong bisimilarity relation from the perspective of the underlying Markov process, both as a model-to-model equivalence and as a state-to-state equivalence. In particular we examine what the relation $P \sim Q$ tells us about the Markov processes generated by P and Q. The partition induced by $\sim$ on the state space of a model is considered but found, in general, to be an unsuitable basis for exact aggregation.

As explained in Chapter 5, two Markov processes are considered to be equivalent if they have the same number of states and the same transition rates between those states. Unlike isomorphic components, strongly bisimilar components will not necessarily generate equivalent Markov processes. For example, consider the components A and B shown in Figure 7.1 and the strong bisimulation in equation 3.2. Here, just as A and B could not be isomorphic because the derivative sets did not have the same number of elements, the corresponding Markov processes cannot be equivalent as they do not have the same number of states.

We will sometimes find it useful to consider a weaker form of equivalence between Markov processes, *lumpable equivalence*.

Definition 7.5.1 *Two Markov processes, $\{X_i\}$ and $\{Y_j\}$, are* lumpably equivalent *if there is a lumpable partition of $\{X_i\}$, $\{X_{[i]}\}$, and a lumpable partition of $\{Y_j\}$, $\{Y_{[j]}\}$ such that there is an injective function f which satisfies*

$$q(X_{[k]}, X_{[l]}) = q(Y_{f([k])}, Y_{f([l])}).$$

Thus two Markov processes are lumpably equivalent if they have lumpable partitions with the same number of elements and there is a one-to-one correspondence between the partitions such that the aggregated transition rates between partitions are also matched. Note that for any process there is a trivial lumpable partition in which every state forms a partition on its own. We do not allow the degenerate partition in which all the states are taken to form a single partition.

If we consider again the strongly bisimilar components A and B, shown in Figure 7.1, we can see that the states corresponding to B_0 and B_2, and B_1 and B_2 may be combined to form a lumpable partition of the underlying state space. Moreover using this partition and the trivial partition on A, it is clear that the Markov processes underlying A and B are lumpably equivalent.

However, strong bisimilarity does not imply even this weaker form of equivalence between the corresponding Markov processes. For example, if we consider the state spaces underlying the components P and Q shown in Figure 7.2, the only possible partitions are the trivial or degenerate ones. Since the transition rates between strongly bisimilar derivatives are not the same it follows that the Markov processes cannot be lumpably equivalent. Therefore we conclude that strong bisimilarity between components does not provide sufficient information for us to deduce any relation between the corresponding Markov processes.

Strong bisimilarity is an equivalence relation over the set of all components and as such will induce an equivalence relation over the derivative set of any component. Thus we also consider how strong bisimilarity between the derivatives of a single component relates to the structure of the Markov process generated by the component. To examine strong bisimilarity as a state-to-state equivalence we consider the partition induced by $\sim$ over the derivative set of a component. Only if the partition is lumpable will the aggregated process be a Markov process.

Recall that a partition is lumpable if for any two states within a partition class their aggregated transition rates to any other partition class are the same. However we have already seen that strong bisimilarity between components does not guarantee that the transition rates to matching derivatives are matched. If we consider strongly bisimilar components within a derivative set they will be elements within the same partition class induced by $\sim$. Thus it follows that it is possible to form such a partition so that elements within the same class have different transition rates to other partition classes. For example, consider the component C shown in Figure 7.3. Partitioning the derivative set by $\sim$ we obtain the

$$C_0 \stackrel{\text{def}}{=} a.C_1 + a.C_2$$

$$C_1 \stackrel{\text{def}}{=} b.C_1 + b.C_3 + b.C_4$$

$$C_2 \stackrel{\text{def}}{=} b.C_2 + b.C_2 + b.C_4$$

$$C_3 \stackrel{\text{def}}{=} c.C_0$$

$$C_4 \stackrel{\text{def}}{=} c.C_0$$

Figure 7.3: Example of $\sim$ inducing a non-lumpable partition

following partition:

$$C_{[0]} = \{C_0\} \qquad C_{[1]} = \{C_1, C_2\} \qquad C_{[2]} = \{C_3, C_4\}$$

This is not a lumpable partition since

$$q(C_1, C_{[2]}) = q(C_1, C_3) + q(C_1, C_4) = 2r_b$$
$$q(C_2, C_{[2]}) = q(C_2, C_3) + q(C_2, C_4) = r_b$$

It follows that, in general, $\sim$ cannot be used to form lumpable partitions over the state space of a component as a basis for exact aggregation. Of course the partitions formed by $\sim$ on the state space of a model could be used for aggregation but some method for calculating the conditional probability of each of the states within each partition would have to be used before the aggregated process could be formed.

Finally we consider whether equivalence between the underlying Markov processes allows us to conclude anything about the strong bisimilarity, or otherwise, of the corresponding PEPA components. As we saw in Section 6.5, a PEPA component contains information about the action types of activities as well as activity rates and so there will always be a loss of information in going from the PEPA component to the underlying Markov process. Therefore it is trivial to construct components which will generate the same Markov process but which are not strongly bisimilar. For example, consider again T_1 and T_2,

$$T_1 \stackrel{\text{def}}{=} (task_1, r).T_1 \qquad\qquad T_2 \stackrel{\text{def}}{=} (task_2, r).T_2$$

T_1 and T_2 generate the same Markov process although they are not strongly bisimilar—they are not even isomorphic. Similarly we can construct processes which generate lumpably equivalent Markov processes but which are not strongly bisimilar.

Augmenting the Markov process does not solve the problem since more than one activity in the PEPA component may be represented as a single transition in the annotated Markov process, annotated by the types of all the activities. Defining equivalent augmented Markov processes and lumpably equivalent augmented Markov processes in the obvious way, we can see that such processes may arise from components which are not strongly bisimilar. For example, consider the components X and Y shown in Figure 7.4 (and Figure 6.1). Here X and Y generate equivalent augmented Markov processes but there is no strong bisimulation relating them.

Hence equivalences between the Markov processes, even if augmented by action types, do not allow us to infer a strong bisimulation between the corresponding components. More significantly, strong bisimilarity does not, in general, provide us with sufficient information about the probabilistic behaviour of components to deduce any relation between, or within, their underlying Markov processes.

$$X_0 \stackrel{\text{def}}{=} (\alpha, r).X_1 + (\beta, s).X_1 \qquad\qquad Y_0 \stackrel{\text{def}}{=} (\alpha, s).Y_1 + (\beta, r).Y_1$$
$$X_1 \stackrel{\text{def}}{=} (\gamma, t).X_0 \qquad\qquad\qquad Y_1 \stackrel{\text{def}}{=} (\gamma, t).Y_0$$

Figure 7.4: Components which generate the same Markov process

7.6   Strong Bisimilarity for Model Simplification

In this section we outline the use of strong bisimilarity as a model simplification technique. It was shown in Section 7.4 that strong bisimilarity alone is not sufficient to ensure that components will exhibit exactly the same behaviour if observed over time. However, we present a simple additional condition, which may be easily tested, which guarantees that this problem with transition rates does not occur. The approach to model simplification, based on strong bisimilarity and this condition, is outlined in Section 7.6.1 and illustrated in Section 7.6.2.

In Section 7.4 it was remarked that a mismatch of transition rates in strongly bisimilar components can only occur when, in at least one of the components, for some activity a, there is more than one a-derivative and at least one of those derivatives results from more than one a activity. The different transition rates occur because these multiple instances of a occur with different derivatives in the two components. Thus we see that if two strongly bisimilar components also satisfy the following condition, Condition 1, then the relative frequencies of activity sequences within the components will be the same.

Condition 1   *P satisfies the condition if, for all $P' \in ds(P)$, for all $a \in \mathcal{A}ct(P')$, either*

- there is only one a-derivative of P'; *or*
- there is only one instance of the activity a resulting in each a-derivative of P'.

It is straightforward to verify that if two components are strongly bisimilar and both satisfy Condition 1 then the transition rates to derivatives which are strongly bisimilar will be the same in the two components. Thus it follows that the probabilistic behaviour of the two components will be the same. In particular the relative frequency of activity sequences in the two components will be matched.

7.6.1   An Approach to Model Simplification

The approach to model simplification which we propose involves replacing a top-level component in a PEPA model by another component which has a smaller derivative set but equivalent behaviour. The replacement component must be strongly bisimilar to the original component and both components must satisfy Condition 1. Since $\sim$ is a congruence relation the modified model is strongly bisimilar to the original model. Also the modified model will satisfy Condition 1 if the original model did. Thus the behaviour of the model is preserved, and an alternative representation of the system has been found. Moreover since the activities of the two models are the same the reward structure will be unaffected. Modifying the model in this way cannot increase the size of the state space of the underlying Markov process and in most cases it will be reduced.

Thus a model may be constructed in a naïve way with each of the components of the model represented explicitly, as in the examples shown in Chapter 4. This might result in a model which has a large state space but using this approach it may subsequently be possible to replace some components of the model and reduce the state space.

7.6.2   Simplifying an MSMQ Model using Strong Bisimilarity

We now illustrate the approach outlined in the previous section, using one of the case studies presented in Chapter 4, the asymmetric MSMQ system. We reduce the state space of the

$$Node_{j0} \stackrel{def}{=} (in, \lambda).Node_{j1} + (walk\_E_j, \top).Node_{j0} \qquad 1 \le j \le N$$
$$Node_{j1} \stackrel{def}{=} (walk\_F_j, \top).Node_{j2}$$
$$Node_{j2} \stackrel{def}{=} (serve_j, \mu_j).Node_{j0} + (walk\_E_j, \top).Node_{j2}$$
$$\text{where } \mu_j = \begin{cases} \mu & \text{if } j = 1 \\ m\mu & \text{if } 1 < j \le N \end{cases}$$

$$S_j \stackrel{def}{=} (walk\_F_j, \omega).(serve_j, \top).S_{j+1} + (walk\_E_j, \omega).S_{j+1}$$
$$\text{where } j + 1 = 1 \text{ when } j = N$$

when $N = 4$:
$$Asym \stackrel{def}{=} (Node_{10} \parallel Node_{20} \parallel Node_{30} \parallel Node_{40}) \underset{\substack{\{walk\_F_j, \\ walk\_E_j, serve_j\}}}{\bowtie} (S_1 \parallel S_1)$$

$$SS_{\{i,j\}} \stackrel{def}{=} (walk\_F_i, \omega).SS_{\{i+,j\}} + (walk\_E_i, \omega).SS_{\{i+1,j\}}$$
$$+ (walk\_F_j, \omega).SS_{\{i,j+\}} + (walk\_E_j, \omega).SS_{\{i,j+1\}}$$
$$SS_{\{i+,j\}} \stackrel{def}{=} (serve_i, \top).SS_{\{i+1,j\}} + (walk\_E_j, \omega).SS_{\{i+,j+1\}} + (walk\_F_j, \omega).SS_{\{i+,j+\}}$$
$$SS_{\{i,j+\}} \stackrel{def}{=} (walk\_E_i, \omega).SS_{\{i+1,j+\}} + (walk\_F_i, \omega).SS_{\{i+,j+\}} + (serve_j, \top).SS_{\{i,j+1\}}$$
$$SS_{\{i+,j+\}} \stackrel{def}{=} (serve_i, \top).SS_{\{i+1,j+\}} + (serve_j, \top).SS_{\{i+,j+1\}}$$
$$\text{where } j + 1 = 1 \text{ when } j = N;$$
$$\text{and } i + 1 = 1 \text{ when } i = N.$$

when $N = 4$:
$$Asym' \stackrel{def}{=} (Node_{10} \parallel Node_{20} \parallel Node_{30} \parallel Node_{40}) \underset{\substack{\{walk\_F_j, \\ walk\_E_j, serve_j\}}}{\bowtie} SS_{\{1,1\}} \qquad \text{for } 1 \le j \le 4$$

Figure 7.5: Original and modified PEPA models of the asymmetric MSMQ system with four nodes

underlying Markov process by finding a simpler, strongly bisimilar, replacement for the component representing the two servers in the system. The original and modified PEPA models of the system are presented in Figure 7.5.

In the original model each server is modelled explicitly as a component, S_j.

$$S_j \stackrel{def}{=} (walk\_F_j, \omega).(serve_j, \top).S_{j+1} + (walk\_E_j, \omega).S_{j+1}$$

The two servers in the system are then represented as a top-level component which is the parallel combination of two such components: $S_1 \parallel S_1$. It is this top-level component which we replace. We take advantage of the fact that the activities which the combination of the two servers can undertake is determined by the present location of the two servers, but not which of them is at which location. We replace $S_i \parallel S_j$ by a single component $SS_{\{i,j\}}$ defined as follows:

$$SS_{\{i,j\}} \stackrel{def}{=} (walk\_F_i, \omega).SS_{\{i+,j\}} + (walk\_E_i, \omega).SS_{\{i+1,j\}} +$$
$$(walk\_F_j, \omega).SS_{\{i,j+\}} + (walk\_E_j, \omega).SS_{\{i,j+1\}}$$
$$SS_{\{i+,j\}} \stackrel{def}{=} (serve_i, \top).SS_{\{i+1,j\}} + (walk\_E_j, \omega).SS_{\{i+,j+1\}} + (walk\_F_j, \omega).SS_{\{i+,j+\}}$$
$$SS_{\{i,j+\}} \stackrel{def}{=} (walk\_E_i, \omega).SS_{\{i+1,j+\}} + (walk\_F_i, \omega).SS_{\{i+,j+\}} + (serve_j, \top).SS_{\{i,j+1\}}$$
$$SS_{\{i+,j+\}} \stackrel{def}{=} (serve_i, \top).SS_{\{i+1,j+\}} + (serve_j, \top).SS_{\{i+,j+1\}}$$

Although at first sight the component $SS_{\{i,j\}}$ appears to be more complex than $S_i \parallel S_j$ it generates a smaller derivative set. For example, in the case $N = 4$, the derivative set of $S_1 \parallel S_1$ has 64 elements, of which 56 are exhibited in the derivatives of *Asym*. Not all the derivatives are exhibited, e.g. $(serve_1, \top).S_2 \parallel (serve_1, \top).S_2$, because to arrive at such a derivative in *Asym* there would need to be more than one customer present at Node 1, contrary to the definition of the node. In contrast $SS_{\{1,1\}}$ has just 36 elements, 32 of which are exhibited in the derivatives of *Asym*.

If we consider the relation $\mathcal{R}$,

$$\mathcal{R} = \left\{ \left((S_i \| S_j), SS_{\{i,j\}}\right),\ \left((S_j \| S_i), SS_{\{i,j\}}\right),\ \left(((serve_i, \top).S_{i+1} \| (serve_j, \top).S_{j+1}), SS_{\{i+,j+\}}\right),\right.$$
$$\left. \left(((serve_i, \top).S_{i+1} \| S_j), SS_{\{i+,j\}}\right),\ \left((S_i \| (serve_j, \top).S_{j+1}), SS_{\{i,j+\}}\right) \ \middle|\ 1 \le i, j \le N \right\}$$

it is easy to verify that it is a strong bisimulation. Moreover, we can see by inspection that both $S_1 \parallel S_1$ and $SS_{\{1,1\}}$ satisfy Condition 1.

Thus we replace $(S_1 \parallel S_1)$ in the model of the asymmetric MSMQ system by the new top-level component $SS_{\{1,1\}}$, to form the modified model *Asym'*. It follows from Proposition 7.3.1 that *Asym* $\sim$ *Asym'*.

$$Asym \stackrel{\text{def}}{=} (N_1 \parallel \cdots \parallel N_N) \underset{\substack{\{walk\_F_j, \\ walk\_E_j, serve_j\}}}{\bowtie} (S_1 \parallel S_1) \qquad Asym' \stackrel{\text{def}}{=} (N_1 \parallel \cdots \parallel N_N) \underset{\substack{\{walk\_F_j, \\ walk\_E_j, serve_j\}}}{\bowtie} (SS_{\{1,1\}})$$

Recall that in Section 4.4 we saw that the Markov process for the model *Asym* with four nodes had 560 states in the state space. The modified model, *Asym'*, when $N = 4$, has 312 states. However the performance measures extracted from the models are exactly the same as the reward structure is unaffected by the simplification.

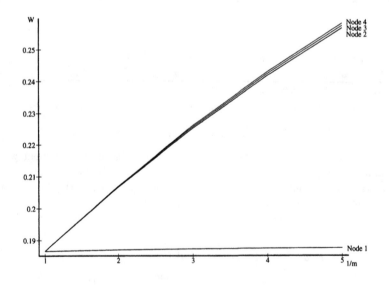

Figure 7.6: Mean customer waiting times as service demand at Node 1 increases, calculated from the modified asymmetric MSMQ model, *Asym'*

Chapter 8

Strong Equivalence

8.1 Introduction

In this chapter an alternative notion of equivalence for PEPA components is developed. This equivalence, *strong equivalence*, is defined in Section 8.2. It is developed in the style of Larsen and Skou's probabilistic bisimulation which was discussed in Section 5.2.3. Here transition rates, already embedded in the PEPA labelled transition system as activity rates, are used instead of probabilities. As with strong bisimulation the relation aims to capture a notion of equivalent behaviour between components. However, observation now occurs without detailed knowledge of the individual transitions involved. Strong equivalence, unlike strong bisimulation, is unable to distinguish between a single $(\alpha, 2r)$ activity and two simultaneously enabled instances of the (α, r) activity.

Some properties of the relation from a process algebra perspective are examined in Section 8.3. Like strong bisimulation, strong equivalence is found to be a congruence relation for PEPA. In Section 8.4 we discuss some of the implications of strong equivalence for the system components being represented, and in Section 8.5 the implications for the underlying Markov processes are reviewed. Finally, in Section 8.6, we outline the use of strong equivalence as a state-to-state equivalence forming the basis of exact aggregation. An alternative approach to the generation of the Markov process underlying a PEPA model is also discussed. These ideas are illustrated in Section 8.6.3 with an example taken from Section 4.4.4.

8.2 Definition of Strong Equivalence

In PEPA two components are strongly bisimilar if any a activity of one can be matched by an a activity of the other, and every a-derivative of one is strongly bisimilar to some a-derivative of the the other. Furthermore the apparent rates of all action types are the same in the two components. We saw in Section 7.4 that although this relation ensures that the sequences of activities which can result from strongly bisimilar components are matched, the relative frequencies of such sequences occurring in the two components are not necessarily the same.

The probabilistic bisimulation of Larsen and Skou [38] forms equivalence classes such that, for any two agents within a class, the probabilities of them performing a given action, α, and resulting in α-derivatives which lie within a given equivalence class, are the same. To apply a similar notion of equivalence to PEPA we consider the *conditional transition rates* rather than the conditional transition probabilities.

The conditional transition rate between two components C_i and C_j, via a given action type α, denoted $q(C_i, C_j, \alpha)$ was defined in Section 3.5.2. It is the rate at which a system behaving as component C_i evolves to behave as component C_j as a result of completing an activity of action type α. It is the sum of activity rates, labelling arcs of type α, connecting the nodes corresponding to C_i and C_j in the derivation graph. If we consider a set of possible derivatives S, the *total conditional transition rate* from C_i to S, denoted $q[C_i, S, \alpha]$, is defined to be

$$q[C_i, S, \alpha] = \sum_{C_j \in S} q(C_i, C_j, \alpha)$$

Two PEPA components are strongly equivalent if there is an equivalence relation between them such that, for any action type α, the total conditional transition rates from those components to any equivalence class, via activities of this type, are the same.

Definition 8.2.1 *An equivalence relation $\mathcal{R} \subseteq \mathcal{C} \times \mathcal{C}$, is a* strong equivalence *if whenever $(P, Q) \in \mathcal{R}$ then for all $\alpha \in \mathcal{A}$ and for all $S \in \mathcal{C}/\mathcal{R}$,*

$$q[P, S, \alpha] = q[Q, S, \alpha] \tag{2.1}$$

It is clear that the identity relation trivially satisfies Definition 8.2.1, and so all components are members of some strong equivalence. As with strong bisimulation we will be interested in the relation which is the largest strong equivalence, formed by the union of all strong equivalences. However it is not straightforward to see that this will indeed be a strong equivalence. First we prove the following proposition, showing that the transitive closure of a union of such relations, is itself a strong equivalence.

Proposition 8.2.1 *Let each $\mathcal{R}_i$, $i \in I$ for some index set I, be a strong equivalence. Then $\mathcal{R} = \left(\bigcup_{i \in I} \mathcal{R}_i \right)^*$, the transitive closure of their union, is also a strong equivalence.*

Proof   Since each $\mathcal{R}_i$ is an equivalence relation, it follows from the definition of $\mathcal{R}$ that $\mathcal{R}$ is also an equivalence relation.

Any equivalence relation over $\mathcal{C}$ will partition the set into equivalence classes. Let $\mathcal{C}/\mathcal{R}$ and $\mathcal{C}/\mathcal{R}_i$ denote these sets of equivalence classes for $\mathcal{R}$ and each $\mathcal{R}_i$ respectively. By definition $(P, Q) \in \mathcal{R}_i$ implies that $(P, Q) \in \mathcal{R}$, and so any equivalence class $S_j^i \in \mathcal{C}/\mathcal{R}_i$ is wholly contained within some equivalence class $T_k \in \mathcal{C}/\mathcal{R}$. Moreover, it follows that there is some set J_k^i such that $T_k = \bigcup_{j \in J_k^i} S_j^i$.

Consider $(P, Q) \in \mathcal{R}$, then $(P, Q) \in \left(\bigcup_{i \in I} \mathcal{R}_i \right)^n$ for some $n > 0$. We will show that $\mathcal{R}$ satisfies equation 2.1 by induction over n. Let $\mathcal{R}_n$ denote $\left(\bigcup_{i \in I} \mathcal{R}_i \right)^n$. For an arbitrary element $T_k \in \mathcal{C}/\mathcal{R}$ and any $\alpha \in \mathcal{A}$, we consider the total conditional transition rates from P and Q into T_k given that $(P, Q) \in \mathcal{R}_n$.

When $n = 1$, $(P, Q) \in \mathcal{R}_1$ implies that $(P, Q) \in \mathcal{R}_i$ for some $i \in I$, and by the argument above,

$$q[P, T_k, \alpha] = \sum_{j \in J_k^i} q[P, S_j^i, \alpha] = \sum_{j \in J_k^i} q[Q, S_j^i, \alpha] = q[Q, T_k, \alpha].$$

For $n > 1$ we assume that for all $\mathcal{R}_m$, where $m < n$, if $(P, Q) \in \mathcal{R}_m$ then,

$$q[P, T_k, \alpha] = q[Q, T_k, \alpha]$$

Now $(P, Q) \in \mathcal{R}_n$ implies that $(P, Q) \in \mathcal{R}_i; \mathcal{R}_{n-1}$, i.e. there is some $C \in \mathcal{C}$ such that $(P, C) \in \mathcal{R}_i$ for some $i \in I$ and $(C, Q) \in \mathcal{R}_{n-1}$. But then it follows by the same argument as above that $q[P, T_k, \alpha] = q[C, T_k, \alpha]$, and by the induction hypothesis, $q[C, T_k, \alpha] = q[Q, T_k, \alpha]$. Thus we can see that $q[P, T_k, \alpha] = q[Q, T_k, \alpha]$ as required.

Therefore $\mathcal{R}$ is a strong equivalence relation. $\square$

Definition 8.2.2 *We say P and Q are* strongly equivalent, *written $P \cong Q$, if $(P, Q) \in \mathcal{R}$ for some strong equivalence $\mathcal{R}$, i.e.*

$$\cong = \bigcup \{\mathcal{R} \mid \mathcal{R} \text{ is a strong equivalence}\}$$

It is clear from the definition that $\cong$ is at least as large as the largest strong equivalence, and it follows from Proposition 8.2.1 that $\cong$ is a strong equivalence itself. Thus we state the following proposition:

Proposition 8.2.2 $\cong$ *is the largest strong equivalence.*

In order to show that $P \cong Q$ we must find a strong equivalence relation $\mathcal{R}$ such that $(P, Q) \in \mathcal{R}$. Alternatively we can regard this as finding partitions of the derivative sets of P and Q satisfying equation 2.1, and a one-to-one correspondence between them.

We can also define a weaker relation, *strong equivalence up to* $\cong$. As with strong bisimilarity and strong bisimulation up to $\sim$, in order to exhibit strong equivalence between two components it is sufficient to find a strong equivalence up to $\cong$ between them. This result is stated in Proposition 8.2.3.

Definition 8.2.3 $\mathcal{R}$ *is a* strong equivalence up to $\cong$ *if $\mathcal{R}$ is an equivalence relation over $\mathcal{C}$ and $(P, Q) \in \mathcal{R}$ implies that for all $\alpha \in \mathcal{A}$, and for all $T \in \mathcal{C}/(\cong\mathcal{R}\cong)$,*

$$q[P, T, \alpha] = q[Q, T, \alpha]$$

Let us consider, for any equivalence relation $\mathcal{R}$, what equivalence classes of the form $T \in \mathcal{C}/(\cong\mathcal{R}\cong)$ represent. Recall that $(P, Q) \in \cong\mathcal{R}\cong$ if there exist P_1 and Q_1 such that $P \cong P_1$, $P_1 \mathcal{R} Q_1$ and $Q_1 \cong Q$. For all $P \in \mathcal{C}$. let S_P denote the equivalence class in $\mathcal{C}/\cong$ which contains P, R_P the corresponding equivalence class in $\mathcal{C}/\mathcal{R}$ and T_P the corresponding equivalence class in $\mathcal{C}/(\cong\mathcal{R}\cong)$. Then we can see that

$$T_P = \{Q \mid P \cong \mathcal{R} \cong Q\} = \bigcup \{S_{Q_1} \mid Q_1 \in \{R_{P_1} \mid P_1 \in S_P\}\}$$

It follows that any $T_P \in \mathcal{C}/(\cong\mathcal{R}\cong)$ is a union of equivalence classes $S_{Q_1} \in \mathcal{C}/\cong$.

Lemma 8.2.1 *If $\mathcal{R}$ is a strong equivalence up to $\cong$, then the relation $\cong\mathcal{R}\cong$ is a strong equivalence.*

Proof Let $P \cong \mathcal{R} \cong Q$. Then there are components P_1 and Q_1 such that $P \cong P_1 \mathcal{R} Q_1 \cong Q$. Moreover for all $S \in \mathcal{C}/\cong$

$$q[P, S, \alpha] = q[P_1, S, \alpha] \qquad q[Q_1, S, \alpha] = q[Q, S, \alpha]$$

and for all $T \in \mathcal{C}/(\cong\mathcal{R}\cong)$, $q[P_1, T, \alpha] = q[Q_1, T, \alpha]$.
Since any $T \in \mathcal{C}/(\cong\mathcal{R}\cong)$ is a union of $S \in \mathcal{C}/\cong$ it follows that for all such T,

$$q[P, T, \alpha] = q[Q, T, \alpha].$$

$\square$

Proposition 8.2.3 *If $\mathcal{R}$ is a strong equivalence up to $\cong$ then $\mathcal{R} \subseteq \cong$.*

Proof This follows immediately from Lemma 8.2.1, by similar reasoning to the proof of Proposition 7.2.2.

$\square$

8.3 Properties of the Strong Equivalence Relation

In this section we investigate the properties of the strong equivalence relation $\cong$ from a process algebra perspective. We show that strong equivalence is a congruence. We also show that isomorphic components are strongly equivalent and examine the relationship between strong bisimilarity and strong equivalence.

8.3.1 Strong Equivalence as a Congruence

We establish that $\cong$ is a congruence for PEPA by showing, in Proposition 8.3.1, that the relation is preserved by the combinators, and in Proposition 8.3.2, that it is preserved by recursive definitions. The proofs are similar to those for strong bisimilarity, although somewhat more intricate.

Proposition 8.3.1 (Preservation by Combinators)
If $P_1 \cong P_2$ then

1. $a.P_1 \cong a.P_2$;

2. $P_1 + Q \cong P_2 + Q$;

3. $P_1 \bowtie_L Q \cong P_2 \bowtie_L Q$;

4. $P_1/L \cong P_2/L$.

Proof We show only the proofs of 2. and 3.—the proof of 1. is straightforward and the proof of 4. is similar to 3.

2. Since $P_1 \cong P_2$ it follows that for all $\alpha \in \mathcal{A}$, and for all $S \in \mathcal{C}/\!\cong$,

$$q[P_1, S, \alpha] = q[P_2, S, \alpha].$$

Consider $P_1 + Q$. By the definition of $q[\cdot]$ and the definition of choice, it follows that for all $\alpha \in \mathcal{A}$ and for all $S \in \mathcal{C}/\!\cong$,

$$q[P_1 + Q, S, \alpha] = q[P_1, S, \alpha] + q[Q, S, \alpha] =$$
$$q[P_2, S, \alpha] + q[Q, S, \alpha] = q[P_2 + Q, S, \alpha].$$

Thus we conclude that $P_1 + Q \cong P_2 + Q$.

3. Consider $\mathcal{R} = \{(Q_1 \bowtie_L Q, Q_2 \bowtie_L Q) \mid Q_1 \cong Q_2\}$. We extend this to a relation $\mathcal{R}^+$ over all components, where $\mathcal{R}^+ = \mathcal{R} \cup Id$. We will show that $\mathcal{R}^+$ is a strong equivalence. Since $\cong$ is an equivalence relation $\mathcal{R}$ is symmetric and transitive, and it follows that $\mathcal{R}^+$ is an equivalence relation.

   Suppose $(Q_1, Q_2) \in \mathcal{R}^+$. Then either $(Q_1, Q_2) \in Id$, i.e. $Q_1 \equiv Q_2$, or $(Q_1, Q_2) \in \mathcal{R}$, i.e. $Q_1 \equiv P_1 \bowtie_L Q$ and $Q_2 \equiv P_2 \bowtie_L Q$ where $P_1 \cong P_2$. In the first case, it is trivially true that for all $T \in \mathcal{C}/\mathcal{R}^+$ and for all $\alpha \in \mathcal{A}$,

$$q[Q_1, T, \alpha] = q[Q_2, T, \alpha].$$

   Therefore consider $(P_1 \bowtie_L Q, P_2 \bowtie_L Q) \in \mathcal{R}$. Recall that since $P_1 \cong P_2$ the set of action types enabled in P_1 and P_2 are the same: $\mathcal{A}(P_1) = \mathcal{A}(P_2)$.

Any derivative of a cooperation of components will have the form of a cooperation of components. Thus we only consider the equivalence classes $T \in \mathcal{C}/\mathcal{R}^+$ such that there is some element $P \bowtie_L Q' \in T$. Then, for some $S \in \mathcal{C}/\cong$,

$$T = \{P' \bowtie_L Q' \mid P \cong P'\} = \{P' \bowtie_L Q' \mid P' \in S\}$$

Thus we may denote each such T as $T_{(S,Q')}$. For any equivalence class $T \in \mathcal{C}/\mathcal{R}^+$ which is not of this form, for all $\alpha \in \mathcal{A}$,

$$q[P_1 \bowtie_L Q, T, \alpha] = 0 = q[P_2 \bowtie_L Q, T, \alpha]$$

Now consider $q[P_1 \bowtie_L Q, T_{(S,Q')}, \alpha]$ for arbitrary $T_{(S,Q')} \in \mathcal{C}/\mathcal{R}^+$, and $\alpha \in \mathcal{A}$. We consider the different cases of α with respect to $\mathcal{A}(P_1 \bowtie_L Q)$ separately.

Case 1: $\alpha \notin \mathcal{A}(P_1 \bowtie_L Q)$
It follows that $\alpha \notin \mathcal{A}(P_2 \bowtie_L Q)$ and so trivially, for all $T_{(S,Q')} \in \mathcal{C}/\mathcal{R}^+$,

$$q[P_1 \bowtie_L Q, T_{(S,Q')}, \alpha] = 0 = q[P_2 \bowtie_L Q, T_{(S,Q')}, \alpha]$$

Case 2: $\alpha \notin L, \ \alpha \in \mathcal{A}(P_1) \setminus \mathcal{A}(Q)$
Only P_1 can complete activities of type α and so for all $T_{(S,Q)} \in \mathcal{C}/\mathcal{R}^+$

$$q[P_1 \bowtie_L Q, T_{(S,Q)}, \alpha] = \sum_{P'_1 \in S} q(P_1, P'_1, \alpha) = q[P_1, S, \alpha]$$

α must be an individual action type of P_2 in $P_2 \bowtie_L Q$, and by similar reasoning $q[P_2 \bowtie_L Q, T_{(S,Q)}, \alpha] = q[P_2, S, \alpha]$. Therefore it follows that,

$$q[P_1 \bowtie_L Q, T_{(S,Q)}, \alpha] = q[P_1, S, \alpha] = q[P_2, S, \alpha] = q[P_2 \bowtie_L Q, T_{(S,Q)}, \alpha]$$

Case 3: $\alpha \notin L, \ \alpha \in \mathcal{A}(Q) \setminus \mathcal{A}(P_1)$
Only Q can complete activities of type α so $P_1 \bowtie_L Q \xrightarrow{(\alpha,r)} P_1 \bowtie_L Q'$ for some Q' and similarly for $P_2 \bowtie_L Q \xrightarrow{(\alpha,r)} P_2 \bowtie_L Q'$. By the definition of $\mathcal{R}$ these will lie within the same equivalence class, and so, for all $T_{(S,Q')} \in \mathcal{C}/\mathcal{R}^+$,

$$q[P_1 \bowtie_L Q, T_{(S,Q')}, \alpha] = q[P_2 \bowtie_L Q, T_{(S,Q')}, \alpha]$$

Case 4: $\alpha \notin L, \ \alpha \in \mathcal{A}(P_1) \cap \mathcal{A}(Q)$
Both P_1 and Q have individual activities of type α. Either P_1 or Q may perform an activity of this type, but not both, and so only one component will change. Thus if we consider any appropriate equivalence class $T_{(S,Q')}$ in $\mathcal{C}/\mathcal{R}'$ we see that the total conditional transition rate $q[P_1 \bowtie_L Q, T_{(S,Q')}, \alpha]$ is

$$\sum_{P' \bowtie_L Q' \in T_{(S,Q')}} q(P_1 \bowtie_L Q, P' \bowtie_L Q', \alpha) = \begin{cases} \sum_{P' \in S} q(P_1, P', \alpha) & \text{if } Q' \equiv Q \\ q(Q, Q', \alpha) & \text{otherwise} \end{cases}$$

Similarly

$$q[P_2 \bowtie_L Q, T_{(S,Q')}, \alpha] = \begin{cases} \sum_{P' \in S} q(P_2, P', \alpha) & \text{if } Q' \equiv Q \\ q(Q, Q', \alpha) & \text{otherwise} \end{cases}$$

Thus it follows that for any $T_{(S,Q')} \in \mathcal{C}/\mathcal{R}^+$,

$$q[P_1 \bowtie_L Q, T_{(S,Q')}, \alpha] = q[P_2 \bowtie_L Q, T_{(S,Q')}, \alpha].$$

Case 5: $\alpha \in L$, $\alpha \in \mathcal{A}(P_1 \underset{L}{\bowtie} Q)$

α is a shared activity of P_1' and Q. In general, for a shared action type α,

$$q(P \underset{L}{\bowtie} Q, P' \underset{L}{\bowtie} Q', \alpha) = \frac{q(P, P', \alpha)}{q(P, \alpha)} \times \frac{q(Q, Q', \alpha)}{q(Q, \alpha)} \min(r_\alpha(P), r_\alpha(Q))$$

and $\min(r_\alpha(P), r_\alpha(Q)) = r_\alpha(P \underset{L}{\bowtie} Q)$.

Since $P_1 \cong P_2$, it follows that $q(P_1, \alpha) = q(P_2, \alpha)$, $r_\alpha(P_1) = r_\alpha(P_2)$, and for all $S \in \mathcal{C}/\cong$, $q[P_1, S, \alpha] = q[P_2, S, \alpha]$.

Now we consider $q[P_1 \underset{L}{\bowtie} Q, T_{(S,Q')}, \alpha]$ for arbitrary $T_{(S,Q')} \in \mathcal{C}/\mathcal{R}^+$:

$$
\begin{aligned}
q[P_1 \underset{L}{\bowtie} Q, T_{(S,Q')}, \alpha] &= \sum_{P' \underset{L}{\bowtie} Q' \in T_{(S,Q')}} q(P_1 \underset{L}{\bowtie} Q, P' \underset{L}{\bowtie} Q', \alpha) \\
&= \frac{q(Q, Q', \alpha)}{q(Q, \alpha)} \times \left(\sum_{P' \in S} \frac{q(P_1, P', \alpha)}{q(P_1, \alpha)} \right) \times r_\alpha(P_1 \underset{L}{\bowtie} Q) \\
&= \frac{q(Q, Q', \alpha)}{q(Q, \alpha)} \times \frac{q[P_1, S, \alpha]}{q(P_1, \alpha)} \times r_\alpha(P_1 \underset{L}{\bowtie} Q) \\
&= \frac{q(Q, Q', \alpha)}{q(Q, \alpha)} \times \frac{q[P_2, S, \alpha]}{q(P_2, \alpha)} \times r_\alpha(P_2 \underset{L}{\bowtie} Q) \\
&= \sum_{P' \underset{L}{\bowtie} Q' \in T_{(S,Q')}} q(P_2 \underset{L}{\bowtie} Q, P' \underset{L}{\bowtie} Q', \alpha) = q[P_2 \underset{L}{\bowtie} Q, T_{(S,Q')}, \alpha]
\end{aligned}
$$

Thus we have shown that for all $\alpha \in \mathcal{A}$ and for all $T \in \mathcal{C}/\mathcal{R}^+$

$$q[P_1 \underset{L}{\bowtie} Q, T, \alpha] = q[P_2 \underset{L}{\bowtie} Q, T, \alpha]$$

and we conclude that $\mathcal{R}^+$ is a strong equivalence as required.
Therefore $P_1 \underset{L}{\bowtie} Q \cong P_2 \underset{L}{\bowtie} Q$.   □

We extend the notion of strong equivalence to component expressions in the obvious way:

Definition 8.3.1 *Let E and F be component expressions, containing variables $\tilde{X}$ at most. Then $E \cong F$ if, for all indexed sets of components $\tilde{P}$, $E\{\tilde{P}/\tilde{X}\} \cong F\{\tilde{P}/\tilde{X}\}$.*

Since most PEPA models are defined in terms of sets of recursive definitions we would like to show that strong equivalence is preserved by such definitions. That is, replacing a subexpression by a strongly equivalent subexpression, will result in a component expression which is strongly equivalent to the original. The following proposition proves that this is indeed the case.

Proposition 8.3.2 (Preservation by Recursive Definition)
Let $\tilde{E}$ and $\tilde{F}$ contain variables $\tilde{X}$ at most. Let $\tilde{A} \stackrel{\text{def}}{=} \tilde{E}\{\tilde{A}/\tilde{X}\}$, $\tilde{B} \stackrel{\text{def}}{=} \tilde{F}\{\tilde{B}/\tilde{X}\}$ and $\tilde{E} \cong \tilde{F}$. Then $\tilde{A} \cong \tilde{B}$.

Proof As in Proposition 7.3.2, it is sufficient to show the result for single recursion equations E and F such that $E \cong F$, $A \stackrel{\text{def}}{=} E\{A/X\}$ and $B \stackrel{\text{def}}{=} F\{B/X\}$. We construct a relation $\mathcal{R}$ as follows,

$$\mathcal{R} = \{(G\{A/X\}, G\{B/X\}) \mid G \text{ contains at most variable } X\}$$

and let $\mathcal{R}^*$ be the transitive, symmetric closure of $\mathcal{R}$. Clearly $\mathcal{R}^*$ is an equivalence relation. We will show that $\mathcal{R}^*$ is a strong equivalence up to $\cong$, using transition induction on the maximal depth of inference by which an activity by $G\{A/X\}$ can be inferred. Let α be an arbitrary activity type, $\alpha \in \mathcal{A}(G\{A/X\})$, $G\{A/X\} \xrightarrow{(\alpha,r)} P'$. We will use induction to show that for all $T \in \mathcal{C}/(\cong\mathcal{R}^*\cong)$,

$$q[G\{A/X\}, T, \alpha] = q[G\{B/X\}, T, \alpha]$$

We assume that if $\alpha \notin \mathcal{A}(G\{A/X\})$ then the maximal depth of inference of α in $G\{A/X\}$ is -1. In this case $q[G\{A/X\}, T, \alpha] = 0$ for any set $T \in \mathcal{C}/(\cong\mathcal{R}^*\cong)$.

Base Case: maximal depth of inference is zero—$G \equiv (\alpha, r).G'$.

$$G\{A/X\} \equiv (\alpha, r).G'\{A/X\} \qquad\qquad G\{B/X\} \equiv (\alpha, r).G'\{B/X\}$$

By the definition of $\mathcal{R}$, $(G'\{A/X\}, G'\{B/X\}) \in \mathcal{R}^*$ and there exists $T' \in \mathcal{C}/(\cong\mathcal{R}^*\cong)$ such that $G'\{A/X\}, G'\{B/X\} \in T'$. Thus it follows that for all $T \in \mathcal{C}/(\cong\mathcal{R}^*\cong)$,

$$q[G\{A/X\}, T, \alpha] = q[G\{B/X\}, T, \alpha] = \begin{cases} r & \text{if } T = T' \\ 0 & \text{otherwise} \end{cases}$$

We now assume that the maximal depth of inference by which an α type activity can be inferred in $G\{A/X\}$ is N, and that $\mathcal{R}^*$ is a strong equivalence up to $\cong$ over components with maximal depth of inference $< N$, i.e. if $G'\{A/X\}$ has maximal depth of inference for activities of type α of $< N$, then for all $T \in \mathcal{C}/(\cong\mathcal{R}^*\cong)$,

$$q[G'\{A/X\}, T, \alpha] = q[G'\{B/X\}, T, \alpha].$$

The possible forms of G are considered separately.

Case 1: $G \equiv X$

$G\{A/X\} \equiv A$, and so $A \xrightarrow{(\alpha,r)} P'$. Also $E\{A/X\} \xrightarrow{(\alpha,r)}$ by a shorter maximal depth of inference, so by the induction hypothesis, for all $T \in \mathcal{C}/(\cong\mathcal{R}^*\cong)$,

$$q[E\{A/X\}, T, \alpha] = q[E\{B/X\}, T, \alpha]$$

Since $E \cong F$, it follows that $E\{B/X\} \cong F\{B/X\}$ and for all $S \in \mathcal{C}/\cong$,

$$q[E\{B/X\}, S, \alpha] = q[F\{B/X\}, S, \alpha].$$

Since any $T \in \mathcal{C}/(\cong\mathcal{R}^*\cong)$ is a union of elements of $\mathcal{C}/\cong$, for all $T \in \mathcal{C}/(\cong\mathcal{R}^*\cong)$,

$$q[E\{B/X\}, T, \alpha] = q[F\{B/X\}, T, \alpha].$$

As $A \stackrel{\text{def}}{=} E\{A/X\}$, $B \stackrel{\text{def}}{=} F\{B/X\}$ and $G \equiv X$, it follows that for any set $U \subseteq \mathcal{C}$,

$$q[G\{A/X\}, U, \alpha] = q[E\{A/X\}, U, \alpha], \quad q[G\{B/X\}, U, \alpha] = q[F\{B/X\}, U, \alpha].$$

Hence we may conclude that for all $T \in \mathcal{C}/(\cong\mathcal{R}^*\cong)$,

$$q[G\{A/X\}, T, \alpha] = q[G\{B/X\}, T, \alpha]$$

Case 2: $G \equiv G_1 + G_2$

Then $G\{A/X\} \equiv G_1\{A/X\} + G_2\{A/X\}$, so for any set $U \subseteq \mathcal{C}$,

$$q[G\{A/X\}, U, \alpha] \;=\; q[G_1\{A/X\}, U, \alpha] + q[G_2\{A/X\}, U, \alpha]$$

and similarly, $G\{B/X\} \equiv G_1\{B/X\} + G_2\{B/X\}$ and

$$q[G\{B/X\}, U, \alpha] \;=\; q[G_1\{B/X\}, U, \alpha] + q[G_2\{B/X\}, U, \alpha].$$

Now both G_1 and G_2 have a shorter maximal depth of inference for inferring an activity of type α, and therefore by induction, for all $T \in \mathcal{C}/(\cong\mathcal{R}^*\cong)$,

$$q[G_1\{A/X\}, T, \alpha] = q[G_1\{B/X\}, T, \alpha] \qquad q[G_2\{A/X\}, T, \alpha] = q[G_2\{B/X\}, T, \alpha]$$

Thus it follows that for all $T \in \mathcal{C}/(\cong\mathcal{R}^*\cong)$,

$$
\begin{aligned}
q[G\{A/X\}, T, \alpha] &= q[G_1\{A/X\}, T, \alpha] + q[G_2\{A/X\}, T, \alpha] \\
&= q[G_1\{B/X\}, T, \alpha] + q[G_2\{B/X\}, T, \alpha] = q[G\{B/X\}, T, \alpha]
\end{aligned}
$$

Case 3: $G \equiv G_1 \bowtie_L G_2$

Clearly $G_1\{A/X\}$ and $G_2\{A/X\}$ both have maximal depth of inference, to infer an activity of type α, $< N$, and by induction, for all $T \in \mathcal{C}/(\cong\mathcal{R}^*\cong)$,

$$q[G_1\{A/X\}, T, \alpha] = q[G_1\{B/X\}, T, \alpha] \qquad q[G_2\{A/X\}, T, \alpha] = q[G_2\{B/X\}, T, \alpha]$$

From this we can deduce that

$$
\begin{aligned}
q(G_1\{A/X\}, \alpha) = q(G_1\{B/X\}, \alpha) && r_\alpha(G_1\{A/X\}) = r_\alpha(G_1\{B/X\}) \\
q(G_2\{A/X\}, \alpha) = q(G_2\{B/X\}, \alpha) && r_\alpha(G_2\{A/X\}) = r_\alpha(G_2\{B/X\}).
\end{aligned}
$$

When the activity $G\{A/X\} \xrightarrow{(\alpha,r)} P'$ is an individual activity the proof is similar to Case 2 above. We present the case of a shared activity: $\alpha \in L$, $\alpha \in \mathcal{A}(G_1\{A/X\}) \cap \mathcal{A}(G_2\{A/X\})$, $G_1\{A/X\} \xrightarrow{(\alpha,r_1)} P_1'$, $G_2\{A/X\} \xrightarrow{(\alpha,r_2)} P_2'$, and $P' \equiv P_1' \bowtie_L P_2'$. Consider the conditional transition rate to P':

$$q(G\{A/X\}, P', \alpha) = \frac{q(G_1\{A/X\}, P_1', \alpha)\, q(G_2\{A/X\}, P_2', \alpha)}{q(G_1\{A/X\}, \alpha)\, q(G_2\{A/X\}, \alpha)}\, \min(r_\alpha(G_1\{A/X\}), r_\alpha(G_2\{A/X\}))$$

For any $T \in \mathcal{C}/(\cong\mathcal{R}^*\cong)$ the total conditional transition rate is

$$q[G\{A/X\}, T, \alpha] \;=\; \sum_{P' \in T} q(G\{A/X\}, P', \alpha)$$

where $P' \equiv P_1' \bowtie_L P_2'$, if $q(G\{A/X\}, P', \alpha) \neq 0$. Since $\cong\mathcal{R}^*\cong$ partitions $\mathcal{C}$, there are equivalence classes $T_1, T_2 \in \mathcal{C}/(\cong\mathcal{R}^*\cong)$, such that $P_1' \in T_1$ and $P_2' \in T_2$. Moreover, since the relation $\cong\mathcal{R}^*\cong$ is preserved by the combinator $\bowtie_L$, it follows that $P_1' \bowtie_L P_2' \in T$, $P_1' \in T_1$, implies that $Q_1 \bowtie_L P_2' \in T$ for all $Q_1 \in T_1$. Similarly $P_1' \bowtie_L Q_2 \in T$, for all $Q_2 \in T_2$. Thus the total conditional transition rate is:

$$\frac{\sum\limits_{Q_1 \in T_1} \left(q(G_1\{A/X\}, Q_1, \alpha) \sum\limits_{Q_2 \in T_2} q(G_2\{A/X\}, Q_2, \alpha) \right)}{q(G_1\{A/X\}, \alpha) \, q(G_2\{A/X\}, \alpha)} \min(r_\alpha(G_1\{A/X\}), r_\alpha(G_2\{A/X\}))$$

$$= \frac{q[G_1\{A/X\}, T_1, \alpha]}{q(G_1\{A/X\}, \alpha)} \frac{q[G_2\{A/X\}, T_2, \alpha]}{q(G_2\{A/X\}, \alpha)} \min(r_\alpha(G_1\{A/X\}), r_\alpha(G_2\{A/X\}))$$

$$= \frac{q[G_1\{B/X\}, T_1, \alpha]}{q(G_1\{B/X\}, \alpha)} \frac{q[G_2\{B/X\}, T_2, \alpha]}{q(G_2\{B/X\}, \alpha)} \min(r_\alpha(G_1\{B/X\}), r_\alpha(G_2\{B/X\}))$$

$$= \sum_{Q' \in T} q(G\{B/X\}, Q', \alpha) = q[G\{B/X\}, T, \alpha]$$

Hence we can conclude that for all $T \in \mathcal{C}/(\cong\mathcal{R}^*\cong)$,

$$q[G\{A/X\}, T, \alpha] \ = \ q[G\{B/X\}, T, \alpha]$$

Case 4: $G \equiv G_1/L$
As $G\{A/X\}$ can infer an activity of type α, with maximal depth of inference N, it follows that $\alpha \notin L$. Moreover since the maximal depth of inference of α in $G_1\{A/X\} < N$ by the induction hypothesis we see that, for all $T \in \mathcal{C}/(\cong\mathcal{R}^*\cong)$,

$$q[G_1\{A/X\}, T, \alpha] \ = \ q[G_1\{B/X\}, T, \alpha]$$

$$q[G\{A/X\}, T, \alpha] = \begin{cases} q[G_1\{A/X\}, T, \alpha] & \text{if } \alpha \neq \tau \\ q[G_1\{A/X\}, T, \tau] + \sum\limits_{\beta \in L} q[G_1\{A/X\}, T, \beta] & \text{if } \alpha = \tau \end{cases}$$

It follows that, for all $T \in \mathcal{C}/(\cong\mathcal{R}^*\cong)$, $\quad q[G\{A/X\}, T, \alpha] \ = \ q[G\{B/X\}, T, \alpha]$.

Case 5: $G \equiv C$ where C is a constant
C is associated with some definition $C \stackrel{\text{def}}{=} P$. Since X does not appear in G, $G\{A/X\}$ and $G\{B/X\}$ are both identical to C. They will have exactly the same transitions, so it follows trivially that, for all $T \in \mathcal{C}/(\cong\mathcal{R}^*\cong)$,

$$q[G\{A/X\}, T, \alpha] \ = \ q[P, T, \alpha] \ = \ q[G\{B/X\}, T, \alpha].$$

Since the choice of $\alpha \in \mathcal{A}$ was arbitrary, it follows that for all $\alpha \in \mathcal{A}$, for all $T \in \mathcal{C}/(\cong\mathcal{R}^*\cong)$,

$$q[G\{A/X\}, T, \alpha] \ = \ q[G\{B/X\}, T, \alpha].$$

Thus, for $\mathcal{R} \equiv \{(G\{A/X\}, G\{B/X\}) \mid G \text{ contains at most variable } X\}$, we have shown that $\mathcal{R}^*$ is a strong equivalence up to $\cong$.

Consequently if we take $G \equiv X$, then $A \cong B$ as required. $\qquad\square$

8.3.2 Isomorphism and Strong Equivalence

Recall that in Section 7.3.2 we showed that isomorphism between components was a stronger relation than strong bisimilarity. In this section we show that it is also a stronger relation than strong equivalence, i.e. $= \ \subset \ \cong$.

Proposition 8.3.3 *If P and Q are isomorphic components then $P \cong Q$.*

Proof Recall that $P = Q$ if there is a component isomorphism $\mathcal{F} : \mathcal{C} \longrightarrow \mathcal{C}$, an injective function, such that $Act(P) = Act(\mathcal{F}(P))$, where for all $a \in Act$ the a-derivatives of $\mathcal{F}(P)$ are the same as the $\mathcal{F}$-images of the a-derivatives of P, and $Q \equiv \mathcal{F}(P)$. We will show that $=$ is a strong equivalence. It is trivial to see that $=$ is an equivalence relation. Let T be any equivalence class in $\mathcal{C}/{=}$, then for all $\alpha \in \mathcal{A}$,

$$q[P,T,\alpha] \;=\; \sum_{P' \in T} q(P,P',\alpha) \;=\; \sum_{P' \in T} q(\mathcal{F}(P),\mathcal{F}(P'),\alpha) \;=\; \sum_{P' \in T} q(Q,P',\alpha) \;=\; q[Q,T,\alpha]$$

Thus we see that $=$ is a strong equivalence, and we conclude that if $P = Q$ then $P \cong Q$. $\qquad\Box$

As for strong bisimilarity, the equational laws stated earlier for isomorphic components, may now be restated with "$=$" replaced by "$\cong$".

Proposition 8.3.4 (Choice)

1. $P + Q \cong Q + P$

2. $P + (Q + R) \cong (P + Q) + R$

Proposition 8.3.5 (Hiding)

1. $(P + Q)/L \cong P/L + Q/L$

2. $((\alpha,r).P)/L \cong \begin{cases} (\tau,r).P/L & \alpha \in L \\ (\alpha,r).P/L & \alpha \notin L \end{cases}$

3. $(P/L)/K \cong P/(L \cup K)$

4. $P/L \cong P$ if $L \cap \vec{A}(P)$

Proposition 8.3.6 (Cooperation)

1. $P \underset{L}{\bowtie} Q \cong Q \underset{L}{\bowtie} P$

2. $P \underset{L}{\bowtie} (Q \underset{L}{\bowtie} R) \cong (P \underset{L}{\bowtie} Q) \underset{L}{\bowtie} R$

3. $(P \underset{L}{\bowtie} Q)/(K \cup M) \cong \Big((P/K) \underset{L}{\bowtie} (Q/K)\Big)\Big/M$ where $K \cap M = K \cap L = \emptyset$

4. $P \underset{K}{\bowtie} Q \cong P \underset{L}{\bowtie} Q$ if $K \cap (\vec{A}(P) \cup \vec{A}(Q)) = L$

5. $(P \underset{L}{\bowtie} Q) \underset{K}{\bowtie} R \cong \begin{cases} P \underset{L}{\bowtie} (Q \underset{K}{\bowtie} R) & \text{if } \vec{A}(R) \cap L \setminus K = \emptyset \wedge \vec{A}(P) \cap K \setminus L = \emptyset \\ Q \underset{L}{\bowtie} (P \underset{K}{\bowtie} R) & \text{if } \vec{A}(R) \cap L \setminus K = \emptyset \wedge \vec{A}(Q) \cap K \setminus L = \emptyset \end{cases}$

Proposition 8.3.7 (Constant)
If $A \overset{\text{def}}{=} P$ then $A \cong P$.

$$A \overset{\text{def}}{=} (\alpha, r).A + (\alpha, r).A \qquad\qquad B \overset{\text{def}}{=} (\alpha, 2r).B$$

Figure 8.1: Strong equivalence does not imply strong bisimilarity

Proposition 8.3.8 (Expansion Law) *Let* $P \equiv (P_1 \bowtie_L P_2)/K$ *with* $L, K \subset \mathcal{A}$. *Then*

$$
\begin{aligned}
P \;\cong\; & \sum\{(\alpha, r).(P_1' \bowtie_L P_2)/K \mid P_1 \xrightarrow{(\alpha, r)} P_1' ; \; \alpha \notin L \cup K\} \\
+ \; & \sum\{(\alpha, r).(P_1 \bowtie_L P_2')/K \mid P_2 \xrightarrow{(\alpha, r)} P_2' ; \; \alpha \notin L \cup K\} \\
+ \; & \sum\{(\tau, r).(P_1' \bowtie_L P_2)/K \mid P_1 \xrightarrow{(\alpha, r)} P_1' ; \; \alpha \in K \setminus L\} \\
+ \; & \sum\{(\tau, r).(P_1 \bowtie_L P_2')/K \mid P_2 \xrightarrow{(\alpha, r)} P_2' ; \; \alpha \in K \setminus L\} \\
+ \; & \sum\{(\alpha, r).(P_1' \bowtie_L P_2')/K \mid P_1 \xrightarrow{(\alpha, r_1)} P_1' ; \; P_2 \xrightarrow{(\alpha, r_2)} P_2' ; \; \alpha \in L \setminus K \; ; \\
& \qquad\qquad\qquad r = \frac{r_1}{r_\alpha(P_1)} \frac{r_2}{r_\alpha(P_2)} \min(r_\alpha(P_1), r_\alpha(P_2))\} \\
+ \; & \sum\{(\tau, r).(P_1' \bowtie_L P_2')/K \mid P_1 \xrightarrow{(\alpha, r_1)} P_1' ; \; P_2 \xrightarrow{(\alpha, r_2)} P_2' ; \; \alpha \in L \cap K \; ; \\
& \qquad\qquad\qquad r = \frac{r_1}{r_\alpha(P_1)} \frac{r_2}{r_\alpha(P_2)} \min(r_\alpha(P_1), r_\alpha(P_2))\}
\end{aligned}
$$

8.3.3 Strong Bisimilarity and Strong Equivalence

In this section we investigate the relation between strong bisimilarity and strong equivalence. It is straightforward to construct components A and B such that $A \cong B$ but $A \nsim B$. For example, consider A and B shown in Figure 8.1. Incidentally, this simple example also shows that $A \cong B$ does not imply $A = B$.

Both strong bisimilarity and strong equivalence are implied by component isomorphism and we might expect to be able to deduce that $\sim \, \subset \, \cong$. However we can construct components, such as P and Q shown in Figure 8.2, which are strongly bisimilar but not strongly equivalent.

Thus we conclude that it is not the case that $\sim \, \subset \, \cong$, or $\cong \, \subset \, \sim$.

$$
\begin{aligned}
P &\overset{\text{def}}{=} a.P + a.P + a.P' & Q &\overset{\text{def}}{=} a.Q + a.Q' + a.Q' \\
P' &\overset{\text{def}}{=} b.P & Q' &\overset{\text{def}}{=} b.Q
\end{aligned}
$$

Figure 8.2: Strong bisimilarity does not imply strong equivalence

8.4   Strong Equivalence and System Components

In this section we consider the implications for the system components modelled by PEPA components P and Q when $P \cong Q$. As previously, let Sys_P and Sys_Q denote the system components modelled by P and Q respectively.

From the definition of strong equivalence it is clear that the action sets of the two components are equal, i.e. $\mathcal{A}(P) = \mathcal{A}(Q)$. Moreover, since the equivalence classes $S \in \mathcal{C}/\cong$ partition the set $\mathcal{C}$, it follows that the conditional exit rates, and the exit rates from the two components are the same:

$$q(P, \alpha) = q(Q, \alpha) \quad \text{for all } \alpha \in \mathcal{A}, \quad \text{and} \quad q(P) = q(Q).$$

As the conditional exit rates are equivalent to the apparent action rates it also follows that $r_\alpha(P) = r_\alpha(Q)$ for all $\alpha \in \mathcal{A}$.

We can deduce that the system components, Sys_P and Sys_Q, appear to perform the same actions, at the same rates, and that their expected delay before performing some action will be the same. Thus, as with strong bisimilarity, an external observer would be unable to distinguish between them on the basis of a memoryless observation. As when $P \sim Q$, it also follows that the probability (or relative frequency) that the action performed will have a given type will be the same in the two components, Sys_P and Sys_Q.

Although $P \sim Q$ implies that Sys_P and Sys_Q are capable of exactly the same sequences of actions we saw in Section 7.4 that it does not ensure that they will occur with the same relative frequency in the two components. Hence prolonged or repeated observation might distinguish between Sys_P and Sys_Q. If we think of these sequences of actions as patterns of behaviour, then for strongly bisimilar components the *possible* patterns of behaviour are the same but the *predominant* ones may differ.

This is not the case when $P \cong Q$. The strong equivalence relation ensures that the conditional probability of completing an activity of type α and resulting in a derivative within a given equivalence class, S, denoted $p[P, S, \alpha]$, is the same in the two components.

$$p[P, S, \alpha] = \frac{q[P, S, \alpha]}{q(P)} = \frac{q[Q, S, \alpha]}{q(Q)} = p[Q, S, \alpha] \tag{4.4}$$

Similarly the unconditional probability of any activity by the component resulting in a derivative within the equivalence class S, $p[P, S]$, will also be matched by P and Q:

$$p[P, S] = \frac{\sum_{\alpha \in \mathcal{A}} q[P, S, \alpha]}{q(P)} = \frac{\sum_{\alpha \in \mathcal{A}} q[Q, S, \alpha]}{q(Q)} = p[Q, S] \tag{4.5}$$

The implication of this is that Sys_P and Sys_Q are indistinguishable even under extended observation.

To see this consider the equivalence classes $S \in \mathcal{C}/\cong$. $P \cong Q$ implies that Sys_P and Sys_Q are capable of the same patterns of behaviour. It follows that each equivalence class S is a set of components all exhibiting the same patterns of behaviour. The example in Figure 8.1 shows that this behaviour may be achieved differently by different components within the class, for example in terms of the number of activities instantiating any action type. However, viewed externally the behaviour of all the components is the same. Moreover, by equation 4.4, the probabilities of Sys_P and Sys_Q completing an α type activity and then exhibiting the behaviour represented in S are the same. Thus, the probabilities, or relative frequencies, of patterns of behaviour in Sys_P and Sys_Q are equal.

This suggests that it might be more appropriate to generate an underlying stochastic process for the PEPA model in terms of these sets of equivalent behaviours. Instead of having a state corresponding to each derivative within the derivative set of a component, we would have a state corresponding to each of the equivalence classes, $S \in \mathcal{C}/\cong$, suitably restricted to the derivative set. This is discussed in more detail in Section 8.6.

8.5 Strong Equivalence and the Markov Process

In this section we examine the strong equivalence relation from the perspective of the underlying Markov process. We consider what we can deduce about the corresponding Markov processes when $P \cong Q$, and whether any relation between Markov processes allows us to deduce this relation between PEPA components. We also consider the use of strong equivalence to induce a state-to-state equivalence on the state space of a model. The properties of the partition generated by this equivalence are presented.

The relation $\cong$ partitions the set of components $\mathcal{C}$, and it is easy to see that if restricted to the derivative set of any component P, the relation partitions this set. Let $ds(P)/\cong$ denote the set of equivalence classes generated in this way.

As a preliminary we state the following proposition.

Proposition 8.5.1 *For any component P, $ds(P)/\cong$ induces a lumpable partition on the state space of the Markov process corresponding to P.*

Proof Let S_i and S_j denote arbitrary elements of $ds(P)/\cong$, and consider any two elements of S_i, P_{i_k} and P_{i_ℓ}. Then since $P_{i_k} \cong P_{i_\ell}$, by equation 4.5,

$$q[P_{i_k}, S_j] = q[P_{i_\ell}, S_j]$$

Thus, it follows immediately that the partition $ds(P)/\cong$ induces a lumpable partition on the state space of the Markov process underlying P. □

Now, if we consider the strict form of equivalence between Markov processes, introduced in Section 5.3, it is easy to see that strongly equivalent components do not necessarily give rise to equivalent Markov processes. Two Markov processes are considered to be equivalent in this way if they have the same number of states and the same transition rates between those states.

$$
\begin{array}{ll}
& D_0 \overset{\text{def}}{=} (\alpha, 2r).D_1 \\
C_0 \overset{\text{def}}{=} (\alpha, 2r).C_1 & D_1 \overset{\text{def}}{=} (\beta, s).D_2 \\
C_1 \overset{\text{def}}{=} (\beta, s).C_0 & D_2 \overset{\text{def}}{=} (\alpha, r).D_3 + (\alpha, r).D_1 \\
& D_3 \overset{\text{def}}{=} (\beta, s).D_0
\end{array}
$$

Figure 8.3: Strong equivalence does not imply equivalent Markov processes

For example, consider the components C and D shown in Figure 8.3. It is straightforward to verify that $\mathcal{R}$,

$$\mathcal{R} = \{(C_0, D_0), (C_0, D_2), (C_1, D_1), (C_1, D_3)\}$$

$$X_0 \stackrel{\text{def}}{=} (\alpha, r).X_1 + (\beta, s).X_1 \qquad\qquad Y_0 \stackrel{\text{def}}{=} (\alpha, s).Y_1 + (\beta, r).Y_1$$

$$X_1 \stackrel{\text{def}}{=} (\gamma, t).X_0 \qquad\qquad\qquad\qquad Y_1 \stackrel{\text{def}}{=} (\gamma, t).Y_0$$

Figure 8.4: Components which generate the same Markov process

is a strong equivalence, giving rise to the partitions:

$$[C_0] = \{C_0\}, \quad [C_1] = \{C_1\}, \qquad [D_0] = \{D_0, D_2\}, \quad [D_1] = \{D_1, D_3\} \tag{5.6}$$

on the derivative sets of C and D respectively. However the Markov processes corresponding to C and D cannot be equivalent as they do not have the same number of states.

Recall from Section 7.5 that two Markov processes are lumpably equivalent if they have lumpable partitions, generating the same number of equivalence classes and there is a one-to-one correspondence between the equivalence classes such that the aggregated transition rates are also matched. If we consider the partitions of $ds(C)$ and $ds(D)$ shown in equation 5.6 it is clear that the Markov processes underlying C and D are lumpably equivalent.

In general, for any two components X and Y such that $X \cong Y$, any equivalence class $S \in \mathcal{C}/\cong$ will induce corresponding equivalence classes, S_X and S_Y in $ds(X)/\cong$ and $ds(Y)/\cong$ respectively. By Proposition 8.5.1 these correspond to lumpable partitions in the underlying state spaces. Moreover, by the strong equivalence relation, these partitions are in one-to-one correspondence with matching total transition rates. Thus we state the following corollary to Proposition 8.5.1.

Corollary 8.5.1 *For any $X, Y \in \mathcal{C}$ if $X \cong Y$ then the Markov processes underlying X and Y respectively are lumpably equivalent.*

It also follows immediately from Proposition 8.5.1 and the definition of lumpability (Definition 5.4.1) that if strong equivalence over the derivative set of a component is used to induce a partition of the state space of the Markov process then the corresponding aggregation will result in a Markov process. Thus the aggregated process may be solved exactly to find the steady state distribution. This use of strong equivalence as a model simplification technique based on aggregation is discussed in detail in Section 8.6 and illustrated by one of the models presented earlier in Section 4.4.

Finally we consider whether equivalence between the underlying Markov processes allows us to conclude anything about the strong equivalence, or otherwise, of the corresponding PEPA components. We consider only the augmented Markov processes introduced in Section 7.5, in which each transition is annotated by the action types of the corresponding activities.

Equivalences between the underlying Markov processes, even if augmented by the action types, do not allow us to infer strong equivalence between the corresponding PEPA components. As previously, this is due to the loss of information in going from the derivation graph of the component to the corresponding Markov process, even if it is augmented. For example, consider the components X and Y shown in Figure 8.4. X and Y generate equivalent, and therefore lumpably equivalent, Markov processes. However there is no strong equivalence relation containing them.

8.6 Strong Equivalence for Aggregation

In this section we present an alternative approach to generating a Markov process corresponding to a PEPA model. In Section 3.5 we explained how the derivation graph of a PEPA model is used to directly generate a representation of the system as a Markov process. This approach is straightforward but may result in a process with a large state space even for moderately simple models. It does not take advantage of any symmetries which might exist within the model.

The alternative approach now presented aims to take advantage of symmetries and other patterns of repeated behaviour within the derivative set of a model. We recall that each equivalence class $S \in ds(P)/\cong$ represents a set of derivatives which all exhibit the same behaviour. Moreover this corresponds to a lumpable partition within the state space of the Markov process generated in the naïve way. Instead of having a state corresponding to each derivative within the derivative set of a component, we generate a state corresponding to each of the equivalence classes induced on the derivative set by strong equivalence, $S \in ds(P)/\cong$. This new process will be a Markov process by Proposition 8.5.1, and in many cases it will have a smaller state space than the original model.

For any PEPA component S, let the set of equivalence classes, $ds(S)/\cong$, induced on the derivative set by the strong equivalence relation, be called the *lumped derivative set*. For any element, T, of this set we can construct the *lumped activity set*, $Act_\cong(T)$.

Definition 8.6.1 *Suppose that P is an arbitrary element of $T \in ds(S)/\cong$, then the lumped activity set of T, $Act_\cong(T)$ is*

$$Act_\cong(T) = \{(\alpha, q') \mid r_\alpha(P) \neq 0, q' = q[P, S, \alpha] \text{ for some } S \in ds(S)/\cong\}$$

Moreover the complete lumped activity set of the component S is,

$$\vec{Act}_\cong(S) = \bigcup_{T \in ds(S)/\cong} Act_\cong(T)$$

Based on this we can also define the *lumped derivation graph*.

Definition 8.6.2 *Given a PEPA component S, and its lumped derivative set $ds(S)/\cong$, the lumped derivation graph, $\mathcal{D}_\cong(S)$, is the labelled directed graph whose set of nodes is $ds(S)/\cong$ and whose set of arcs, $A_\cong$ is defined as follows:*

- *The elements of $A_\cong$ are taken from the set $ds(S)/\cong \times ds(S)/\cong \times \vec{Act}_\cong(S)$;*
- *$\langle T_i, T_j, (\alpha, q') \rangle \in A_\cong$ if $(\alpha, q') \in Act_\cong(T_i)$ and $q' = q[P_i, T_j, \alpha]$ for all $P_i \in T_i$.*

The node T_0, where $S \in T_0$, is taken to be the initial node of the graph.

8.6.1 Basic Application of Strong Equivalence Aggregation

The most straightforward way to apply strong equivalence aggregation is at the level of a complete PEPA model of a system. Instead of the derivation graph, we now use the lumped derivation graph to generate the Markov process representation of the model. A state of this process is associated with each node in the lumped derivation graph, and the transition rate between any two nodes is the sum of the total conditional transition rates attached to the arcs connecting them. In effect strong equivalence is used to induce a state-to-state equivalence which gives an exact aggregation of the original Markov process, although this process is not constructed.

Performance measures are derived from a reward structure defined at the level of the PEPA model in terms of the derivative set and enabled activities. If the integrity of these measures is to be maintained by the strong equivalence aggregation, it must be possible to derive the same reward from the lumped derivation graph. This is analogous to Nicola's extension of strong lumpability to Markov reward processes, presented in [103]:

Definition 8.6.3 *A Markov reward process is strongly lumpable with respect to a reward R in the context of a partition χ, if, for every starting distribution, the aggregated process is a Markov reward process which results in the same reward.*

We can define the lumped reward for any element $T_j \in ds(\mathcal{S})/\cong$ in the intuitive way, in terms of the conditional steady state probabilities for each component within the equivalence class. If $\widehat{R}$ denotes the lumped reward function, corresponding to the reward function R, and Π_j is the conditional steady state probability,

$$\widehat{R}(T_j) = \sum_{C_i \in T_j} R(C_i)\, \Pi_j(C_i) \qquad \text{for all } T_j \in ds(\mathcal{S})/\cong \qquad (6.7)$$

However this implies that when the steady state distribution of the lumped process has been found disaggregation must be performed in order to find the rewards. Clearly we would like to be able to derive the reward directly from the Markov process based on the lumped derivation graph. This will be possible in some cases. The following proposition provides a sufficient condition which can be easily verified.

Proposition 8.6.1 *The strong equivalence aggregation of $\mathcal{S}$ is strongly lumpable with respect to some reward defined by R, if for all $T_j \in ds(\mathcal{S})/\cong$, for all $C_i \in T_j$, $R(C_i) = \rho$. Then $\widehat{R}(T_j) = \rho$.*

Proof The aggregation is strongly lumpable, and results in a Markov process, by Proposition 8.5.1. It remains to show that the reward R is maintained, but this follows immediately since,

$$R = \sum_{C_i \in ds(\mathcal{S})} \rho_i \Pi(C_i) = \sum_{T_j \in ds(\mathcal{S})/\cong} \left(\sum_{C_i \in T_j} \rho_i \Pi(C_i) \right) = \sum_{T_j \in ds(\mathcal{S})/\cong} \rho\, \widehat{\Pi}(T_j)$$

where $\widehat{\Pi}(\cdot)$ is the steady state distribution of the aggregated process.   □

Since rewards are defined in terms of the activities of a component many PEPA models will satisfy the condition of Proposition 8.6.1. For example in order to calculate the throughput of an action within a system a reward equal to the activity rate is attached to all activities of the given action type. As the apparent rate of an action type is the same in all strongly equivalent components, this reward will satisfy the condition of Proposition 8.6.1.

When the condition is not satisfied for all $T_j \in ds(\mathcal{C})/\cong$ it may still be satisfied by some partitions, in particular those which contain no components to which a reward is attached. Thus even if the lumped reward must be kept in the form shown in equation 6.7 selective disaggregation may be carried out to calculate the reward when the steady state distribution has been found. An outline of the procedure implementing this approach is given in Figure 8.5.

1. Construct the model S, combining components until the full functionality of the system is represented.

2. Generate the derivative set, $ds(S)$, corresponding to the model.

3. Find the strong equivalence classes within $ds(S)$ and form the lumped derivative set $ds(S)/\cong$.

4. Form the lumped activity set for each $T \in ds(S)/\cong$ and construct the lumped derivation graph $\mathcal{D}_{\cong}(S)$.

5. Form the aggregated Markov process, associating one state of the process with each node of $\mathcal{D}_{\cong}(S)$, and with transition rates equal to the total transition rates between nodes.

6. Assign lumped rewards to the states of the process corresponding to equivalence classes they represent.

7. Solve the aggregated Markov process and calculate the rewards, disaggregating to find conditional probabilities if necessary, i.e. if the conditions of Proposition 8.6.1 were not satisfied.

Figure 8.5: Outline of a procedure implementing the basic application of strong equivalence aggregation

Note that the state-to-state equivalence induced on the state space of a Markov process by $\cong$ is stronger than the relation generally underlying lumpability. In the partitions based on $ds(S)/\cong$ not only the rates of transitions between partitions are matched but also the action types of the activities involved. Thus there may be a lumpable partition of the Markov process underlying a PEPA component which has fewer elements than the partition induced by $\cong$. However strong equivalence aggregation has the advantage that lumping may be carried out before the full state space is generated, leading to *compositional strong equivalence aggregation*.

8.6.2   Compositional Strong Equivalence Aggregation

The use of strong equivalence over the derivative set of a complete model, to induce a state-to-state equivalence resulting in aggregation, may result in a drastic reduction of the state space of the underlying Markov process. However this approach still necessitates the construction of the full derivative set of the model. In some cases this will be prohibitively large making even aggregation of the model infeasible. In this section we outline an application of strong equivalence aggregation which takes advantage of the fact that strong equivalence is a congruence. We apply strong equivalence as a state-to-state equivalence compositionally, replacing cooperating components by strongly equivalent, *lumped components*.

It is clear from the definition of a derivation graph (Definition 3.4.3) that just as we can form such a multigraph corresponding to any PEPA component, so we can also form a PEPA component corresponding to any derivation multigraph. Furthermore if we consider a lumped derivation graph, as defined in Definition 8.6.2, we can see that it has labelled nodes, and arcs connecting them which are labelled by an action type and a transition rate. Thus each lumped derivation graph may be regarded as a derivation graph. For any lumped derivation graph we can form a lumped PEPA component.

Definition 8.6.4 *The lumped component of P, $\widehat{P}$, is formed from the lumped derivation graph, $\mathcal{D}_{\cong}(P)$ in the natural way: we associate a component $\widehat{P}_j$ with each $T_j \in ds(P)/\cong$ such that*

$$\mathcal{A}ct(\widehat{P}_j) = \mathcal{A}ct_{\cong}(T_j)$$

In particular we associate $\widehat{P}_0$ with T_0, the initial node of $\mathcal{D}_{\cong}(P)$. Then $\widehat{P} \stackrel{\text{def}}{=} \widehat{P}_0$.

Proposition 8.6.2 *Any PEPA component P is strongly equivalent to its lumped component, $\widehat{P}$, i.e. $P \cong \widehat{P}$.*

Proof   By definition, $ds(\widehat{P})/\cong = ds(\widehat{P}) = ds(P)/\cong$. The result follows immediately.
$\square$

Since strong equivalence is a congruence this means that if we replace one component within a model by the equivalent lumped component, the new model will be strongly equivalent to the original one. In most cases the derivative set of a lumped component will be smaller than the derivative set of the component it replaces, and it will never be larger, i.e. $|ds(\widehat{P})| \leq |ds(P)|$. Also, since the lumped derivation graph is a *graph* and not a multigraph, the number of transitions generated by the lumped component will also usually be reduced.

To apply strong equivalence aggregation compositionally we replace components which represent separately resourced components of the system, the components combined by the

---

1. Construct the model S, combining components until the full functionality of the system is represented.

2. Identify the atomic cooperating components of the model, X and Y, by unfolding. Apply strong equivalence aggregation to the cooperation of these components, $P \equiv X \underset{L}{\bowtie} Y$, to form $\widehat{P}$:

   2.1 Form the derivative set of the component P, $ds(P)$.
   2.2 Find the strong equivalence classes within $ds(P)$ and form the lumped derivative set $ds(P)/\cong$.
   2.3 Form the lumped activity set for each $T \in ds(P)/\cong$ and construct the lumped derivation graph $\mathcal{D}_\cong(P)$.
   2.4 Construct the lumped component $\widehat{P}$, based on $\mathcal{D}_\cong(P)$, and replace P by $\widehat{P}$.

   Repeat with all other pairs of atomic components.

3. Consider the next level of the model, i.e. $Q \underset{K}{\bowtie} \widehat{P}$, for some Q. Repeat steps 2.1–2.4 applied to $Q \underset{K}{\bowtie} \widehat{P}$. Continue in this way until $\widehat{S}$ has been formed.

4. Based on the derivation graph of $\widehat{S}$ (this will be the lumped derivation graph of S formed in the previous step) form an aggregated Markov process representing the model, in the usual way.

5. Assign lumped rewards to the states of the process.

6. Solve the aggregated Markov process and calculate the rewards.

Figure 8.6: Outline of a procedure implementing the compositional application of strong equivalence aggregation

cooperation combinator, by their strongly equivalent lumped components. This cannot increase the size of the derivative set of the model, and in most cases will reduce it, sometimes dramatically.

Proposition 8.6.3 *When a lumped component, $\widehat{P}$, replaces a top-level component P, within a model, S, to form a modified model, S', then $|ds(S')| \leq |ds(S)|$.*

Proof P is a top-level component, so S has the form $S \equiv P \underset{L}{\bowtie} Q$ for some other component Q and some cooperation set L. Similarly $S' \equiv \widehat{P} \underset{L}{\bowtie} Q$. By the definition of the cooperation combinator, the derivative set of the cooperation of two components is no larger than the product of the derivative sets of those components, i.e.

$$|ds(S)| \leq |ds(P)| \times |ds(Q)| \qquad \text{and} \qquad |ds(S')| \leq |ds(\widehat{P})| \times |ds(Q)|$$

Since $|ds(\widehat{P})| \leq |ds(P)|$ it follows immediately that $|ds(S')| \leq |ds(S)|$. $\qquad \square$

   Thus we can systematically simplify a model, by considering each of its top-level components in turn. Each of these is itself treated as a separate model, and its top-level components are identified and so on. At some level the identified top-level components will be atomic, in the sense that they cannot themselves be broken down into cooperating components. The strong equivalence aggregation is applied to the cooperation of these atomic components, resulting in a lumped component which replaces them. At each level of the model the aggregation procedure is applied, until a lumped version of the complete original model is formed. The outline of a procedure to implement this approach to model simplification is shown in Figure 8.6. Note that the full derivative set of the original model does not need to be constructed. No Markov process is constructed until the aggregation procedure is complete.

As with the basic application of strong equivalence aggregation, we must consider the implication of compositional aggregation for the performance measures to be extracted from the model. One alternative is to postpone the definition of the reward structure until the lumped model has been formed. Rewards would then be attached to the elements of the complete lumped activity set, and associated with derivatives of the model in the usual way. This is a straightforward approach but it requires the modeller to keep track of the aggregation of the model. Thus it eliminates the possibility of the technique being automated and applied without the intervention of the modeller.

A preferable alternative is to define the reward structure, R, over the full model as previously, but to restrict the aggregation to components where the resulting partition will be strongly lumpable with respect to R. For example, this will be the case if aggregation is only applied to components which satisfy the condition of Proposition 8.6.1. This may mean that some components for which a strong equivalence aggregation exists, are left unlumped, but it has the consequence that lumped rewards are easy to derive and no disaggregation is necessary. Moreover the approach has potential to be automated and carried out without the participation of the modeller. It also implies that the form of the lumped model may be dependent on the performance measure, and reward structure, under consideration.

8.6.3   Aggregating an MSMQ Model using Strong Equivalence

To illustrate the compositional application of strong equivalence aggregation we consider the faulty $M_i/M_i/M/(2,1,1,1)/Q \times S/L$ MSMQ system with random polling shown in Figure 8.7, similar to the system presented in Section 4.4.4. This model, with four nodes, has 1170 states and 5865 transitions. It would be extremely time consuming to solve using the techniques and equipment used to solve the models presented in Chapter 4. Using compositional strong equivalence aggregation we can reduce the state space of the underlying Markov process to 191 states and 745 transitions. This smaller model can be easily solved in a matter of minutes.

We consider two separate reward structures. The first is used to calculate the expected waiting time for customers at $Node_1$ and concerns only activities associated with that node. Similarly the second reward structure only attaches rewards to activities of $Node_4$ as it is used to calculate the expected waiting time for customers at any of the single place buffers.

The top-level components of the model are the parallel composition of the servers, and the parallel composition of the nodes. The atomic components are the individual servers and nodes. Let us consider the component representing the two servers in the system, $S\|S$. Note that there are no rewards directly associated with the activities of this component although rewards are attached to activities which will be carried out with the cooperation

$$Node'_{100} \overset{\text{def}}{=} (in, 2\lambda).Node'_{110} + (pass_1, 2e).Node'_{100}$$
$$Node'_{110} \overset{\text{def}}{=} (in, \lambda).Node'_{111} + (engage_1, e).Node'_{120} + (pass_1, e).Node'_{110}$$
$$Node'_{111} \overset{\text{def}}{=} (engage_1, 2e).Node'_{121}$$
$$Node'_{120} \overset{\text{def}}{=} (in, \lambda).Node'_{121} + (pass_1, 2e).Node'_{120} + (serve, \top).Node'_{100}$$
$$Node'_{121} \overset{\text{def}}{=} (engage_1, e).Node'_{122} + (pass_1, e).Node'_{121} + (serve, \top).Node'_{110}$$
$$Node'_{122} \overset{\text{def}}{=} (pass_1, 2e).Node'_{120} + (serve, \top).Node'_{120}$$

$$Node_{j0} \overset{\text{def}}{=} (in, \lambda).Node_{j1} + (pass_j, e).Node_{j0} \qquad\qquad \text{for } j = 2, 3, 4$$
$$Node_{j1} \overset{\text{def}}{=} (engage_j, e).Node_{j2}$$
$$Node_{j2} \overset{\text{def}}{=} (serve, \top).Node_{j0} + (pass_j, e).Node_{j2}$$

$$S \overset{\text{def}}{=} (walk, \omega/4).S_1 + (walk, \omega/4).S_2 + (walk, \omega/4).S_3 + (walk, \omega/4).S_4$$
$$S_j \overset{\text{def}}{=} (pass_j, \top).S + (engage_j, \top).(serve, \mu).S \qquad\qquad 1 \le j \le 4$$

$$MSMQwf \overset{\text{def}}{=} (Node'_{100} \parallel Node_{20} \parallel Node_{30} \parallel Node_{40}) \underset{L}{\bowtie} (S \parallel S)/K$$
$$\text{where } L = \{engage_j, pass_j, serve \mid 1 \le j \le 4\} \text{ and } K = \{pass_j, engage_j \mid 1 \le j \le 4\}$$

Figure 8.7: Asymmetric MSMQ model with faulty connector to $Node_1$

of this component.

$$ds(S \parallel S) = \{S \parallel S,\ S \parallel S_j,\ S_j \parallel S,\ S_j \parallel S_i,\ S \parallel (serve, \mu).S,\ (serve, \mu).S \parallel S,$$
$$S_j \parallel (serve, \mu).S,\ (serve, \mu).S \parallel S_j,\ (serve, \mu).S \parallel (serve, \mu).S \mid 1 \le i, j \le 3\}$$

Recall that since isomorphism implies strong equivalence, for any components X and Y, $X \parallel Y \cong Y \parallel X$. Hence, partitioning this derivative set by strong equivalence we obtain:

$$ds(S \parallel S)/\cong\ =\ \{\{S \parallel S\},\ \{S \parallel (serve, \mu).S,\ (serve, \mu).S \parallel S,\},\ \{S \parallel S_j,\ S_j \parallel S\},$$
$$\{S_j \parallel S_i,\ S_i \parallel S_j\},\ \{S_j \parallel (serve, \mu).S,\ (serve, \mu).S \parallel S_j\},$$
$$\{S_j \parallel S_j\},\ \{(serve, \mu).S \parallel (serve, \mu).S\} \mid 1 \le j, i \le 3, i < j\}$$

Since no rewards are directly associated with activities of the servers we can form the lumped component, denoted SS, without consideration of the reward structure. We associate one derivative of SS with each node of the lumped derivation graph as follows:

$$SS_0 \leftrightarrow \{S \parallel S\} \qquad SS_{jj} \leftrightarrow \{S_j \parallel S_j\} \qquad SSs_0 \leftrightarrow \{S \parallel (serve, \mu).S,\ (serve, \mu).S \parallel S\}$$
$$SS_j \leftrightarrow \{S \parallel S_j,\ S_j \parallel S\} \qquad\qquad SSss \leftrightarrow \{(serve, \mu).S \parallel (serve, \mu).S\}$$
$$SS_{ij} \leftrightarrow \{S_i \parallel S_j,\ S_j \parallel S_i,\ i < j\} \qquad SSs_j \leftrightarrow \{(serve, \mu).S \parallel S_j,\ S_j \parallel (serve, \mu).S\}$$

Using the lumped activity sets we can define the behaviour of these lumped components:

$$SS_0 \stackrel{\text{def}}{=} \sum_{j=1}^{4}(walk, 2\omega/4).SS_j$$

$$SSs_0 \stackrel{\text{def}}{=} (serve, \mu).SS_0 + \sum_{j=1}^{4}(walk, \omega/s).SSs_j$$

$$SS_{jj} \stackrel{\text{def}}{=} (pass_j, \top).SS_j + (engage_j, \top).SSs_j$$

$$SS_j \stackrel{\text{def}}{=} (pass_j, \top).SS_0 + (engage_j, \top).SSs_0 + \sum_{i=1}^{4}(walk, \omega/4).SS_{ij}$$

$$SSss \stackrel{\text{def}}{=} (serve, 2\mu).SSs_0$$
$$SS_{ij} \stackrel{\text{def}}{=} (pass_j, \top).SS_i + (engage_j, \top).SSs_i + (pass_i, \top).SS_j + (engage_i, \top).SSs_j$$
$$SSs_j \stackrel{\text{def}}{=} (serve, \mu).SS_j + (pass_j, \top).SSs_0 + (engage_j, \top).SSss$$

This component, SS_0, now replaces $S_0 \parallel S_0$ in the complete model.

If we consider the atomic node components $Node_j$ for $1 \leq j \leq 4$, in pairs, we can see that there are no non-trivial strong equivalence partitions of the derivative sets because the activity sets of the components are not the same. The hiding operator, which will make all $engage_j$ and $pass_j$ activities appear as τ type activities does not apply at this level of the model, and cannot be passed through the cooperation since the action types $engage_j$ and $pass_j$ appear in the cooperation set. Therefore the parallel composition of the node components cannot be independently simplified using strong equivalence. Thus we form the final version of the model as:

$$MSMQwf' \stackrel{\text{def}}{=} (Node'_{100} \parallel Node_{20} \parallel Node_{30} \parallel Node_{40}) \bowtie_{L} (SS_0)/K$$

where, as previously, $L = \{serve, engage_j, pass_j\}$, and $K = \{pass_j, engage_j\}$.

If we compare the size of the derivative set $ds(MSMQwf)$ with the size of the derivative set $ds(MSMQwf')$ we can see that it is already considerably reduced.

$$|ds(MSMQwf)| = 1170 \qquad \text{whereas} \qquad |ds(MSMQwf')| = 670$$

Furthermore, we can take advantage of the fact that the action types $pass_j$ and $engage_j$ are hidden, and so all appear as τ type activities. This, together with the fact that the reward structure is defined only over one node at a time, allows us to partition the derivative set of the model. For example when we consider the reward structure defined only over $Node_1$, in order to find the mean waiting time of customers at that node, we can generate a Markov process based on the lumped derivation graph which has only 191 states.

Components which exhibit equivalent behaviour are found by considering the states of the nodes without rewards, $Node_2$, $Node_3$ and $Node_4$, and the positions of the two servers (as represented in the lumped component SS). For example, the following components

$$\{(Node'_{100} \parallel Node_{21} \parallel Node_{30} \parallel Node_{41}) \bowtie_{L} (SS_2)/K,$$
$$(Node'_{100} \parallel Node_{21} \parallel Node_{31} \parallel Node_{40}) \bowtie_{L} (SS_2)/K,$$
$$(Node'_{100} \parallel Node_{20} \parallel Node_{31} \parallel Node_{41}) \bowtie_{L} (SS_3)/K,$$
$$(Node'_{100} \parallel Node_{21} \parallel Node_{31} \parallel Node_{40}) \bowtie_{L} (SS_3)/K,$$
$$(Node'_{100} \parallel Node_{21} \parallel Node_{30} \parallel Node_{41}) \bowtie_{L} (SS_4)/K,$$
$$(Node'_{100} \parallel Node_{20} \parallel Node_{31} \parallel Node_{41}) \bowtie_{L} (SS_4)/K \}$$

are all strongly equivalent and so the corresponding nodes will be amalgamated into a single node in the lumped derivation graph. Similarly

$$\{(Node'_{121} \parallel Node_{20} \parallel Node_{30} \parallel Node_{41}) \underset{L}{\bowtie} (SSs_2)/K,$$
$$(Node'_{121} \parallel Node_{20} \parallel Node_{31} \parallel Node_{40}) \underset{L}{\bowtie} (SSs_2)/K,$$
$$(Node'_{121} \parallel Node_{20} \parallel Node_{30} \parallel Node_{41}) \underset{L}{\bowtie} (SSs_3)/K,$$
$$(Node'_{121} \parallel Node_{21} \parallel Node_{30} \parallel Node_{40}) \underset{L}{\bowtie} (SSs_3)/K,$$
$$(Node'_{121} \parallel Node_{20} \parallel Node_{31} \parallel Node_{40}) \underset{L}{\bowtie} (SSs_4)/K,$$
$$(Node'_{121} \parallel Node_{21} \parallel Node_{30} \parallel Node_{40}) \underset{L}{\bowtie} (SSs_4)/K \}$$

are strongly equivalent and may be represented by a single state in the underlying Markov process. Other examples of the reward preserving, strong equivalence classes are:

$$\{(Node'_{122} \parallel Node_{20} \parallel Node_{30} \parallel Node_{40}) \underset{L}{\bowtie} (SSss)/K\}$$

$$\{(Node'_{111} \parallel Node_{21} \parallel Node_{31} \parallel Node_{42}) \underset{L}{\bowtie} (SSs_4)/K,$$
$$(Node'_{111} \parallel Node_{21} \parallel Node_{32} \parallel Node_{41}) \underset{L}{\bowtie} (SSs_3)/K,$$
$$(Node'_{111} \parallel Node_{22} \parallel Node_{31} \parallel Node_{41}) \underset{L}{\bowtie} (SSs_2)/K \}$$

$$\{(Node'_{120} \parallel Node_{20} \parallel Node_{30} \parallel Node_{40}) \underset{L}{\bowtie} (SSs_0)/K\}$$

Each of these will be represented by a single node, with appropriate arcs, in the lumped derivation graph, and so a single state in the underlying Markov process.

If we consider the reward structure used to derive the expected waiting time of customers at $Node_4$ we can find similar equivalence classes by considering states of $Node_1$, $Node_2$ and $Node_3$, and the positions of the servers. For example, in this case the pairs

$$\{(Node'_{111} \parallel Node_{20} \parallel Node_{31} \parallel Node_{40}) \underset{L}{\bowtie} (SS_{23})/K,$$
$$(Node'_{111} \parallel Node_{21} \parallel Node_{30} \parallel Node_{40}) \underset{L}{\bowtie} (SS_{23})/K \},$$

$$\{(Node'_{121} \parallel Node_{20} \parallel Node_{32} \parallel Node_{41}) \underset{L}{\bowtie} (SSss)/K,$$
$$(Node'_{121} \parallel Node_{22} \parallel Node_{30} \parallel Node_{41}) \underset{L}{\bowtie} (SSss)/K \},$$

and

$$\{(Node'_{100} \parallel Node_{21} \parallel Node_{30} \parallel Node_{42}) \underset{L}{\bowtie} (SSs_2)/K,$$
$$(Node'_{100} \parallel Node_{20} \parallel Node_{31} \parallel Node_{42}) \underset{L}{\bowtie} (SSs_3)/K \}$$

are strongly equivalent components which have the same reward, and so may be represented by a single node in the lumped derivation graph. In this case the state space of the underlying Markov process is reduced to 423 states.

in	*pass$_j$ or engage$_j$*	*serve*	*walk*
λ or 2λ	e or $2e$	μ	ω
$\lambda = 0.1$	$e = 50$	1.0	$4, 8, 12, 16, 20$

Table 8.1: Parameter values assigned to aggregated model of *MSMQwf'*

Figure 8.8 shows how the mean waiting time for customers at $Node_1$ decreases as the walk rate of the servers is varied between 4 and 20. The other values for parameters in the model are shown in Table 8.1. These performance characteristics were calculated using the aggregated model described above, and were verified against values obtained from the simplified model $MSMQwf'$.

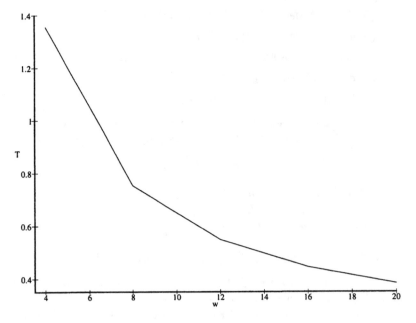

Figure 8.8: Mean waiting time for customers at $Node_1$ in the $MSMQwf'$ system with four nodes.

Chapter 9

Conclusions

9.1 Introduction

In this chapter the main results of the thesis are summarised. The extent to which these address the problems facing performance analysis, identified in Section 2.4, is assessed. In Section 9.4, the direction for further work and future development of PEPA, as it appeared at the end of the thesis, are discussed. The chapter concludes with a review of work which has been developed since the thesis was completed, particularly examining the extent to which the areas outlined in Section 9.4 have been addressed.

9.2 Summary

A compositional approach to performance modelling has been presented. This novel model construction technique, based on the stochastic process algebra PEPA, has been shown to be suitable for specifying a Markov process. This underlying process can subsequently be solved using any appropriate numerical technique. The ease with which models can be constructed and modified using PEPA was demonstrated in the case studies presented in Chapter 4. For example, when the effect of a faulty component was to be investigated, only the relevant component within the model had to be modified.

As outlined in Section 3.6, one of the major advantages of PEPA over the standard paradigms for specifying stochastic performance models is the inherent apparatus for reasoning about the structure and behaviour of models. In the later chapters of the thesis this apparatus has been exploited to define four equivalence relations over PEPA components. Each of these notions of equivalence has intrinsic interest from a process algebra perspective. However, they have also been demonstrated to be useful in a performance modelling context.

Isomorphism is a strong notion of equivalence, defined structurally. It generates equational laws which form the basis of model transformation techniques, based on term rewriting.

Weak isomorphism, in which the observation of internal activities is relaxed, leads to a model simplification technique which is sensitive to the intended use of the model. Via judicious use of the PEPA abstraction mechanisms, weak isomorphism allows a model to be modified to a simpler form, reflecting its current experimental frame. Moreover, although the relation is not a congruence relation, it has been shown to be preserved by cooperation, and so this model simplification technique can be applied compositionally in appropriate circumstances.

Strong bisimilarity, a bisimulation in the style of CCS, captures the notion of equivalence under memoryless observation. It has been shown that this is insufficient to ensure that the systems represented exhibit exactly the same behaviour. However the additional condition which must be satisfied for this to be the case has been identified. The model simplification technique based on strong bisimilarity involves the modeller identifying components of the model which can be replaced by a strongly bisimilar alternative which has a smaller derivative set. This implies that some insight is required on the part of the modeller; such insight is easily developed with experience.

Strong equivalence is also a bisimulation, developed in the style of the probabilistic bisimulation of Larsen and Skou. It has been shown that this relation is sufficient to ensure that the systems represented exhibit exactly the same behaviour. Moreover, when used to induce a state-to-state equivalence in the underlying Markov process, it results in a lumpable partition of the state space. Thus strong equivalence can be used as a basis for exact aggregation of the Markov process, and because it is a congruence this may be systematically applied hierarchically through the component structure of the model. Since this technique can be formally defined it could potentially be applied automatically. A procedure for implementing the compositional application of strong equivalence aggregation has been outlined in Figure 8.6.

Thus the performance modeller is armed with several methods for reducing the state space of the Markov process underlying a PEPA model. Each of these methods can be applied at the level of the PEPA model, without the construction of the state space of the original model. Since the techniques are compositional they can be used simultaneously, with different methods being applied to different components within the same model.

Some of the techniques for model construction and model solution described in the thesis have already been implemented by Gilmore [104], and further development of this tool, the PEPA Workbench, is planned.

9.3   Evaluation

The problems facing performance analysis outlined in Section 2.4 were:

1. Integrating performance analysis into system design;

2. Representing systems as models; and

3. Model tractability.

The use of process algebras as system description formalisms is widely accepted. Therefore PEPA represents a step towards the timely consideration of quantitative characteristics of systems during design, as stochastic process algebras integrate performance analysis into a design methodology. PEPA has been defined so that the additional information which must be included in the model for performance analysis to take place, the activity rates, may be regarded as an annotation of a pure process algebra model. Thus there is the possibility that existing designs may be used to generate performance models. The applicability of such an approach may, however, turn out to be limited. As described in Section 3.5.4, the set of PEPA components which can be considered to specify a performance model is restricted and work needs to be done to investigate how often "satisfactory" designs fall within this set.

PEPA, like all process algebras, exemplifies the *cooperator paradigm* described in Section 2.4. Thus it is an appropriate notation for representing modern computer and communication systems in which components have autonomy. The compositional structure inherent in the process algebra corresponds to the structure of these systems. Furthermore this style of model construction suggests the possibility of a modelling tool based around a library of parameterised components. Such a tool would help to make performance analysis accessible to the non-expert.

Like stochastic Petri net paradigms, PEPA is susceptible to the problem of state space explosion. The size of the state space underlying a model grows extremely rapidly as the size and complexity of the system modelled increases. It has been shown however, that PEPA supports three model simplification techniques which can take advantage of the compositional structure of the model. These have the advantage over standard techniques for tackling state space explosion that they can be applied without the construction of the state space of the original model. In the future it may be possible that the compositional structure of the PEPA models may also be used to inform the solution of the underlying Markov process, enhancing the tractability of these models even further.

9.4 Further Work and Future Directions

The further work and future developments of PEPA will also be motivated by the problems outlined in Section 2.4.

In the examples presented in this thesis we have considered PEPA only as a performance modelling paradigm. However it also has the potential to be used as a design notation, possibly with the activity rates omitted. Constructing performance models directly from designs, using an annotation of the design notation, has a clear intuitive appeal. As well as integrating performance analysis into a design methodology, it has important implications for model verification. However, as already noted, there is potentially a mismatch between the models which can be constructed in this way and the set of models which can be considered to be valid performance models.

Further work is needed to establish the relationship between qualitative, or functional, properties of systems, and quantitative, or performance, characteristics. For example, a *deadlock* or *livelock* will correspond to an absorbing state, or an absorbing set of states, respectively, in the underlying Markov process. A combined qualitative/quantitative analysis of the system could provide measures such as the mean time until a deadlock occurs.

We have established that PEPA may be used to succinctly describe MSMQ systems. However, in its present form PEPA may be regarded as a minimal notation. There is considerable scope for adding more features to the language. Indeed, some applications may require them. The current version of the language was chosen for the work presented in the thesis because it allowed interesting models to be developed, without over-complicating the proofs.

Some features which could be added to the language to enhance modelling convenience include *immediate* activities and *prioritised* activities. It has been shown that the primary importance of these features is to allow models, particularly parameterised ones, to be constructed easily, rather than increasing the expressiveness in SPNs. It is anticipated that similar results could be developed for PEPA.

There are many different ways in which components within a system interact with each other. The form of synchronisation represented by the cooperation combinator of PEPA was chosen because it is general enough to represent many situations, and because its behaviour is fully compositional. However, alternative combinators could be derived or defined to represent other interactions such as the *one-way condition testing* and *loose synchronisation* identified by Ciardo and Trivedi [74]. Modified versions of PEPA could be developed to suit particular applications.

The final, and most interesting, area for future work involves the investigation of the use of the compositional structure of PEPA models to inform model solution. The relationship between this structure and various decompositional approaches to the solution of the underlying Markov process promises to be an interesting and fruitful area for future research.

There has been considerable recent interest in establishing the circumstances under which an SPN model will be amenable to a product form solution [23, 81]. A class of nets which satisfy the required conditions has been identified but the structure of these nets is limited. These results have been considered in the more general framework of Markov processes by Boucherie [80]. His results suggest that a product form solution for PEPA models would only be possible in models in which all cooperation sets are empty. Further work is necessary to extend these results to PEPA.

An alternative compositional approach to the solution of Markov processes is the use of tensor algebra to express the generator matrix of a process. This approach has been proposed by Plateau [82] and Buchholz [83]. Again, this is based on a restricted form of interaction between subsystems within the system. However there appears to be potential for expressing these forms of interaction in PEPA, or a similar stochastic process algebra.

9.5   Developments Since the Completion of the Thesis

In this section, added for the publication of the thesis as a book, we review the developments which have taken place in the area of stochastic process algebra since the thesis was completed. There are now more researchers involved in the development of such formalisms and their application to performance modelling. Since these researchers have diverse backgrounds and motivations some of the recent developments are outside the areas identified in the original conclusions of the thesis. However, particular attention is paid to the directions for future work suggested in the previous section. As in that section, the discussion is structured around the problems facing performance modelling introduced in Section 2.4. First, a general overview of recent work on stochastic process algebras is presented.

9.5.1   Stochastic Process Algebras

There have been no significant changes to PEPA since the thesis was completed, although recently the set of combinators has been extended (see Section 9.5.3). Most of the research effort centred on the language has been directed towards identifying cases when the model structure can be exploited to provide efficient model solution (see Section 9.5.4).

The PEPA Workbench has been developed to address the creation and solution of more sophisticated models. This has led to improvements in the state space storage scheme used and also to the solution methods offered. The symbolic solution methods which are available by using the PEPA Workbench with the Maple computer algebra system can now be supplemented by using the workbench with the high-performance numeric methods from the Matlab computing environment [105]. In addition to efficient numerical solution methods, Matlab also offers sophisticated facilities for visualising matrices. The information obtained in this way may be used to guide a series of experiments which investigate the model, or to provide insight into how the structure at the process algebra level influences the structure of the generator matrix. In addition the workbench can be used with an implementation of the preconditioned biconjugate gradient method for sparse equation solution. This is an iterative solution method which gives very good performance and allows the workbench to be used independently of both Maple and Matlab.

Recent work on TIPP has focussed on a Markovian version of the language, sometimes called MTIPP, and an equivalence relation, *Markovian bisimulation* (strong equivalence). Recognising the usefulness of such relations for model transformation the Erlangen team have been developing a sound and complete set of axioms to capture Markovian bisimulation [106]. The aim is to develop a term-rewriting system based on these axioms that would carry out the aggregation automatically at the syntactic level of models. The equivalence relation has recently been extended to encompass various extensions to the language [107, 108] (see Section 9.5.3).

A tool has also been developed for TIPP [109]. The *TIPP-tool* is similar to the PEPA Workbench. It supports a LOTOS-oriented input language and provides facilities for functional analysis as well as a set of numerical solution modules for the transient and steady state analysis of the underlying Markov process.

In 1994 two new stochastic process algebras appeared in the literature. Markovian Process Algebra (MPA) was developed by Buchholz of the University of Dortmund [110, 111]. The major difference between this language and PEPA or TIPP, is the assumption that all actions of type α proceed at a fixed rate μ_α. Activities are still represented as (α, r) pairs but r now represents the number of concurrently enabled instances of action α, all of which proceed at rate μ_α. These instances are assumed to be competing in the sense that as soon as one of them completes the rest are aborted. This difference has subtle impact on the semantics of the language.

Extended Markovian Process Algebra (EMPA)[1] has been developed by Gorrieri's group at the University of Bologna [112, 113]. Although closer to PEPA than earlier work [62], this language includes a richer set of combinators than either PEPA or TIPP. It was also the first stochastic process algebra to include *immediate* or instantaneous actions. Passive actions play a central role in the theory of EMPA and synchronisation is restricted to involve at most one timed or immediate action. Most of the work on EMPA has focussed on various Petri net based semantics for the language.

There have also recently been some interesting explorations of the next departure after stochastic process algebra. In [114] Priami presents a stochastic extension of the π-calculus. The extension is analogous to the approach taken by the stochastic process algebras and allows Priami to consider the flexibility which process mobility might bring to performance modelling whilst staying within the Markovian framework. In two recent papers [115, 116], Brinksma *et al.* investigate the potential of using a true concurrency approach via stochastic extensions to a simple process algebra in a causality-based setting.

There has been extensive work studying semantic models of stochastic process algebra languages based on SPNs over the last two years [117, 118, 119, 120, 121]. Ribaudo's work [118, 122] makes use of a net-based semantics to compare the approaches to state space aggregation which are available in PEPA and Stochastic Well-formed Nets (SWN), a class of coloured SPN. In particular the semantics is used to establish that the aggregation achieved by strong equivalence in PEPA is more compact than that achieved by symbolic marking in SWN [123].

9.5.2   Integrating Performance Analysis into System Design

The work by Holton *et al.* [124, 125, 126] can be regarded as an initial investigation of how far PEPA provides integration between design and performance modelling. Previous work on the

---

[1]Originally this stochastic process algebra was also called MPA but the authors subsequently changed the name to avoid ambiguity.

performance analysis of robots and production cells has been limited, and mostly focussed on detailed simulation studies. However use of formal methods, such as process algebras, as design tools is better established [127]. The preliminary conclusions of experience of using PEPA in this way are that the reservations about using designs to generate performance models, expressed in Section 9.3, are not unfounded. In particular problems due to state space explosion and transient states have been encountered. However, these problems are not insurmountable and it has been found that designs can be readily modified to produce tractable performance models once the modeller has developed a little experience [125]. In the future it is planned to develop a refinement calculus based on PEPA which allows a model containing only essential detail for performance modelling, to be elaborated through stages of detailed design and implementation.

9.5.3   Representing Systems as Models

In addition to the work on robots and production cells case studies have been published on communication protocols [128, 129], a distributed mail system [130, 131] and a fault tolerant multi-processor [132, 133]. Some of these case studies have particularly aimed to consider the extent to which qualitative and quantitative analysis can be integrated [130, 134]. In the area of performability modelling this has been found to be especially relevant.

As mentioned above EMPA offers the modeller the richest set of combinators. Recently Holton has developed new combinators for PEPA [135]. The impact of such combinators on the transformation from design to performance model is still to be assessed in practice. Application area specific language features have not yet been investigated. This is possibly because except for the work on robots and production cells the case studies are being carried out by language developers themselves.

Recent work on TIPP has aimed to enhance the usefulness of the language by incorporating immediate actions. Here the aim is to offer the modeller a more compact representation of the system. Analysing the role of immediate actions within a modelling paradigm Rettelbach identifies two important ways in which they are used. The first role—representing "management" activities whose duration is negligible—is investigated in [108]. In this paper previous theoretical results on TIPP are extended to a new version of the language which includes such immediate actions. Moreover it is shown that transitions corresponding to these actions can be safely eliminated before the underlying CTMC is generated. Similarly in [107] Rettelbach tackles the second role for immediate actions—representing decisions and choices which do not consume system resources. Here too an equivalence relation is developed which could be used to automatically reduce the transition system, without affecting the integrity of the performance measures, whilst retaining this attractive modelling feature for model development. Thus, as anticipated, the addition of immediate actions, whilst easing model construction does not enhance the expressiveness of the stochastic process algebra.

Preliminary work exploring the more informal relationship between the modelling styles and facilities available in stochastic process algebras and GSPN has recently been published [136, 131]. Paradigms exhibit distinct strengths and weaknesses and a better understanding of the relationships between them can have mutual benefit as characteristics and techniques are imported from one to the other. Indeed the benefits of understanding the relationship between formalisms has become apparent in recent work on efficient solution: the recent results on product form solutions were inspired by earlier work on SPNs and queueing networks.

Little work has yet been done comparing the different stochastic process algebras. However by analysing their GSPN semantics, Ribaudo was able to present a summary of their differing characteristics and facilities [137]. This paper highlights the fact that the most significant difference between the formalisms is their different interpretations of synchronisation or cooperation. This is analysed in some detail in [138].

9.5.4 Model Tractability

Finding ways of exploiting the structure within PEPA models to enhance model tractability was identified as the most compelling problem left unsolved at the end of the thesis. Although the problem is still far from being completely resolved, significant progress has been made. Three distinct strands of research have arisen in this area corresponding to product form solution, near complete decomposability (or time scale decomposition), and tensor algebra and other special matrix representations.

The work on product form solutions aims to take advantage of apparent independence between submodels of a model, so that the submodels can be solved in isolation. Based on Henderson and Taylor's work on product form SPN models, Sereno has developed criteria to recognise a class of PEPA models which exhibit product form solution [139]. In such models the activities themselves are considered to be the states of a Markov chain which may be solved to find the steady state of the complete process. As in the SPN case only limited forms of synchronisation between submodels is allowed.

Similarly the work of Harrison and Hillston [140] derives conditions to recognise a restricted form of interaction between submodels which corresponds to the limited form of interaction between nodes in a queueing network. Efficient product form solution is one of the major attractions of such networks for performance modelling purposes. This work uses the notion of *quasi-reversibility* which had previously only been defined in a queueing network setting [141]. Extending this notion to a Markov process setting, the authors are able to define a form of interaction between PEPA components which ensures apparently independent behaviour. There is a pleasing resonance between the compositionality of the stochastic process algebra models and the modular, hierarchical approach defined by quasi-reversibility.

Note that the classes of models identified by the two approaches are distinct and it is an interesting area for future work to be able to compare them within the common framework of stochastic process algebras.

In contrast to the *exact* solutions obtained by product form methods, time scale decomposition results in an approximate solution. However the loss of accuracy is compensated by a technique which is efficient both in terms of time and storage. The essence of the approach is to identify when the model has a *nearly completely decomposable* structure [97] (see Section 5.3). In [142] Hillston and Mertsiotakis present a class of TIPP models which satisfy this property and give an algorithm to apply time scale decomposition to such models. Similarly to recent work on SPN models [143], each submodel in the decomposition corresponds to a set of derivatives which are reachable via *fast* activities. Transitions between submodels correspond to *slow* activities. A prototype implementation of the algorithm has been developed for the TIPP-tool and this is described in the paper.

Although not decompositional in the sense of the techniques described above work on tensor algebra and spectral expansion allow the generator matrix representing a model to be expressed in a form which facilitates efficient solution. The compositional structure is not used to identify submodels which can be solved in isolation. Instead this structure is used to structure the generator matrix so that specialised efficient solution algorithms can be employed. In [110, 111] and [144] the benefits of recognising the correspondence between operators in the process algebra and tensor operators on the underlying matrices are explored for MPA and a subset of TIPP, respectively. More recently a convenient means of modelling the behaviour of infinite state systems based on TIPP has been developed [145]. The approach allows analysis of the system's underlying Markov chain using the *spectral expansion* solution method [146].

Bibliography

[1] N. Götz, U. Herzog, and M. Rettelbach. TIPP - A Stochastic Process Algebra. In J. Hillston and F. Moller, editors, *Proc. of the Workshop on Process Algebra and Performance Modelling*. Department of Computer Science, University of Edinburgh, May 1993. (pp 1, 14)

[2] N. Götz, U. Herzog, and M. Rettelbach. Multiprocessor and Distributed System Design: The Integration of Functional Specification and Performance Analysis using Stochastic Process Algebras. In *Performance'93*, 1993. (pp 1, 11, 14)

[3] H. Beilner. Structured Modelling - Heterogeneous Modelling. In *Proc. of the European Simulation Multiconference*. Univeristy of Dortmund, Informak IV, SCS, June 1989. (pp 6, 11)

[4] U. Herzog. Formal description, time and performance analysis: A framework. Technical Report 15/90, IMMD VII, Friedrich-Alexander-Universität, Erlangen-Nürnberg, Germany, September 1990. (pp 6, 12, 13)

[5] W.H. Sanders and J.F. Meyer. Reduced base model construction methods for stochastic activity networks. *IEEE Journal on Selected Areas in Communications*, 9(1):25–36, January 1991. (pp 6, 8, 38, 42, 43, 70)

[6] A.L. Opdahl. *Performance Engineering During Information System Development*. PhD thesis, Norwegian Technical High School, Trondheim, 1993. (pp 6, 11)

[7] P. Schweitzer. A Survey of Aggregation-Disaggregation in Large Markov Chains. In W.J. Stewart, editor, *Numerical Solution of Markov Processes*, chapter 4, pages 63–88. Marcel Dekker, 1990. (pp 6, 11, 68, 72)

[8] L. Kleinrock. *Queueing Systems, Volume I: Theory*. John Wiley, New York, 1975. (pp 6, 40)

[9] L. Kleinrock. *Queueing Systems, Volume II: Computer Applications*. John Wiley, New York, 1976. (pp 6, 40)

[10] A. Allen. *Probability, Statistics and Queueing Theory with Computer Science Applications*. Academic Press, second edition, 1990. (p 6)

[11] P.J.B. King. *Computer and Communication Systems Performance Modelling*. Prentice Hall, 1990. (pp 6, 40)

[12] P.G. Harrison and N.M. Patel. *Performance Modelling of Communication Networks and Computer Architectures*. Addison-Wesley, 1992. (pp 6, 40)

[13] F. Baskett, K.M. Chandy, R.R. Muntz, and F.G. Palacios. Open, Closed and Mixed Networks of Queues with Different Classes of Customers. *Journal of the ACM*, 22(2):248–260, April 1975.   (p 7)

[14] J. Stifakis. Use of Petri Nets for Performance Evaluation. In H. Beilner and E. Gelenbe, editors, *Measuring, Modelling and Evaluating Computer Systems,*, pages 75–93. North-Holland, 1977.   (p 8)

[15] W.M. Zuberek. Timed Petri Nets and Preliminary Performance Evaluation. In *Proc. of 7th Annual Symposium on Computer Architecture*, pages 89–96, 1980.   (p 8)

[16] M.K. Molloy. *On the Integration of Delay and Throughput Measures in Distributed Processing Models.* PhD thesis, University of California, Los Angeles, 1981.   (p 8)

[17] M. Ajmone Marsan, G. Conte, and G. Balbo. A Class of Generalised Stochastic Petri Nets for the Performance Evaluation of Multiprocessor Systems. *ACM Transactions on Computer Systems*, 2(2):93–122, May 1984.   (pp 8, 12, 32, 40)

[18] J. Bechta Dugan, K.S. Trivedi, R.M. Geist, and V.F. Nicola. Extended Stochastic Petri Nets: Applications and Analysis. In E. Gelenbe, editor, *Performance '84*, pages 507 – 517. Elsevier Science Publishers, 1984.   (pp 8, 12)

[19] A. Movaghar and J.F. Meyer. Performability Modelling with Stochastic Activity Networks. In *Proc. of 1984 Real-Time Symposium*, Austin, Texas., December 1984.   (pp 8, 40)

[20] M.A. Holliday and M.K. Vernon. A generalised timed petri net model for performance analysis. *IEEE Transactions on Software Engineering*, 13(12):1297–1320, December 1987.   (p 8)

[21] J.K. Muppala and K.S. Trivedi. Composite Performance and Availability Analysis Using a Hierarchy of Stochastic Reward Nets. In G. Balbo and G. Serazzi, editors, *Computer Performance Evaluation: Modelling Techniques and Tools*, pages 335– 349. Elsevier, February 1991.   (pp 8, 38)

[22] M.K. Molloy. Performance analysis using stochastic petri nets. *IEEE Transactions on Computers*, 31(9):913–917, September 1982.   (pp 8, 40)

[23] W. Henderson and P.G. Taylor. Embedded Processes in Stochastic Petri Nets. *IEEE Transactions on Software Engineering*, 17(2):108 – 116, February 1991.   (pp 8, 42, 140)

[24] G. Balbo, S.C. Bruell, and S. Ghanta. Combining Queueing Network and Generalized Stochastic Petri Net Models for the Analysis of some Software Blocking Phenomena. *IEEE Transactions on Software Engineering*, 12(4):561–576, April 1986.   (pp 8, 43)

[25] G. Balbo, S. Bruell, and S. Ghanta. Combining Queueing Networks and Generalized Stochastic Petri Nets for the Solution of Complex Models of System Behaviour. *IEEE Transactions on Computers*, 37(10):1252–1268, October 1988.   (pp 8, 11, 73)

[26] M. Ajmone Marsan, S. Donatelli, and F. Neri. GSPN Models of Markovian Multiserver Multiqueue Systems. *Performance Evaluation*, 11:227–240, 1990.   (pp 8, 45, 49, 50, 52, 53, 56)

[27] G. Chiola, S. Donatelli, and G. Franceschinis. GSPNs versus SPNs: What is the actual role of immediate transitions? In *Petri Nets and Performance Models*, PNPM, pages 20–31, Melbourne, Australia, December 1991. IEEE Computer Society Press.   (pp 8, 41, 42, 43, 70)

[28] J.F. Meyer, A. Movaghar, and W.H. Sanders. Stochastic activity networks: Structure, behavior and application. In *Proc of Int. Workshop on Timed Petri Nets*, pages 106–115, Torino, Italy., 1985. IEEE Computer Society Press.   (pp 8, 12, 18, 40)

[29] R. Milner. *Communication and Concurrency*. Prentice-Hall, 1989.   (pp 9, 67)

[30] C.A.R. Hoare. *Communicating Sequential Processes*. Prentice-Hall, 1985.   (p 9)

[31] J.A. Bergstra and J.W. Klop. Algebra for Communicating Processes with Abstraction. *Journal of Theoretical Computer Science*, 37:77–121, 1985.   (p 9)

[32] G.D. Plotkin. A Structured Approach to Operational Semantics. Technical Report DAIMI FM-19, Computer Science Department, Aarhus University, 1981.   (pp 9, 28)

[33] R. Milner. Calculi for synchrony and asynchroni. *Theoretical Computer Science*, 25(3):267–310, 1983.   (p 9)

[34] F. Moller and C. Tofts. A Temporal Calculus for Communicating Systems. In J.C.M. Baeten and J.W. Klop, editors, *CONCUR'90*, volume 458 of *LNCS*, pages 401–415. Springer-Verlag, August 1989.   (pp 10, 67)

[35] J. Baeten and J. Bergstra. Real Time Process Algebra. *Formal Aspects of Computing*, 3(2):142–188, 1991.   (p 10)

[36] C-C. Jou and S.A. Smolka. Equivalences, Congruences and Complete Axiomatizations of Probabilistic Processes. In J.C.M. Baeten and J.W. Klop, editors, *CONCUR'90*, volume 458 of *LNCS*, pages 367–383. Springer-Verlag, August 1990.   (pp 10, 67, 68)

[37] C. Tofts. Describing Social Insect Behaviour Using Process Algebra. *Transactions of the Society for Computer Simulation*, 9(4):227–283, December 1992.   (p 10)

[38] K. Larsen and A. Skou. Bisimulation through Probabilistic Testing. *Information and Computation*, 94(1):1–28, September 1991.   (pp 10, 67, 68, 113)

[39] L. Christoff. *Specification and Verification Methods for Probabilistic Process*. PhD thesis, Department of Computer Science, Uppsala University, March 1993.   (p 10)

[40] Y. Yemini and J. Kuros. Towards the Unification of the Functional and Performance Analysis of Protocols, or Is the Alternating-Bit Protocol Really Correct? In C. Sunshine, editor, *Protocol Specification, Testing and Verification*, volume II. North Holland (IFIP), 1982.   (p 11)

[41] C. Harvey. Performance Engineering as an Integral Part of System Design. *BT Technology Journal*, 4(3):143–147, July 1986.   (p 11)

[42] G.V. Bochmann and J. Vaucher. Adding Performance Aspects to Specification Languages. In S. Aggarwal and K. Sabnani, editors, *Protocol Specification, Testing and Verification*, volume VIII, pages 19–31. North Holland (IFIP), 1988.   (p 11)

[43] C.U. Smith. *Performance Engineering of Software Systems*. Software Engineering Institute (SEI). Addison-Wesley, 1990. (p 11)

[44] P. Buchholz. Hierarchical Markovian Models - Symmetries and Reduction. In R.J. Pooley and J. Hillston, editors, *Computer Performance Evaluation: Modelling Techniques and Tools*, volume 10 of *EDITS*, pages 234–246. Edinburgh University Press, August 1993. (pp 11, 12, 73)

[45] W. Henderson and D. Lucic. Aggregation and Disaggregation Through Insensitivity in Stochastic Petri Nets. *Performance Evaluation*, 17(2):91–114, March 1993. (pp 11, 92)

[46] I.S.O. LOTOS : A Formal Description Technique Based on the Temporal Ordering of Observational Behaviour. IS 8807, TC97/SC21, 1989. (p 11)

[47] C.J. Koomen. *The Design of Communicating Systems: A System Engineering Approach*. Kluwer, 1991. (p 11)

[48] A. Valderruten, O. Hjiej, A. Benzekri, and D. Gazal. Deriving Queueing Networks Performance Models from Annotated LOTOS Specifications. In R.J. Pooley and J. Hillston, editors, *Computer Performance Evaluation '92: Modelling Techniques and Tools*, pages 167 – 178, 1992. (p 11)

[49] F. Bause and P. Buchholz. Protocol Analysis using a timed version of SDL. In *Proc. of 3rd. International Conference on Formal Description Techniques (FORTE '90)*, Madrid, Spain, November 1990. (p 11)

[50] J.A. Hillebrand. The ABP and the CABP - a comparison of performances in real time process algebra. Technical Report P9211, Programming Research Group, University of Amsterdam, 1992. (p 11)

[51] P. Dembinski and S. Dubkowski. Simulating Estelle Specifications with Time Parameters. In H. Rudin and C.H. West, editors, *Protocol Specification, Testing and Verification*, volume VII, pages 265–279. North Holland (IFIP), 1987. (p 11)

[52] C-Y. Wang and K.S. Trivedi. Integration of Specification for Modelling and Specification for System Design. In M. Ajmone Marsan, editor, *Application and Theory of Petri Nets*, pages 473–492. Springer-Verlag, 1993. (p 11)

[53] R.J. Pooley. Deriving Functional Properties of Process Based Simulation Models. In J. Hillston and F. Moller, editors, *Proceedings of the Workshop on Process Algebra and Performance Modelling*, number CSR-26-93 in Technical Reports. Department of Computer Science, University of Edinburgh, May 1993. (p 11)

[54] Y. Yemini and N. Nounou. CUPID: A Protocol Development Environment. In H. Rudin and C.H. West, editors, *Protocol Specification, Testing and Verification*, volume III, pages 347–355. North Holland (IFIP), 1983. (pp 11, 13)

[55] N. Nounou and Y. Yemini. Algebraic Specification-Based Performance Analysis of Communication Protocols. In Y. Yemini, R. Strom, and S. Yemini, editors, *Protocol Specification, Testing and Verification*, volume IV. North Holland (IFIP), 1985. (pp 11, 13)

[56] J. Hillston. System Description Formalisms and Performance Evaluation. IMSE project deliverable D4.4-2, (Edinburgh University), BNR Europe Ltd, London Road, Harlow, Essex, UK, December 1991. (p 12)

[57] J.J. Zic. Extensions to Communicating Sequential Processes to allow Protocol Performance Specification. *ACM Computer Communication Review*, 17(5):217–227, 1987. Special Issue: SIGCOMM'87 Workshop on Frontiers in Computer Communications Technology. (p 13)

[58] B. Strulo. *Process Algebra for Discrete Event Simulation*. PhD thesis, Imperial College, 1993. (p 14)

[59] R.J. Pooley. *Deriving Functional Properties of Process Based Simulation Models*. PhD thesis, Department of Computer Science, University of Edinburgh, 1995. (p 15)

[60] G. Birtwistle, R.J. Pooley, and C.N.M. Tofts. Characterising the Structure of Simulation Models in CCS. *Transactions of the SCS*, 10(3):205–236, 1993. (p 15)

[61] G. Birtwistle. *DEMOS: Discrete Event Modelling On Simula*. MacMillan, 1978. (p 15)

[62] R. Gorrieri and M. Rocetti. Towards Performance Evaluation in Process Algebras. In *Proc. of the 3rd Int. Conference on Algebraic Methodology and Software Technology*, 1993. (pp 15, 141)

[63] W. Feller. *An Introduction to Probability Theory and Its Applications*, volume I. Wiley, 3rd edition, 1970. (p 36)

[64] B.W. Char, K.O. Geddes, G.H. Gonnet, B.L. Leong, M.B. Monagan, and S.M. Watt. *Maple V Library Reference Manual*. Springer-Verlag, 1992. (p 37)

[65] N. Patel. Structuring Analytical Performance Models Using *Mathematica*. In R. Pooley and J. Hillston, editors, *Computer Performance Evaluation: Modelling Techniques and Tools*, volume 10 of *EDITS*, pages 208–219, 1992. (p 37)

[66] A. Allen and G. Hynes. Solving a Queueing Model with *Mathematica*. *Mathematica Journal*, 1(3):108–112, 1991. (p 37)

[67] A. Allen. *Introduction to Computer Performance Analysis with* Mathematica. Academic Press, 1992. (p 37)

[68] R. Howard. *Dynamic Probabilistic Systems: Semi-Markov and Decision Systems*, volume II. Wiley, 1971. (p 38)

[69] J.F. Meyer. On evaluating the performability of degradable computing systems. *IEEE Transactions on Computers*, 29(8):720–731, August 1980. (p 38)

[70] G. Ciardo, J. Muppala, and K.S. Trivedi. SPNP: Stochastic Petri Net Package. In *Petri Nets and Performance Models*, pages 142–150, Kyoto, Japan, December 1989. IEEE. (p 38)

[71] G. Ciardo, J. Muppala, and K. Trivedi. On the solution of GSPN reward models. *Performance Evaluation*, 12:237–253, 1991. (p 38)

[72] W.H. Sanders and J.F. Meyer. Performance Variable Driven Construction Methods for Stochastic Activity Networks. In G. Iazeolla, P.J. Courtois, and O.J. Boxma, editors, *Computer Performance and Reliability*, pages 383–398. Elsevier Science Publishers, 1988. (p 38)

[73] W. Henderson, D. Lucic, and P.G. Taylor. A Net Level Performance Analysis of Stochastic Petri Nets. *Journal of Australian Mathematical Society Series B*, 31:176–187, 1989. (pp 40, 42)

[74] G. Ciardo and K. Trivedi. A Decomposition Approach for Stochastic Petri Nets. In *Petri Nets and Performance Models*, pages 74–83. IEEE Computer Society, December 1991. (pp 40, 71, 139)

[75] S. Jacobson and E. Lazowska. Analysing queueing networks with simultaneous resource possession. *Communications of the ACM*, 25(2):142–151, February 1982. (p 41)

[76] P. Heidelberger and K. Trivedi. Analytic queueing models of programs with internal concurrency. *IEEE Transactions on Computers*, 32:73–82, 1983. (p 41)

[77] F. Baccelli and Z. Liu. A New Solver for QNET for Parallel Fork-Join Networks. IMSE project deliverable R5.5-7, (INRIA, Sophia Antipolis), BNR Europe Ltd., London Road, Harlow, Essex, UK, December 1989. (p 41)

[78] G. Chiola, C. Dutheillet, G. Franceschinis, and S. Haddad. On Well-Formed Coloured Nets and Their Symbolic Reachability Graph. In K. Jensen and G. Rozenberg, editors, *High-Level Petri Nets. Theory and Application*. Springer Verlag, 1991. (p 42)

[79] A.A. Lazar and T.G. Robertazzi. Markovian Petri Net Protocols with Product Form Solution. *Performance Evaluation*, 12(1):67–77, January 1991. (p 42)

[80] R.J. Boucherie. A Characterisation of Independence for Competing Markov Chains with Applications to Stochastic Petri nets. Technical Report 1880, INRIA, Sophia-Antipolis, 1993. (pp 42, 140)

[81] D. Frosch-Wilkes. An Exact Analysis of Closed Synchronised Systems of Stochastic Sequential Processes. Forschungsbericht, Mathematik/Informatik 93-02, University of Trier, 1993. (pp 42, 140)

[82] B. Plateau, J-M. Fourneau, and K-H. Lee. PEPS: A Package for Solving Complex Markov Models of Parallel Systems. In R. Puigjaner, editor, *Proc. of 4th Int. Conf. on Modelling Techniques and Tools for Computer Performance Evaluation*, pages 341–360. Plenum Press, 1988. (pp 42, 140)

[83] P. Buchholz. Numerical Solution Methods Based on Structured Descriptions of Markovian Models. In G. Balbo and G. Serazzi, editors, *Proc. of 5th Int. conference on Modelling Techniques and Tools for Computer Performance Evaluation*, pages 242–257, February 1991. (pp 42, 140)

[84] T. Raith. Performance Analysis of Multibus Interconnection Networks in Distributed Systems. In M. Akiyama, editor, *Teletraffic Issues in an Advanced Information Society ITC-11*, pages 662–668. Elsevier, 1985. (pp 45, 50, 52, 54)

[85] R.J.T. Morris and Y.T. Wang. Some Results for Multiqueue Systems with Multiple Cyclic Servers. In H. Rudin and W. Bux, editors, *Performance of Computer Communication Systems*, pages 245–258. Elsevier, 1984. (pp 45, 50, 52, 54)

[86] A.E. Kamal and V.C. Hamacher. Approximate Analysis of Non-exhaustive Multiserver Polling Systems with Applications to Local Area Networks. *Computer Networks and ISDN Systems*, 17(1):15–27, 1989. (pp 45, 50, 52, 53)

[87] Q. Yang, D. Ghosal, and L. Bhuyan. Performance Analysis of Multiple Token Ring and Multiple Slotted Ring Networks. In *Proceedings of Computer Network Symposium*, pages 79–86, Washington DC, 1986. IEEE. (pp 45, 50, 52, 54)

[88] T.I. Yuk and J.C. Palais. Analysis of Multichannel Token Ring Networks. In *Proceedings of the International Conference on Communication Systems*, pages 907–911, 1988. (pp 45, 50, 54)

[89] H. Takagi. Queueing Analysis of Polling Models: An Update. In H. Takagi, editor, *Stochastic Analysis of Computer and Communication Systems*, pages 267 – 318. IFIP/ North Holland, 1990. (pp 45, 47, 49, 62)

[90] H. Choi and K.S. Trivedi. Approximate Performance Models of Polling Systems Using Stochastic Petri Nets. In *Proceedings of INFOCOM' 92*, 1992. (p 49)

[91] O.C. Ibe and K.S. Trivedi. Stochastic Petri Net Models of Polling Systems. *IEEE Journal on Selected Areas of Communication*, 8(9), 1990. (p 49)

[92] D. Grillo. Polling Mechanism Models in Communication Systems - Some Application Examples. In H. Takagi, editor, *Stochastic Analysis of Computer and Communication Systems*, pages 659 – 698. IFIP/North Holland, 1990. (p 50)

[93] M. Ajmone Marsan, S. Donatelli, F. Neri, and U. Rubino. On The Construction of Abstract GSPNs: An Exercise in Modelling. In J. Billington and W. Henderson, editors, *Petri Nets and Performance Modelling*, pages 2–17. IEEE, December 1991. (p 50)

[94] B.D. Bunday and E. Khorram. The Efficiency of Uni-directionally Patrolled Machines with Two Robot Repairmen. *European Journal of Operational Research*, 39(1):32–39, 1989. (p 52)

[95] F. Moller. *The Edinburgh Concurrency Workbench (Version 6.0)*. LFCS, Dept. of Computer Science, University of Edinburgh., August 1991. (p 68)

[96] B.P. Zeigler. *Theory of Modelling and Simulation*. Krieger, 1976. (p 69)

[97] P.J. Courtois. *Decomposability: Queueing and Computer System Applications*. ACM Series. Academic Press, New York, 1977. (pp 71, 143)

[98] P. Buchholz. Exact and Ordinary Lumpability in Finite Markov Chains. *Journal of Applied Probability*, 31(1):59–75, 1994. (p 71)

[99] G. Rubino and B. Sericola. Sojourn Times in Finite Markov Processes. *Journal of Applied Probability*, 27:744–756, 1989. (p 72)

[100] J.G. Kemeny and J.L. Snell. *Finite Markov Chains*. Van Nostrand, 1960. (p 72)

[101] P. Schweitzer. Aggregation Methods for Large Markov Chains. In G. Iazeolla, P.J Courtois, and A. Hordijk, editors, *Mathematical Computer Performance and Reliability*. North Holland, 1984.   (p 72)

[102] K. Matthes. Zur Theorie der Bedienungsprozesse. In *3rd Prague Conf. on Information Theory, Statistical Decision Functions and Random Processes*, pages 513–528, 1962. (p 91)

[103] V. Nicola. Lumping in Markov Reward Processes. Research Report RC 14719, IBM, 1989. IBM Thomas Watson Research Centre, P.O. Box 704, Yorktown Heights, NY 10598.   (p 128)

[104] S. Gilmore and J. Hillston. The PEPA Workbench: A Tool to Support a Process Algebra-based Approach to Performance Modelling. In G. Haring and G. Kotsis, editors, *Proceedings of the Seventh International Conference on Modelling Techniques and Tools for Computer Performance Evaluation*, volume 794 of *LNCS*, pages 353–368. Springer-Verlag, 1994.   (p 138)

[105] The MathWorks Inc. *The Matlab manual*, 1994.   (p 140)

[106] H. Hermanns and M.L. Rettelbach. Syntax, Semantics, Equivalences and Axioms for MTIPP. In U. Herzog and M. Rettelbach, editors, *Proc. of 2nd Process Algebra and Performance Modelling Workshop*, 1994.   (p 141)

[107] M. Rettelbach. Probabilistic Branching in Markovian Process Algebras. *The Computer Journal*, 38(6), 1995. Special Issue: Proc. of 3rd Process Algebra and Performance Modelling Workshop.   (pp 141, 142)

[108] H. Hermanns, M. Rettelbach, and T. Weiß. Formal Characterisation of Immediate Actions in SPA with Nondeterministic Branching. *The Computer Journal*, 38(6), 1995. Special Issue: Proc. of 3rd Workshop on Process Algebras and Performance Modelling. (pp 141, 142)

[109] H. Hermanns and V. Mertsiotakis. A Stochastic Process Algebra Based Modelling Tool. In *Proc. of the 11th UK Performance Engineering Workshop for Computer and Telecommunication Systems*. Springer, 1995.   (p 141)

[110] P. Buchholz. On a Markovian Process Algebra. Technical Report 500/194, Informatik IV, Universität Dortmund, April 1994.   (pp 141, 143)

[111] P. Buchholz. Compositional Analysis of a Markovian Process Algebra. In U. Herzog and M. Rettelbach, editors, *Proc. of 2nd Process Algebra and Performance Modelling Workshop*, 1994.   (pp 141, 143)

[112] M. Bernardo, R. Gorrieri, and L. Donatiello. MPA: A Stochastic Process Algebra. Technical Report UBLCS-94-10, Laboratory of Computer Science, University of Bologna, May 1994.   (p 141)

[113] M. Bernardo, L. Donatiello, and R. Gorrieri. Modelling and Analyzing Concurrent Systems with MPA. In U. Herzog and M. Rettelbach, editors, *Proc. of 2nd Process Algebra and Performance Modelling Workshop*, 1994.   (p 141)

[114] C. Priami. Stochastic π-Calculus. *The Computer Journal*, 38(6), 1995. Special Issue: Proc. of 3rd Process Algebra and Performance Modelling Workshop.   (p 141)

[115] E. Brinksma, J-P. Katoen, R. Langerak, and D. Latella. Performance Analysis and True Concurrency Semantics. In U. Herzog and M. Rettelbach, editors, *Proc. of 2nd Process Algebra and Performance Modelling Workshop*, 1994. (p 141)

[116] E. Brinskma, J-P. Katoen, R. Langerak, and D. Latella. A Stochastic Causality-Based Process Algebra. *The Computer Journal*, 38(6), 1995. Special Issue: Proc. of 3rd Process Algebra and Performance Modelling Workshop. (p 141)

[117] M. Bernardo, R. Gorrieri, and L. Donatiello. Operational GSPN Semantics of MPA. Technical Report UBLCS-94-12, Laboratory of Computer Science, University of Bologna, May 1994. (p 141)

[118] M. Ribaudo. *On the Relationship between Stochastic Petri Nets and Stochastic Process Algebras*. PhD thesis, Dipartimento di Informatica, Università di Torino, May 1995. (p 141)

[119] M. Ribaudo. Stochastic Petri Net Semantics for Stochastic Process Algebras. In *Proc. 6th International Workshop on Petri Nets and Performance Models*, pages 148,157, Durham, NC, 1995. (p 141)

[120] M. Bernardo, L. Donatiello, and R. Gorrieri. Giving a Net Semantics to Markovian Process Algebras. In *Proc. 6th International Workshop on Petri Nets and Performance Models*, pages 169,178, Durham, NC, 1995. (p 141)

[121] M. Bernardo, N. Busi, and R. Gorrieri. A Distributed Semantics for EMPA Based on Stochastic Contextual Nets. *The Computer Journal*, 38(6), 1995. Special Issue: Proc. of 3rd Process Algebra and Performance Modelling Workshop. (p 141)

[122] M. Ribaudo. On the Aggregation Techniques in Stochastic Petri Nets and Stochastic Process Algebras. *The Computer Journal*, 38(6), 1995. Special Issue: Proc. of 3rd Process Algebra and Performance Modelling Workshop. (p 141)

[123] G. Chiola, C. Dutheillet, G. Franceschinis, and S. Haddad. Stochastic Well-Formed Coloured Nets and Symmetric Modelling Applications. *IEEE Transactions on Computers*, 42(11):1343–1359, November 1993. (p 141)

[124] S. Gilmore, J. Hillston, R. Holton, and M. Rettelbach. Specifications in Stochastic Process Algebra for a Robot Control Problem. *International Journal of Production Research*, December 1995. (p 141)

[125] D.R.W. Holton. A PEPA Specification of and Industrial Production Cell. *The Computer Journal*, 38(6), 1995. Special Issue: Proc. of 3rd Process Algebra and Performance Modelling Workshop. (pp 141, 142)

[126] D.R.W. Holton and J.P.N. Glover. An SPA Performance Model of a Production Cell. Submitted to the Second World Automation Congress, Montpellier, France, December 1995. (p 141)

[127] D.R.W. Holton. *A Rigorous Approach to Robot Programming*. PhD thesis, The Queen's University of Belfast, 1991. (p 142)

[128] N. Götz. *Stochastische Prozeßalgebren – Integration von funktionalem Entwurf und Leistungsbewertung Verteilter Systeme*. PhD thesis, Universität Erlangen–Nürnberg, Martensstraße 3, 91058 Erlangen, April 1994. (p 142)

[129] H. Hermanns, V. Mersiotakis, and M. Rettelbach. Performance analysis of distributed systems using TIPP—a case study. In J. Hillston and R. Pooley, editors, *Proc. of 10th UK Computer and Telecommunications Performance Engineering Workshop*, 1994. (p 142)

[130] J. Hillston, H. Hermanns, U. Herzog, V. Mertsiotakis, and M. Rettelbach. Integrating Qualitative and Quantitative Modelling with Stochastic Process Algebras. Technical report, IMMD VII, Universität Erlangen-Nürnberg, May 1994. (p 142)

[131] S. Donatelli, H. Hermanns, J. Hillston, and M. Ribaudo. GSPN and SPA Compared in Practice: Modelling a Distributed Mail System. In F. Baccelli, A. Jean-Marie, and I. Mitrani, editors, *Quantitative Methods in Parallel Systems*, pages 38–51. Springer, 1995. (p 142)

[132] U. Herzog and V. Mertsiotakis. Stochastic Process Algebras Applied to Failure Modelling. In U. Herzog and M. Rettelbach, editors, *Proc. of 2nd Process Algebra and Performance Modelling Workshop*, 1994. (p 142)

[133] H. Hermanns, U. Herzog, and V. Mertsiotakis. Stochastic Process Algebras as a Tool for Performance and Dependability Modelling. In *Proc. of IEEE International Computer Performance and Dependability Symposium*, pages 102–111, Erlangen, April 1995. IEEE Computer Society Press. (p 142)

[134] J. Hillston, H. Hermanns, U. Herzog, V. Mersiotakis, and M. Rettelbach. Stochastic process algebras: Integrating qualitative and quantitative modelling. In *Proc. of FORTE'94*, 1994. position statement. (p 142)

[135] D.R.W. Holton. Defining New Combinators for PEPA. Technical report, Department of Computing, The University of Bradford, 1995. (p 142)

[136] S. Donatelli, J. Hillston, and M. Ribaudo. A Comparison of Performance Evaluation Process Algebra and Generalized Stochastic Petri Nets. In *Proc. of the 6th Petri Nets and Performance Models Workshop*, pages 158–168, October 1995. (p 142)

[137] M. Ribaudo. Understanding Stochastic Process Algebras via their Stochastic Petri Net Semantics. In U. Herzog and M. Rettelbach, editors, *Proc. of 2nd Process Algebra and Performance Modelling Workshop*, 1994. (p 143)

[138] J. Hillston. The Nature of Synchronisation. In U. Herzog and M. Rettelbach, editors, *Proc. of 2nd Process Algebra and Performance Modelling Workshop*, 1994. (p 143)

[139] M. Sereno. Towards a Product Form Solution of Stochastic Process Algebras. *The Computer Journal*, 38(6), 1995. Special Issue: Proc. of 3rd Process Algebra and Performance Modelling Workshop. (p 143)

[140] P. Harrison and J. Hillston. Exploiting Quasi-reversible Structures in Markovian Process Algebra Models. *The Computer Journal*, 38(6), 1995. Special Issue: Proc. of 3rd Process Algebra and Performance Modelling Workshop. (p 143)

[141] F. Kelly. *Reversibility and Stochastic Processes*. Wiley, 1979. (p 143)

[142] J. Hillston and V. Mertsiotakis. A Simple Time Scale Decomposition Technique for Stochastic Process Algebras. *The Computer Journal*, 38(6), 1995. Special Issue: Proc. of 3rd Process Algebra and Performance Modelling Workshop. (p 143)

[143] A. Blakemore and S. Tripathi. Automated Time Scale Decomposition of SPNs. In *Proc. of 5th Int. Workshop on Petri Nets and Performance Models (PNPM '93)*, Toulouse, 1993.   (p 143)

[144] M.L. Rettelbach and M. Siegle. Compositional Minimal Semantics for the Stochastic Process Algebra TIPP. In U. Herzog and M. Rettelbach, editors, *Proc. of 2nd Process Algebra and Performance Modelling Workshop*, 1994.   (p 143)

[145] I. Mitrani, A. Ost, and M. Rettelbach. *Quantitative Methods in Parallel Systems*, chapter TIPP and the Spectral Expansion Method. Springer, 1995.   (p 144)

[146] I. Mitrani and D. Mitra. A Spectral Expansion Method for Random Walks on Semi-Infinite Strips. In *Proc. of the IMACS Symposium on Iterative Methods in Linear Algebra*. Springer, 1991.   (p 144)

Index